ULTIMATE

WORD

SUCCESS

2nd Edition

Laurie Rozakis, Ph.D.

PETERSON'S
A nelnet COMPANY

About Peterson's
To succeed on your lifelong educational journey, you will need accurate, dependable, and practical tools and resources. That is why Peterson's is everywhere education happens. Because whenever and however you need education content delivered, you can rely on Peterson's to provide the information, know-how, and guidance to help you reach your goals. Tools to match the right students with the right school. It's here. Personalized resources and expert guidance. It's here. Comprehensive and dependable education content—delivered whenever and however you need it. It's all here.

For more information, contact Peterson's, 2000 Lenox Drive, Lawrenceville, NJ 08648; 800-338-3282; or find us on the World Wide Web at www.petersons.com/about.

Contents

Contents

Part III Build Your Word Bank

Part IV Unlock Key Words

Part V Collect More Valuable Words

Part VI Go for the Gold! Puzzles and Games to Win with Words

Introduction

Frequently Asked Questions

Let's start by exploring some frequently asked questions about learning words for standardized exams. Then, we'll take a look at strategies for using this book to your best advantage.

Q: *How is vocabulary measured on standardized exams?*

A: The SAT*, PSAT/NMSQT*, GED, ACT®, and TOEFL® all test your vocabulary. For example, the SAT includes "vocabulary-in-context" questions, in which you must determine the meaning of words as used in specific sentences. If you know the meaning of every word in the question, you'll probably get the answer right. The more words you know, the better your chances of narrowing down the choices to the correct one. In addition, standardized tests assess your vocabulary indirectly through the use of reading comprehension passages and questions. Test takers with a strong vocabulary have an advantage in answering these questions.

Q: *How do the test makers choose words for the exams?*

A: The test makers want to determine whether you possess a well-rounded, "educated" vocabulary—the kind of vocabulary you need to read, write, and speak effectively in college and beyond. Test-worthy words include those that any educated person might use in speaking or writing, as well as those that are quite specific to particular academic fields.

Q: *What kind of words won't be on the exam or in this book?*

A: The following types of words are excluded from this book because they're not likely to appear on a standardized test:

- Relatively common words that most high school students already know

- Highly technical words understood only by specialists or experts in certain academic fields and professions

- Non-English words that are not widely used among English speakers

- Informal jargon, slang, or colloquialisms

- Words no longer in common use

1

Q: *Does this book include all of the words I need to know for my exam?*

A: Of course not—the English language includes thousands of test-worthy words. The *Oxford English Dictionary* lists more than 600,000 words; German has fewer than one-third that number, French fewer than one-sixth. No matter how thoroughly you've prepared for the test, you will most likely encounter new and unfamiliar words on the exam.

Q: *Can I learn the words I need to know by taking simulated practice tests?*

A: Unfortunately, no. You'll learn a few new words this way but not nearly enough. Simulated testing is more useful for learning test-taking "skills"—analyzing questions and developing strategies for responding to them—than for improving vocabulary.

Definitions and Phonetic Spellings in This Book

A phonetic spelling "spells out" a word just the way it sounds when spoken, without the confusing marks that you find in dictionaries. The syllable receiving primary emphasis is spelled with *italics* or capital letters. Here's an example of a word with its phonetic spelling as used in this book:

ideology (*eye*-dee-ol-oh-jee)

You can tell that the first syllable receives the emphasis because it is written in italics.

Here's a guide to help you properly interpret the phonetic spellings used in this book:

Phonetic Spelling	Sample Word	Pronunciation
a	**c**at	*k*at
ah	**o**tter	*ah*-ter
ay	st**a**te	st*ay*t
	airplane	*ayr*-playn
aw	**aw**esome	*aw*-sum
ee	n**ea**t	n*ee*t
e or eh	n**e**cklace	*nek*-lis
	espouse	eh-*spowz*
i or ih	**i**ndicate	*in*-dih-kayt
y or eye	k**i**te	k*yt*
	idea	eye-*dee*-ah
oh	**o**pen	*oh*-pin
oo	b**eau**tiful	*byoo*-tih-ful
ow	c**ou**ch	*kowch*
u or uh	st**u**ck	st*uk*
	appreciate	uh-*pree*-shee-ayt
	bull**y**	*bul*-ee
zh	excur**s**ion	ek-*sker*-zhun

Part I

Get the Edge!

Day 1:
Take a Pretest

Day 2:
Discover the Secret to a High Score on Standardized Vocabulary Tests

Day 3:
Master the Top Ten Tips for Learning (and Remembering) New Words

Day 1

Take a Pretest

Before you can determine where you have to go, you need to figure out where you are. Take the following pretest to see how your vocabulary measures up to that of other test takers. The following pretest conforms to the format of the vocabulary portion of the SAT. This format will help you assess your current knowledge of vocabulary and standardized test-taking format for this all-important college admissions test.

Directions: For each question in this section, select the best answer from among the choices given. Circle your answer or write your choice on a separate sheet of paper.

Each sentence below has one or two blanks, each blank indicating that something has been omitted. Beneath each sentence are five words or sets of words labeled (A) through (E). Choose the word or set of words that, when inserted in the sentence, *best* fits the meaning of the sentence as a whole.

Example:

A pidgin is a(n) _____ jargon containing words of various languages and little in the way of grammar.

- **(A)** precise
- **(B)** explicit
- **(C)** demanding
- **(D)** makeshift
- **(E)** anecdotal

The correct answer is (D).

---

1. By working a great deal of overtime, Hector gave the boss a(n) _____ reason to give him a raise.

    (A) autocratic (*aw*-toh-krah-tic)
    (B) despotic (des-*pah*-tic)
    (C) compelling (kum-*pel*-ing)
    (D) dogged (*dog*-id)
    (E) intrepid (in-*treh*-pid)

2. Records were made _____ by CDs, but now they are making a comeback among collectors.

    (A) popular
    (B) obsolete (awb-suh-*leet*)
    (C) standard
    (D) sought
    (E) recommend

3. The referee's _____ behavior angered the players because he was inconsistent in his calls.

    (A) capricious (kuh-*pree*-shus)
    (B) apathetic (a-puh-*thet*-ic)
    (C) inconsequential (in-kahn-suh-*kwen*-shul)
    (D) superficial (soo-per-*fish*-ul)
    (E) trivial (*trih*-vee-ul)

4. The girl's expression was _____, so the painter had a difficult time capturing it on canvas.

    (A) affable (*af*-uh-bul)
    (B) facetious (fuh-*see*-shus)
    (C) cordial (*kor*-jul)
    (D) truncated (*trun*-kay-tid)
    (E) elusive (ee-*loo*-sive)

5. Professor Herman was a _____ teacher who rarely took time to listen to his students.

    (A) brusque (brusk)
    (B) caustic (*kaw*-stik)
    (C) feral (*feh*-rul)
    (D) notorious (no-*tor*-ee-us)
    (E) pugnacious (pug-*nay*-shus)

6. I had a _____ professor who said that it's man's ability to use language that makes him the dominant species on the planet.

    (A) sentimental
    (B) gruesome (*grew*-some)
    (C) commodious
    (D) linguistics
    (E) crepuscular (kreh-*pews*-kyoo-ler)

7. The goldsmith seemed to work by _____, constructing jewelry with gems that almost seemed to float in the air.

    (A) cupidity (kyoo-*pid*-ih-tee)
    (B) serendipity (sayr-en-*dip*-uh-tee)
    (C) verisimilitude (vayr-ih-*sim*-ih-lih-tood)
    (D) machinations (mak-uh-*nay*-shins)
    (E) artifice (*ar*-tuh-fis)

8. Sad because of the inclement weather, the dog cast a(n) _____ glance at his master.

    (A) baleful (*bayl*-ful)
    (B) vivacious (vi-*vay*-shush)
    (C) inchoate (in-*koh*-ayt)
    (D) indefatigable (in-dih-*fa*-tih-guh-bul)
    (E) nefarious (neh-*fayr*-ee-us)

9. The teacher had an unfortunate habit of _____ a point over and over to make sure her students understood it.

    (A) devouring
    (B) castigating (*kas*-tuh-gayt-ing)
    (C) belaboring (buh-*lay*-ber-ing)
    (D) assimilating
    (E) proliferating (pro-*liff*-er-ayt-ing)

10. The drunken revelers made such a loud _____ that police had to be called.

   (A) functionary (*funk*-shun-ayr-ee)
   (B) fracas (*fray*-kus)
   (C) imbroglio (im-*broh*-lee-oh)
   (D) machination (mak-uh-*nay*-shin)
   (E) obsequies (*ahb*-seh-kweez)

11. The child's wound was _____ and barely bled; as a result, his mother knew it was a(n) _____ injury.

   (A) superficial (soo-per-*fish*-ul).. inconsequential (in-kahn-suh-*kwen*-shul)
   (B) symbiotic (sim-bee-*ah*-tik).. indifferent
   (C) spontaneous (spon-*tay*-nee-us).. apathetic (ap-uh-*thet*-ic)
   (D) quixotic (kwik-*zah*-tik).. obstinate (*ahb*-stin-ut)
   (E) intrepid (in-*treh*-pid).. incumbent (in-*kum*-bunt)

12. The critic neither _____ nor _____ the director's latest film: she evaluated the film's strengths and weaknesses carefully and fairly.

   (A) aggrandized (uh-*gran*-dyzd).. favored
   (B) maligned (*mah*-lynd)..criticized
   (C) celebrated..adapted
   (D) lauded (*law*-did)..derided (dee-*ri*-ded)
   (E) disregarded (dis-ree-*gar*-ded).. showcased

13. Tragically, so many marshes and wetlands are _____ by agricultural overdevelopment and technological encroachment (in-*kroach*-ment) that they may _____ by the next century.

   (A) sequestered (see-*kwest*-erd).. separate
   (B) threatened..vanish
   (C) consumed..augment (*awg*-ment)
   (D) embellished (em-*bell*-ishd).. dwindle (*dwin*-dul)
   (E) rejuvenated (ree-*joo*-vih-nay-ted).. dissolve

14. As a museum archivist who restores ancient documents, Matt Hijing protested an art council policy that resulted in the wholesale _____ of clearly _____ records.

   (A) extermination..inconsequential
   (B) leveling..derelict (*der*-eh-likt)
   (C) protection..venerable (*veh*-ner-ah-bul)
   (D) destruction..salvageable (*salv*-ah-jah-ble)
   (E) indemnity (in-*dem*-nih-tee).. grimy

15. It would be _____ for any aspiring office seeker to _____ such a powerful group of voters.

   (A) intelligent..aggravate
   (B) senseless..irritate
   (C) astute (ah-*stoot*)..infuriate (in-*fyoor*-e-ate)
   (D) discerning (dis-*surn*-ing).. provoke
   (E) preposterous (pre-*pos*-tur-us).. abet (ah-*bet*)

Answers in Brief

1. C	6. D	11. A
2. B	7. E	12. D
3. A	8. A	13. B
4. E	9. C	14. D
5. A	10. B	15. B

Answers Explained

You can often figure out what a new word means by seeing it in *context*, the surrounding words and phrases. That way, you can still get the *gist* (jist) of the conversation or reading, even if you have never seen the word before. Sentence completion questions build on this skill by requiring you to fill in one or two words that have been removed from a sentence.

1. **The correct answer is (C).** *By working a great deal of overtime, Hector gave the boss a compelling reason to give him a raise. Compelling* means "forceful; urgently demanding attention."

   (A) *autocratic* means "tyrannical"
   (B) *despotic* means "dictatorial, oppressive"
   (D) *dogged* means "stubbornly persevering"
   (E) *intrepid* means "courageous, fearless"

2. **The correct answer is (B).** *Records were made obsolete by CDs, but now they are making a comeback among collectors. Obsolete* means "out-of-date, antiquated."

   (A) *popular* means "sought after"
   (C) *standard* means "regular"
   (D) *sought* means "desired"
   (E) *recommend* means "endorsed"

3. **The correct answer is (A).** *The referee's capricious behavior angered the players because he was inconsistent in his calls. Capricious* means "fickle, inconstant."

   (B) *apathetic* means "impassive"
   (C) *inconsequential* means "not important"
   (D) *superficial* means "shallow"
   (E) *trivial* means "unimportant"

4. **The correct answer is (E).** *The girl's expression was elusive, so the painter had a difficult time capturing it on canvas. Elusive* means "intangible, hard to grasp."

   (A) *affable* means "friendly"
   (B) *facetious* means "sarcastic"
   (C) *cordial* means "friendly"
   (D) *truncated* means "shortened"

5. **The correct answer is (A).** *Professor Herman was a brusque teacher who rarely took time to listen to his students. Brusque* means "abrupt, harsh."

   (B) *caustic* means "bitter, cutting, sardonic"
   (C) *feral* means "wild, savage"
   (D) *notorious* means "infamous"
   (E) *pugnacious* means "belligerent, combative"

6. **The correct answer is (D).** *I had a linguistics professor who said that it's man's ability to use language that makes him the dominant species on the planet. Linguistics* is the study of language.

   (A) *sentimental* means "romantic"
   (B) *gruesome* means "gory"
   (C) *commodious* means "large, spacious, holding a great deal"
   (E) *crepuscular* means "pertaining to twilight"

7. **The correct answer is (E).** *The goldsmith seemed to work by artifice, constructing jewelry with gems that almost seemed to float in the air. Artifice* means "cunning or craftiness." It can also mean "a clever and deceptive trick."

   (A) *cupidity* means "greed; avarice"
   (B) *serendipity* means "accidental good fortune or luck"
   (C) *verisimilitude* means "the appearance of truth"
   (D) *machinations* means "a plot or scheme, especially a wily or deceptive one; ploy; ruse; sham; chicanery"

8. **The correct answer is (A).** *Sad because of the inclement weather, the dog cast a baleful glance at his master. Baleful* means "sorrowful." It can also mean "evil; destructive."

   (B) *vivacious* means "lively, animated, spirited"
   (C) *inchoate* means "just begun; incipient; elementary; rudimentary"
   (D) *indefatigable* means "tireless; inexhaustible; unflagging"
   (E) *nefarious* means "wicked; iniquitous; abominable"

9. **The correct answer is (C).** *The teacher had an unfortunate habit of belaboring a point over and over to make sure her students understood it. Belaboring* means "to repeat, reiterate, or go over again and again, to the point of being tiresome."

   (A) *devouring* means "consuming"
   (B) *castigating* means "to punish, chastise, or criticize severely"
   (D) *assimilating* means "to make part of the whole"
   (E) *proliferating* means "to grow or increase rapidly"

10. **The correct answer is (B).** *The drunken revelers made such a loud fracas that police had to be called. Fracas* is "a loud disturbance, a melee."

    (A) *functionary* means "an official; a person holding an office or position of authority"
    (C) *imbroglio* means "a perplexing situation; entanglement; dilemma."
    (D) *machination* means "a plot or scheme, especially a wily or deceptive one; ploy; ruse; sham; chicanery"
    (E) *obsequies* means "funeral rites"

11. **The correct answer is (A).** *The child's wound was superficial and barely bled; as a result, his mother knew it was an inconsequential injury. Superficial* means "surface"; *inconsequential* means "not important or significant."

    (B) *symbiotic* means "characterized by a mutually beneficial relationship; interdependent"; *indifferent* means "not caring one way or the other"
    (C) *spontaneous* means "unplanned"; *apathetic* means "feeling or showing little emotion"
    (D) *quixotic* means "idealistic but impractical"; *obstinate* means "stubborn"
    (E) *intrepid* means "fearless"; *incumbent* means "required"

12. **The correct answer is (D).** *The critic neither lauded nor derided the director's latest film: she evaluated the film's strengths and weaknesses carefully and fairly.* Lauded means "praised"; *derided* means "ridiculed."

    (A) *aggrandized* means "increase; expand"; *favored* means "prefer"
    (B) *maligned* means "disparaged; defamed"; *criticized* means "condemned; denounced"
    (C) *celebrated* means "honored"; *adapted* means "fashioned to one's own needs"
    (E) *disregarded* means "ignored"; *showcased* means "set off for display"

13. **The correct answer is (B).** *Tragically, so many marshes and wetlands are threatened by agricultural overdevelopment and technological encroachment that they may vanish by the next century.* Threatened means "having an uncertain chance of continued survival"; *vanish* means "to pass quickly from sight; to disappear."

    (A) *sequestered* means "isolating jurors"; *separate* means "to set or keep apart"
    (C) *consumed* means "used up, ate"; *augment* means "to add to; to enlarge"
    (D) *embellished* means "decorated"; *dwindle* means "decline, diminish"
    (E) *rejuvenated* means "restored to youth"; *dissolve* means "to cause to disappear"

14. **The correct answer is (D).** *As a museum archivist who restores ancient documents, Matt Hijing protested an art council policy that resulted in the wholesale destruction of clearly salvageable records.* Destruction means "having destroyed or ruined"; *salvageable* means "can be saved."

    (A) *extermination* means "destruction"; *inconsequential* means "minor, not important"
    (B) *leveling* means "making flat; knocking down"; *derelict* means "neglected"
    (C) *protection* means "support of one that is smaller or weaker"; *venerable* means "esteemed"
    (E) *indemnity* means "compensation, payment"; *grimy* means "dirty"

15. **The correct answer is (B).** *It would be senseless for any aspiring office seeker to irritate such a powerful group of voters.* Senseless means "foolish, stupid"; *irritate* means "to provoke impatience, anger, or displeasure in."

    (A) *intelligent* means "revealing good thought or judgment"; *aggravate* means "to make worse." It is only used in relation to conditions, as in "Wet weather aggravates my bad back." It is not used as a synonym for annoy, as in "He annoys me." (Not "He aggravates me.")
    (C) *astute* means "wise"; *infuriate* means "make very angry"
    (D) *discerning* means "having good judgment"; *provoke* means "annoy"
    (E) *preposterous* means "absurd"; *abet* means "aid, help"

Day 2

Discover the Secret to a High Score on Standardized Vocabulary Tests

Different standardized tests include different types of vocabulary questions, depending on the test's purpose. Sentence completions and vocabulary in context are the most common types. Let's analyze both types of questions now so you can learn the test-taking strategies you need to succeed.

Conquer Sentence Completion Vocabulary Tests

On Day 1, you took a pretest involving sentence completions. This type of vocabulary test question appears on many standardized tests, especially the GED, ACT, SAT, PSAT/NMSQT, and TOEFL. As a result, it is important to know how to approach these test items.

You can often figure out what a new word means by seeing it in *context*, the surrounding words and phrases. That way, you can still get the *gist* (jist) of the conversation or reading, even if you have never seen the word before. Sentence completion questions build on this skill by requiring you to fill in one word or two words that have been removed from a sentence.

What NOT to Do . . .

Don't just plug in answers and choose the one that sounds best. Consider the following sentence completion test item:

Increasingly, the previously _____ sources of disease have now been recognized through current research and analysis.

(A) perspicacious
(B) mysterious
(C) familiar
(D) remarkable
(E) salutary

11

The temptation is strong just to plug in each answer choice and choose the one that seems to fit and that sounds best. If you do this, here's what you'll get:

(A) Increasingly, the previously *perspicacious* sources of disease have now been recognized through current research and analysis. Sounds good, especially if you don't know what "perspicacious" means.

(B) Increasingly, the previously *mysterious* sources of disease have now been recognized through current research and analysis. This sounds good, too.

(C) Increasingly, the previously *familiar* sources of disease have now been recognized through current research and analysis." Nothing wrong here . . . or is there?

(D) Increasingly, the previously *remarkable* sources of disease have now been recognized through current research and analysis. This one sounds just as good as the previous choices.

(E) Increasingly, the previously *salutary* sources of disease have now been recognized through current research and analysis. This also makes perfect sense grammatically, and if you don't know what the word "salutary" means, you've got nothing to go on but sound and grammatical form.

The correct answer is (B). *Increasingly, the previously mysterious sources of disease have now been recognized through current research and analysis.*

(A) *Perspicacious* means "perceptive, keen, acute." This question tests your knowledge of test-worthy words.

(C) *Familiar* does not make sense in context because it is the exact opposite of the meaning you need. If the sources were already "familiar," why would they now "be recognized"?

(D) *Remarkable* is a weak choice because why would sources be "remarkable"? Logic says that most diseases come from the same sources: bacteria, viruses, and poor sanitation.

(E) *Salutary* means "healthy, wholesome." The "previously healthy sources of disease" is illogical. This question obviously tests your knowledge of test-worthy words.

What to Do . . .

If you start by trying to plug in the words that you have been given, you'll waste valuable time and confuse yourself. That's because the test writers are on to this approach. Try the following techniques instead.

To solve a one-blank sentence completion test item, follow these five steps:

1. Cover the answers. Read the sentence and substitute the word *blank* for the blank. Look for links in ideas and clues in the sentence that show how the sentence makes sense when complete.

2. Without looking at the answer choices, predict the word that would best complete the sentence.

3. Read the answer choices. Choose the one that best matches your choice. Use process of elimination to narrow the field. If you are very confused, start with the familiar, easier words and work toward the unfamiliar, difficult words.

4. Check your answers by reading the entire sentence. Rereading the answer you have chosen can help you decide if it makes sense. If not, revise your answer.

5. Use common sense to make sure your answer is logical. If your answer doesn't match what you already know, make another choice.

To solve a two-blank sentence completion test item, follow these five steps:
1. Cover the answers, read the sentence, and focus on the blank that you find easier. Look for hints that point out the word needed to fill in the easier blank.

2. Provide your own answer, without looking at the choices.

3. Look at the answers, pick the one that best matches your word, and fill in the easier blank.

4. Follow the same process for the second blank.

5. Be sure to use process of elimination. As you read the answer choices, knock out the ones that are obviously incorrect.

Ace Critical Reading Tests

Practice is the best way to boost your critical reading comprehension skills, so read every minute you can. "I don't have the time to read," you say. Think about little bits of time that are otherwise wasted. Use the time you spend waiting in line at the bus stop, sitting in the dentist's office, or waiting for class to start. You can use all of these "lost minutes" to read. Fifteen minutes here, 10 minutes there—by the end of the day, it adds up to at least an hour that you can use to sharpen your vocabulary and reading skills by *actually* reading.

Boost Your Vocabulary

When people say "I can't read well," what they often mean is "I get stuck on the hard words." A bigger vocabulary and strong reading skills go hand-in-hand. The more words you know and understand, the more easily you will comprehend what you read. Since reading will be easier, you'll do better on standardized tests, too. When you study words in this book as well as in other sources, mentally arrange them in these three categories:

1. Words you know

These are the words you can *define*. You should know secondary as well as primary definitions. You can comfortably use these words in a sentence, too.

For example:

behemoth (bi-*hee*-muhth; *bee*-uh-muhth)

n. something of monstrous size; a mighty animal:
My neighbor's new car is a behemoth that takes up two parking spaces!

2. Words you think you know

These are words that you have seen before and perhaps even used in conversation and speech. However, you're not exactly sure what they mean. As you read, you usually figure out these words by their *context,* the surrounding words and phrases. As you will learn on Day 3, there are three main types of context clues: *restatement clues* (there's a synonym in the passage), *inferential clues* (you have to "read between the lines" to figure out the meaning), and *contrast clues* (the opposite of the unfamiliar word).

For example:

diligent (*dil*-i-jehnt)

adj. constant effort to accomplish something; done with attention; painstaking:
The diligent student conducted a diligent search of the library for the book.

3. Words you've seen only once or never

On every standardized test, you'll find words that are completely new to you. Try to figure out these words through context clues, roots, suffixes, and prefixes, especially if the words are crucial to meaning. Being an involved reader will greatly increase your grasp of the writer's point as well as the subtle elements of his or her style.

For example:

frugal (*froo*-guhl)

adj. economical, entailing little expense:
The frugal accountant brought her lunch to work every day.

Be an Active Reader

As an active reader, link what you read to what you already know—your *prior knowledge*—to clarify confusing ideas. The process looks like this:

Story Clues + What I Know = Inference

Below are some sample questions you can ask yourself as you read:

- What does this unfamiliar word mean? How can I use prefixes, roots, and suffixes to define the word? How can I use context clues?
- Am I confused because the word has multiple meanings? If so, which meaning is being used here?
- What point is the author making in this passage? Where is the topic sentence or main idea?
- What is the author's purpose? Is it to tell a story? To explain or inform? To persuade? To describe?
- How is this passage organized? How is the text organization linked to the author's purpose?
- Which details in the passage help me visualize or imagine the scene I'm reading?

Be Test-Smart

Standardized tests are similar to classroom tests in many ways, but they have a few significant differences. These differences change the strategies you use. First off, the test items on standardized tests are often arranged from easier to more difficult. As you work through the test, the questions will get more and more challenging. Therefore, you will have to budget your time differently. Spend less time on the first questions and more time on the last questions.

Be prepared not to know everything you'll be asked on a standardized test. You can (and do!) study for a classroom test. As a result, you're able to ace the test because you know the material and test-taking strategies. This is not true with most standardized tests. You can prepare by learning the types of information you can expect, but you can't study the specific material because the content isn't released beforehand. As a result, there will most likely be questions you can't answer. Don't be upset; this is the way the test is designed.

The Question of Guessing

Some tests penalize you for guessing, while others don't. In general, many standardized tests try to discourage guessing by taking off points for incorrect answers. The PSAT/NMSQT, SAT, and SAT Subject Tests penalize you for guessing. On the other hand, most state assessments do not penalize you for guessing.

If there is *no* penalty for guessing, fill in every single answer—even if you have to guess. After all, you have nothing to lose and everything to gain!

If there *is* a penalty for guessing, try to reduce the odds. For example, if every multiple-choice question gives you four possible answers, you have a 25 percent chance of being right (and a 75 percent chance of being wrong) each time you have to guess. But if you can eliminate a single answer, your chance of being correct rises to 33 percent. And if you can get your choices down to two answers, you have a 50 percent chance of being right. Even if there is a penalty for guessing, pick one answer if you can reduce your choices to two. Fifty percent odds are good enough to chance a guess.

Before you give up on any question, always try to eliminate one or more of the answer choices. Remember: the more choices you can eliminate, the better your odds of choosing the right answer.

Dealing with Panic

Panic is a natural reaction to a pressure situation. Nonetheless, panic can prevent you from doing your best on tests, so let's reduce or banish it. Here are some techniques that can help you deal with panic:

Don't panic if some questions seem much harder than others.
They probably are! That's the way the test was designed. This is especially true on standardized tests. Accept this and do the best you can. On standardized tests, you don't have to answer each question to do well. That's because you're not being marked against yourself; rather, you're being judged against all other test takers. They're feeling the same way you are.

Don't panic if you can't get an answer.
Just skip the question and move on. If you have enough time, you can come back to it later. If you run out of time before you can return to it, you were still better off answering more questions than wasting time on a question you didn't know.

Don't panic if you blow the test all out of proportion.
It is true that some tests are more important than others, especially standardized college admission tests. But any test is only one factor in your overall education. Remind yourself that you have been working hard in class and keeping up with all your homework. Keep in mind that how you do on one test will not affect your entire academic career.

Don't panic if you freeze and just can't go on.
If this happens, remind yourself that you have studied and so you are well prepared. Remember that every question you have answered is worth points. Reassure yourself

that you're doing just fine. After all, you are! Stop working and close your eyes. Take two or three deep breaths. Breathe in and out to the count of five. Then, go on with the test.

And remember: A minor case of nerves can actually help you do well on a standardized test because it keeps you alert and focused.

Day 3

Master the Top Ten Tips for Learning (and Remembering) New Words

By opening this book, you've taken an important first step toward mastering the difficult vocabulary words that appear on standardized tests such as the SAT, GED, PSAT/NMSQT, ACT, and TOEFL. That's because this book was designed to give you the vocabulary you need to do your very best on standardized tests.

This book is packed with 100 percent "test-worthy" words. These are the words that the test makers include on standardized exams—especially on exam questions involving sentence completions, analogies, and antonyms, which test vocabulary directly.

To unlock the secret to a wide and useful vocabulary, you need to do more than memorize lists of words. Your goal should be to . . .

- Develop a system that will help you remember the vocabulary words you'll learn; and
- Increase your chances of correctly defining and using many other words that you've yet to encounter on standardized tests and in life.

The following twelve tips (the Top Ten and two bonuses!) can help you develop just such a strategy. Whatever your level of skill, you can benefit from the following time-tested vocabulary techniques. They're easy—and they work.

To get the greatest benefit from this section, read the guidelines several times. Practice them with the vocabulary words provided later in this chapter. Then, use the guidelines as you work your way through this book.

Tip 1: Read

Reading is probably the single best way to improve your vocabulary. When you're preparing for standardized tests, read material that contains words you are most likely to encounter. Possibilities include classic novels such as *Pride and Prejudice* by Jane Austen, *A Tale of Two Cities* by Charles Dickens, and *The Sound and The Fury* by William Faulkner.

Don't have the time or inclination to read? All is not lost. In this chapter, you'll learn some effective and enjoyable ways to increase the number of test-worthy words you know.

Tip 2: Use a Dictionary and a Thesaurus

If you're serious about improving your test-worthy vocabulary, you must have (and use!) a good dictionary. (A good thesaurus also helps a lot, but more on that later.)

A dictionary entry always includes the following components:

- Spelling
- Pronunciation
- Part(s) of speech
- Irregular forms of the word
- Definition
- Etymology (the derivation and development of words).

An entry may also contain synonyms and antonyms of the word; prefixes, suffixes, and other elements in word formation; and abbreviations.

An *abridged* dictionary contains only the most common words that people use every day. These are the dictionaries you'll use in your daily life. An *unabridged* dictionary contains all the words in English. Unabridged dictionaries come in many volumes, like a set of encyclopedias.

Most people think that all dictionaries are the same. After all, all dictionaries are chock full of words listed in alphabetical order. They all have pronunciation guides, word definitions, and word histories. However, all dictionaries are *not* the same. Different types of dictionaries fit different needs.

For example, some dictionaries have been written just for scholars. The most famous scholarly dictionary is *The Oxford English Dictionary (OED)*. An unabridged dictionary, *OED* contains more than 500,000 entries. Don't rush right out to buy one to stash in your bookcase, however, because *OED* now contains about 60 million words in twenty volumes.

Dictionaries also have been created just for adults, college students, high school students, and elementary school students. The following list includes the bestselling general dictionaries and the Web addresses for the online versions, when available:

- *The American Heritage Dictionary of the English Language* (Houghton Mifflin Co.: www.bartleby.com/61)
- *Merriam-Webster's Collegiate Dictionary* (Merriam-Webster, Inc.: www.m-w.com/dictionary.htm)
- *Merriam-Webster's Pocket Dictionary* (Merriam-Webster, Inc.)
- *The New Shorter Oxford English Dictionary* (Oxford University Press, Inc.)
- *The Random House College Dictionary* (Random House, Inc.)
- *Webster's New World College Dictionary* (Hungry Minds, Inc.)

Which dictionary should you purchase and use? Since more than 30,000 dictionaries are currently offered for sale online, you've got some shopping to do. Here's what you need:

- A dictionary that contains all the words that you are likely to encounter on standardized tests. This will most likely be the same dictionary that you can use in school, in your personal life, and in your professional life.

- A dictionary that explains the words in terms you can understand.

- A dictionary in a size that fits your needs. You might wish to buy a hardbound dictionary to use at home when you study and a smaller paperback to keep in your backpack or briefcase for immediate reference.

An online dictionary can't fulfill all your needs, unless you like to tote around your laptop all the time. Always have a print dictionary to use—even if you like to use an online version.

When you're trying to find a word in the dictionary, always begin by making an educated guess as to its spelling. The odds are in your favor. However, the more spelling patterns you know for a sound, the better your chances for finding the word quickly. You can find a pronunciation chart in the beginning of any dictionary. Once you've narrowed down your search and you're flipping through the pages, use the *guide words*, located on the upper corners of the pages, to guide your search. Then, follow strict alphabetical order.

The following diagram shows how to read a sample entry.

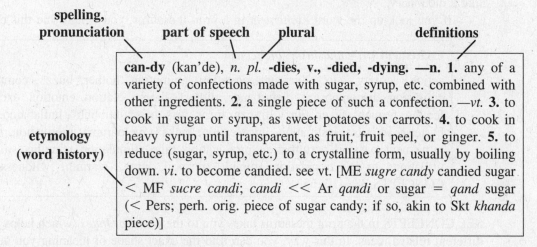

Let's look a little closer at the entry:

- Notice the pronunciation comes right after the entry word. It's in parentheses—(kan'de).

- The part of speech is indicated by the **n.** It's an abbreviation for "noun." Look at the third entry. The **vt.** right before the 3. shows that the word can be used as a transitive verb (a verb that must be followed by a direct object). The **vi.** at the end of the fifth entry shows that the word can also be used as an intransitive verb (a verb that does not need a direct object to make sense in a sentence).

- The **pl.** at the beginning of the entry shows how you can make the word plural. Here, the singular "candy" becomes the plural "candies."

- The definitions follow the plural forms of the word. The word "candy" has several different meanings. They are arranged by the part of speech: the first definitions show what "candy" means when used as a noun; the second group shows what "candy" means when used as a verb.

- The information at the very end of the entry is the etymology or history of the word. This shows how the word was formed and came into English.

A *thesaurus* is a reference book that contains synonyms and antonyms. The word *thesaurus* comes from a Greek word that means "collection" or "treasure." A thesaurus is especially helpful when you're trying to express an idea but you don't know how to phrase it. It is also a helpful reference book when you are trying to find a better word than the one you've been using. This helps you state exact shades of meaning rather than approximations. As a result, your vocabulary increases by heaps and heaps of words. This is clearly a big advantage when it comes to preparing for a standardized test.

In a thesaurus, words with similar meanings are grouped together. To find a synonym for a word in a traditional print thesaurus, you must use the index at the back of the book. However, new editions and online versions of a thesaurus are arranged in alphabetical order like a dictionary.

If you look up the word *excitement* in a print thesaurus, you would find this entry:

---

excitement [*n*] *enthusiasm; incitement*

action, activity, ado, adventure, agitation, animation, bother, buzz*, commotion, confusion, discomposure, disturbance, dither*, drama, elation, emotion, excitation, feeling, ferment, fever, flurry, frenzy, furor, fuss, heat*, hubbub*, hullabaloo, hurry, hysteria, impulse, instigation, intoxication, kicks*, melodrama, motivation, motive, movement, passion, perturbation, provocation, rage, stimulation, stimulus, stir, thrill, titillation, to-do, trepidation, tumult, turmoil, urge, warmth, wildness. SEE CONCEPTS 38, 410, 633.

SEE CONCEPTS in the print thesaurus takes you to the *Concept Index,* which helps you link different related ideas. In this way, you can find the exact shade of meaning you need. Use the key in the beginning of the print thesaurus to understand different symbols. In this entry, for example, the * shows that a word is colloquial or the slang level of usage.

Online thesaurus programs are especially useful for distinguishing among homonyms. If you intended to type "*whether*" but instead keyboarded "*weather*," the thesaurus will give you synonyms like *atmospheric conditions, climate, meteorology,* and *the elements.* This can help you keep your homonyms straight.

Both the print thesaurus and the online thesaurus will unquestionably help you beef up your vocabulary; however, in general, the print thesaurus will offer you more options. That's because the print versions have more words in them. Chances are, even if you like using an online version, you will need to use a print thesaurus when your writing requires a wider variety of word choices.

Tip 3: Pronounce Words Correctly

Knowing the meaning of a word is only half the battle; you also have to know how to pronounce it. It's astonishing how many words are misunderstood simply because they are mispronounced. Words get mangled in surprisingly inventive ways. For example, people often switch letters. For example, *abhor* (hate) becomes uh-*bor* rather than ab-*hor*.

People have also been known to drop letters. For instance, the food poisoning known as *salmonella* is correctly pronounced sal-muh-*nel*-uh. Dropping the *l* results in sam-uh-*nel*-uh.

The pronunciation problem is especially acute with words that can function as more than one part of speech. The word *ally* is a case in point. As a noun, it's pronounced *al*-eye. As a verb, it's pronounced uh-*leye*.

In addition, people often insert an extra letter or two, which can make the word unrecognizable. For instance, *ambidextrous* (able to use either hand) has four syllables and is correctly pronounced am-bi-*deks*-trus. But sometimes speakers add an extra syllable to get am-bi-*deks*-tree-us or am-bi-*deks*-tru-us.

Even the lowly word *picture* can get warped as *pitcher*. As a result, no one knows what anyone else is talking about. Incorrect pronunciations can make it impossible to define the word, too.

The most effective way to learn how to pronounce new words is by using a dictionary. Get a reliable desk or pocket dictionary. It's the best source for the words you need to get you where you want to go.

How well do you pronounce test-worthy words? Take the following self-test to see. Cover the third column with a piece of paper. Then read each word and its definition. Pronounce each word. Last, check the third column to see how well you did.

Word	Meaning	Pronunciation
Amish	Pennsylvania Dutch	*ah*-mish
aplomb	assurance	uh-*plahm*
awry	wrong, crooked	uh-*ry*
banquet	feast	*bang*-kwit
buffet	self-service meal	buh-*fay*
buoy	floating marker	*boo*-ee
Celtic	Irish	*kel*-tik
denouement	conclusion	day-*noo*-mah
entrepreneur	businessperson	ahn-truh-pruh-*nur*
fracas	noisy fight	*fray*-kis
hegemony	leadership	hi-*jem*-uh-nee
insouciant	carefree	in-*soo*-see-int
khaki	light brown	*kak*-ee
larynx	voice box	*lar*-inks
mausoleum	tomb	maw-suh-*lee*-um
niche	corner	*nich* (rhymes with "itch")
penchant	inclination	*pen*-chint

Pronounce Words Correctly—*continued*

Word	Meaning	Pronunciation
posthumous	after death	*pahs*-chuu-mus
quagmire	swamp	*kwag*-myr
remuneration	payment	ri-myoo-nuh-*ray*-shin
shallot	onion	*shal*-it or shuh-*laht*
toupee	hairpiece	too-*pay*
vehement	fiery, passionate	*vee*-uh-mint
verbiage	wordy	*vur*-bee-ij
worsted	yarn	*wuus*-tid

Tip 4: Use Word Cards

One of the most effective ways to make a word your own is through repetition. Going over the word can help you master its meaning as well as its pronunciation and usage. Try this idea: buy a stack of 3 × 5 index cards.

As you read through the following chapters, write each difficult test-worthy word on the front of an index card, one word per card. Then, write the definition on the back. Here's a sample:

FRONT:

matriarch

BACK:

the female head of
a family or tribe

We've already done some for you—turn to the back of the book. Study the cards every chance you get. Take them with you on the bus, train, or plane; hide them in your lap and sneak a peek during dull meetings. Be sure to rotate the cards so you learn many different words. Also, turn to the back of this book. We've gotten you started with 216 vocab words.

Word games are another great way to learn test-worthy words. There are lots of games and puzzles in this book to help you out, but why not add Scrabble® and Boggle™ to your repertoire?

Tip 5: Learn Synonyms and Antonyms

Synonyms are words that are nearly the same in meaning as other words. *Antonyms* are words that are opposites. Learning different synonyms and antonyms can help swell your vocabulary. Go ahead and try it now.

Complete the following chart by writing at least one synonym and antonym for each word. Then, see how many more synonyms and antonyms you can brainstorm. The answers appear on page 33.

Word	Synonyms	Antonyms
1. adapt		
2. authentic		
3. chronic		
4. conquer		
5. frustrate		
6. indulge		
7. naïve		
8. punish		
9. relinquish		
10. sullen		

Seventh-Inning Stretch: Word-Definition Match

Take a stretch by completing this easy quiz. Just match each of the twenty vocabulary words with its definition. Write the letter of the definition in the space provided by each word. Use the techniques you learned so far in this chapter as you complete the exercise below. The answers appear on page 33.

_____	1. inalienable	a.	mistakes
_____	2. crotchety	b.	academic
_____	3. lumbering	c.	thinking
_____	4. hinterlands	d.	not to be taken away
_____	5. endemic	e.	grind
_____	6. kiosk	f.	to give in
_____	7. distraught	g.	left unplanted
_____	8. macerate	h.	moving in a clumsy way
_____	9. cognition	i.	sober, self-restraining
_____	10. abstemious	j.	greatly upset
_____	11. didactic	k.	grouchy
_____	12. capitulate	l.	common in a particular area
_____	13. decadence	m.	decline
_____	14. winsome	n.	great many
_____	15. turbid	o.	lacking firmness
_____	16. myriad	p.	region remote from cities
_____	17. loath	q.	murky
_____	18. fallow	r.	unwilling
_____	19. errata	s.	magazine stand
_____	20. flaccid	t.	charming

Tip 6: Understand a Word's Unstated Meanings

Every word has a *denotation,* its dictionary meaning. In addition, some words have *connotations,* their understood meanings or emotional overtones. For example, both *house* and *home* have the same denotation, a shelter. *Home,* however, carries a connotation of warmth and love not present in *house.*

Slight differences in connotative meaning are important for precise speech and writing. For example, do you *adore, cherish, have affection for, worship, revere, treasure, esteem, honor,* or *prize* your latest sweetie? All these words are synonyms for "love," but I think you'll agree that there's a world of understood difference between saying "I love you" and "I worship you."

Let's take the opposite of love, *hate.* Do you *abhor, despise, scorn, abominate, curse, despise, condemn, shun,* or *spurn* your most bitter foe? *Cursing* is not the same as *shunning* because the former involves foul words, while the latter is silent. Likewise, *scorning* is not the same as *condemning.*

Check out your understanding of connotation and denotation by completing the following chart. Write a plus sign (+) next to any word with a positive connotation and a dash (−) next to any word with a negative connotation. The answers appear on page 33.

Word	Connotation	Word	Connotation
1. emaciated	_____	6. steadfast	_____
2. slender	_____	7. reckless	_____
3. cheap	_____	8. bold	_____
4. thrifty	_____	9. obstinate	_____
5. stubborn	_____	10. constant	_____

Incorporate new words into everyday conversation. Use new words as you converse with friends. As you do so, pause to explain what the word means, and ask your friend if he or she knows any similar or contrary words. You're bound to discover even more test-worthy words this way!

Tip 7: Use Word Parts

A surprisingly large number of words can be divided into parts that you can figure out easily. If you can define the parts, then you can often decode the entire word. This is a crucial skill on standardized tests, when you're under time constraints.

There are three main word parts to know: *prefixes, roots,* and *suffixes*.

- A *prefix* is a letter or a group of letters placed at the beginning of a word to change its meaning. Prefixes are covered in depth in Day 4.

- A *root* is a base or stem form of many words. Roots are covered in depth in Day 5.

- A *suffix* is a letter or a group of letters placed at the end of a word to change its meaning. Suffixes are covered in depth in Day 6.

For example, if you know the Latin root *ami* means "like" or "love," you can easily figure out that *amiable* means "pleasant and friendly." Similarly, you could deduce that *amorous* means "loving." Even if you can't define a word exactly, recognizing the different parts of the word will give you a general idea of the word's meaning.

Tip 8: Use Mnemonics

Mnemonics are memory tricks that help you remember everything from the order of the planets to your grocery list. Mnemonics are another technique you can use to help you distinguish between easily confused words. For example, to remember that *principal* means "main" (as in the principal of a school), look at the last three letters: the *principal* is your *pal*. To remember that *principle* means "rule," remember that both words end in *le*.

Likewise, *stationary* means "standing still" (both *stationary* and *standing* contain an "a") while *stationery* is paper used for writing letters (both *stationery* and *letter* contain "er"). *Desert* and *dessert* become easier to define when you remember that *dessert* has a double "s," like *strawberry shortcake,* or you could remember that *dessert* is *double*-delicious!

Create your own mnemonics to help you remember the easily confused words that you are most likely to encounter on standardized tests.

Tip 9: Use Context Clues

When you take standardized tests, you'll be expected to define unfamiliar words. You can often get clues to the meaning of unfamiliar words by the information surrounding the word, its *context*. When you use *context* and *context clues,* you interpret a word's specific meaning by examining its relationship to other words in the sentence. To figure out the meaning of the unfamiliar word, you make inferences based on what you already know and the details that you are given in the sentence or paragraph. Here's an example:

> Just after midnight on April 15, 1912, one of the most dramatic and famous of all maritime disasters occurred, the sinking of the *Titanic*. The *Titanic* was the most luxurious ship afloat at the time, with its beautifully decorated staterooms, glittering crystal chandeliers, and elaborate food service.

How can you figure out that *maritime* must mean "related to the sea, nautical"? Use clues:

What you already know   The *Titanic* was an ocean liner.

Sentence details   "The *Titanic* was the most luxurious ship afloat . . ."

Try it yourself by defining *futile* as it is used in the following passage:

The "unsinkable" *Titanic* vanished under the water at 2:20 a.m., April 15. There were about 2,200 passengers aboard, and all but about 700 died. The tragedy was made even worse by the crew's futile rescue attempts. Since there were not enough lifeboats, hundreds of people died who could have survived.

Context clues come in different forms. The most common types of context clues include:

- Restatement context clues
- Inferential context clues
- Contrast context clues

Let's look at each type.

Restatement Context Clues

Here's how one writer defined the word *levee* right in the passage:

The Army Corps of Engineers distributed 26 million plastic bags throughout the region. Volunteers filled each bag with 35 pounds of sand and then stacked them to create *levees,* makeshift barriers against the floodwaters.

Right after the word *levee*, readers get the definition: "makeshift barriers against the floodwaters."

You can also use an entire passage to get a general sense of difficult words. For example, define *epidemic* as it is used in the following sentence: "Nearly 40 million Americans are overweight; obesity has become an *epidemic*." Since the sentence describes the epidemic as affecting "40 million people," odds are good that *epidemic* means "something that happens to a large group of people." Sometimes you won't be able to pinpoint the precise meaning. Here, for instance, you might infer that an *epidemic* indicates a widespread threat, but you might miss the subtle connection between epidemic and disease. Nonetheless, this clue might be just enough to help you define a new word that you encounter on a standardized test.

Each of the following sentences contains a restatement context clue. The unfamiliar word is in italics. Write the definition on the line next to each sentence. The answers appear on page 34.

1. Fatty deposits on artery walls combine with calcium compounds to cause *arteriosclerosis,* hardening of the arteries. _____

2. The upper part of the heart, the left *atrium,* receives blood returning from circulation.

    _____

3. In many Native American tribes, the *shaman,* or medicine man, acted as a ceremonial priest. _____

4. I believe that life is short, so we should eat what we enjoy. As a result, I consume mass quantities of *confectioneries*, candies, and keep my dentist on retainer.

    _____

5. She jumped into the *fray* and enjoyed every minute of the fight.

    _____

6. As with all electric *currents* or discharges, lightning will follow the *path of least resistance*. This means that it will take the route that is easiest for it to travel on.

    _____

    _____

7. Many settlers on the vast American plains in the late nineteenth century used *sod*, or earth, as a building material for their houses. _____

8. Then, arrange a handful of *mulch*, dead leaves, on the top of the soil. _____

9. Born in 1831, John Styth Pemberton was a *pharmacist*, a person licensed to dispense drugs and medicines, who moved to Atlanta, Georgia, in 1869.

    _____

10. To make a living, he created so-called *patent medicines,* homemade medicines that were sold without a prescription. _____

Inferential Context Clues

As you have just read, sometimes the unfamiliar word may be defined right in the text. At other times, however, you will have to *infer* the meaning from what you already know and from details you heard or read. This takes a bit of detective work.

When you *make an inference*, you combine what you already know with spoken or textual clues to discover the unstated information. You may have heard this referred to as "reading between the lines" or "putting two and two together." In graphical form, the process of making an inference looks like this:

Text Clues + What I Know = Inference

Try the following example:

In 1862, in order to support the Civil War effort, Congress enacted the nation's first income tax law. It was a <u>forerunner</u> of our modern income tax in that it was based on the principles of graduated, or progressive, taxation and of withholding income at the source.

Context Clue	+	What I Know	=	Inference
It was a *forerunner*	+	*fore* means "before" or "precede"	=	forerunner means "before"

Contrast Context Clues

You can also figure out an unknown word when an opposite or contrast is presented. When you do this, you're making an inference. For example, you can define *literal* by finding its contrast in the sentence:

> It is hard to use *literal* language when talking about nature because people tend to talk about nature using figurative language.

Literal language must be the opposite of "figurative language." If you know that figurative language is words and expressions not meant to be taken at face value, you can infer that "literal" must mean *the strict or exact meaning*. Other synonyms would include *verbatim* or *word-for-word*.

Use contrast clues to infer the meaning of *menace* in the following sentence:

> I was afraid that my mother-in-law would be a <u>menace</u> to our already cranky family, but she turned out to be a great peacemaker.

Menace means "threat." You can infer this from the contrast between "menace" and "peacemaker."

The following words express contrast. Watch for them as you read passages on standardized tests.

Expressions That Show Contrast			
but	conversely	however	in contrast
on the other hand	still	nevertheless	yet

Since using context is such an important way to define unfamiliar words on standardized tests, you'll want some additional practice to help you master this critical skill. Use all the different types of context clues as you decode these unfamiliar words in italics. The answers appear on page 34.

> Most natural hazards can be detected before their threat matures. But *seisms* (from the Greek *seismos*, earthquake) have no known *precursors*, so they come without warning, like the *vengeance* of an ancient warrior. For this reason, they continue to kill in some areas at a level usually reserved for wars and epidemics—the 11,000 deaths in northeastern Iran occurred on August 31, 1968, not in the ancient past. Nor is the horror of the *lethal* earthquake completed with the heavy death toll. The homeless are left to cope with fire, looting, *pestilence*, fear, and the burden of rebuilding what the planet so easily shrugs away.

Word	Pronunciation	Definition
seisms	*si*-zums	
precursors	pree-*ker*-sers	
vengeance	*ven*-jens	
lethal	*lee*-thal	
pestilence	*pes*-til-ens	

The film industry *metamorphosed* from silent films to the "talkies," after the success in 1927 of *The Jazz Singer*. Mickey Mouse was one of the few "stars" who made a smooth *transition* from silent films to talkies with his 1928 cartoon *Steamboat Willie*. Within a year, hundreds of Mickey Mouse clubs had sprung up all across the United States. By 1931, more than a million people belonged to a Mickey Mouse club. The *phenomenon* was not confined to America. In London, Madame Tussaud's *illustrious* wax museum placed a wax figure of Mickey alongside its statues of other *eminent* film stars. In 1933, according to Disney Studios, Mickey received 800,000 fan letters—an average of more than 2,000 letters a day. To date, no "star" has ever received as much fan mail as Mickey Mouse.

Word	Pronunciation	Definition
metamorphosis	meh-tah-*mor*-foh-sis	
transition	tran-*sih*-shun	
phenomenon	fee-*nohm*-ih-nan	
illustrious	ih-*lus*-tree-us	
eminent	*eh*-min-ent	

A worldwide *economic* Depression in the 1930s left many people unemployed. One such person was Charles Darrow of Philadelphia, Pennsylvania, who had lost his job as a heating engineer. To try to make a living, Darrow invented a board game he called "Monopoly." *Initially*, Darrow tried to sell his idea to the leading game manufacturer in America, but Parker Brothers turned the game down because it felt the game was too *elaborate* to play. In *desperation*, Darrow used his own money to have 5,000 games made by a small company. He sold the games himself, and the *craze* spread. Seeing the success of the game, Parker Brothers changed its mind and purchased the game for manufacturing and distribution. In 1975, twice as much Monopoly money was printed in the United States as real money. All told, nearly 100 million Monopoly sets have been sold since 1935.

Word	Pronunciation	Definition
economic	ek-oh-*nah*-mihk	
initially	in-*ih*-shull-ee	
elaborate	ee-*lah*-bor-ayt	
desperation	dehs-per-*ay*-shun	
craze	crayz	

Context clues are especially crucial when you encounter words with more than one meaning. The word *favor,* for example, has many different meanings. Here are six of them: *a kind act, friendly regard, being approved, a gift, to support,* and *to resemble.*

When you read, you often come across a word that you think you know but that doesn't make sense in the sentence you're reading. That's your clue that the word has more than one meaning. In this case, you must choose the meaning that fits the context.

Follow these three simple steps:

1. Read the sentence and find the word with multiple meanings.

2. Look for context clues that tell you which meaning of the word fits.

3. Substitute a synonym for the word and see if it makes sense. If not, try another meaning for the word. Continue until you find the right meaning.

For example: Nico was <u>resigned</u> to working overtime on Friday night.

1. *Resigned* has multiple meanings. *Resigned* means "quitting a job." It also means "giving in unhappily but without resistance."

2. Since Nico is working overtime, he is not quitting his job. Therefore, the second meaning of *resigned* should fit.

3. Using the synonym *agreeable* for *resigned*: Nico was <u>agreeable</u> to working overtime on Friday night. The sentence makes sense, so you have found the correct meaning for *resigned.*

Here are some examples of multiple-meaning words:

Word	Example	Meaning	Example	Meaning
address	home <u>address</u>	residence	graduation <u>address</u>	speech
game	play a <u>game</u>	sport	have a <u>game</u> leg	injured
catholic	<u>catholic</u> tastes	universal, wide	<u>Catholic</u> religion	of the Roman church
rash	have a <u>rash</u>	skin problem	<u>rash</u> action	hasty

Tip 10: Learn Word Histories

In the 1600s, people believed that toads were poisonous, and anyone who mistakenly ate a toad's leg instead of a frog's leg would die. Rather than swearing off frogs' legs, people sought a cure for the "fatal" food poisoning. Performing in public, "quack" healers would sometimes hire an accomplice who would pretend to eat a toad, at which point his employer would whip out an instant remedy and "save" his helper's life. For his duties, the helper came to be called a "toad-eater." Since anyone who would consume anything as disgusting as a live toad must be completely under his master's thumb, "toad-eater" or "toady" became the term for a bootlicking, fawning flatterer.

And that's how the word *toady* came to be. English is a living language. From its Germanic beginnings, English absorbed influences from a wide variety of sources, including classical Greek and Latin to Italian, French, Spanish, and Arabic languages. English continues to absorb new words as our culture changes. In addition, a significant part of our vocabulary is artificially created to meet new situations. Exploring the history of these words, their *etymology*, can help you learn many useful everyday words.

And Two Bonus Tips . . .

Tip 11: Vocalize as You Learn

Saying words aloud or hearing somebody else say them helps you to recall them later. Try reading sample sentences and definitions aloud as well.

Tip 12: Review, Review, Review

It's not enough to "learn" a word once. Unless you review it, the word will soon vanish from your memory banks. This book is packed with quizzes and word games to help refresh your memory.

Answers and Explanations

Synonyms and Antonyms (page 23)

(Possible answers)

Word	Synonyms	Antonyms
1. adapt	adjust, accustom, accommodate	disarrange, dislocate
2. authentic	genuine, real, legitimate	fake, counterfeit, bogus, imitation
3. chronic	habitual, ongoing, constant	one time, single
4. conquer	defeat, vanquish, overwhelm	surrender, yield, forfeit, give up
5. frustrate	baffle, beat, disappoint	facilitate, encourage
6. indulge	tolerate, humor, allow, permit	prohibit, deter, restrain, enjoin
7. naïve	innocent, ingenuous	worldly, urbane, suave
8. punish	discipline, castigate	reward, compensate, remunerate
9. relinquish	quit, renounce	perpetuate, keep
10. sullen	irritable, morose, moody	cheerful, jolly, blithe, happy

Word-Definition Match (page 24)

1. d	6. s	11. b	16. n
2. k	7. j	12. f	17. r
3. h	8. e	13. m	18. g
4. p	9. c	14. t	19. a
5. l	10. i	15. q	20. o

Word Connotations (page 25)

All the even-numbered words have a positive connotation; all the odd-numbered words have a negative connotation—even though the word pairs have basically the same denotations.

Here are some additional examples to swell your vocabulary even more:

Denotation	Positive Connotation	Negative Connotation
confused	puzzled	flustered
without a friend	friendless	reclusive
raw	unrefined	crude
inexperienced	trusting	naïve (ny-*eev*)
fat	plump	obese
underfed	slim	emaciated (ee-*may*-she-ay-tid)
courteous	polite	groveling
civil	considerate	obsequious (ob-*see*-kwe-us)
bent	curved	warped
minor	not significant	petty

Restatement Context Clues (pages 27–28)

1. *Arteriosclerosis* means "hardening of the arteries."

2. *Atrium* means "the upper part of the heart."

3. *Shaman* means "medicine man."

4. *Confectioneries* means "candies."

5. *Fray* means "fight."

6. *Current* means "discharges," and *the path of least resistance* means "the route that is easiest for it to travel on."

7. *Sod* means "earth."

8. *Mulch* means "dead leaves."

9. *Pharmacist* means "a person licensed to dispense drugs."

10. *Patent medicines* means "homemade medicines that were sold without a prescription."

Contrast Context Clues (pages 29–30)

Word	Pronunciation	Definition
seisms	*si*-zums	earthquakes
precursors	pre-*ker*-sers	warnings, forerunners
vengeance	*ven*-jens	revenge, retribution
lethal	*lee*-thal	deadly
pestilence	*pes*-til-ens	a deadly and widespread disease, like the plague

Word	Pronunciation	Definition
metamorphosis	meh-tah-*mor*-foh-sis	change
transition	tran-*sih*-shun	development
phenomenon	fee-*nohm*-ih-nan	event, occurrence
illustrious	ih-*lus*-tree-us	distinguished, celebrated
eminent	*eh*-min-ent	famous

Word	Pronunciation	Definition
economic	ek-oh-*nah*-mihk	having to do with money
initially	in-*ih*-shull-ee	at first
elaborate	ee-*lah*-bor-ayt	complicated
desperation	dehs-per-*ay*-shun	frantically
craze	crayz	fad, fashion

Part II

Find Out That New Words Equal the Sum of Their Parts

Day 4:
Study Prefixes

Day 5:
Branch Out with Word Roots

Day 6:
Master Suffixes

Day 4

Study Prefixes

A *prefix* is a letter or a group of letters placed at the beginning of a word to change the word's meaning. For example, the prefix *in* means "not." Therefore, *inappropriate* means "not appropriate." *Insolvent* means "not solvent" or bankrupt; *insatiable* means "not able to be fully satisfied." (To *sate* or *satiate* is a verb that means "to satisfy fully.")

Knowing common prefixes is a *very* useful skill because it enables you to figure out the meaning of many unfamiliar words. In addition, by discovering the building blocks of words, you easily can master thousands of test-worthy words.

How Prefixes Work

1. Prefixes Are Added to the Front of Roots to Create Many Words.

As just stated, prefixes are placed at the beginning of a word to change its meaning. Therefore, knowing just a handful of prefixes can make it easy for you to figure out many words—without ever having to use a dictionary. Here are some examples with the prefix *re*, which means "to do again."

Prefix +	Root =	Word	Definition
re-	absorb	reabsorb	absorb again
re-	acquaint	reacquaint	meet again
re-	qualify	requalify	qualify again
re-	admit	readmit	admit again
re-	allocate	reallocate	allocate again
re-	appear	reappear	appear again
re-	arrange	rearrange	change the arrangement
re-	attach	reattach	attach again
re-	fasten	refasten	fasten again
re-	copy	recopy	copy again

2. Prefixes Are Most Often Attached to Words Without a Break.

Even though you may have seen the prefix written with a hyphen (as in *pre-*, *re-*, *de-*), the prefix is attached seamlessly. The following chart shows some examples:

Prefix +	Root =	Word	Definition
dis-	inter	disinter	to unearth
dis-	credit	discredit	to cause to be doubted
extra-	terrestrial	extraterrestrial	alien (not of this place)
in-	tractable	intractable	hard to handle; unmanageable
mal-	content	malcontent	a dissatisfied person
multi-	faceted	multifaceted	having many sides or aspects
multi-	form	multiform	having many different forms
phil-	harmonic	philharmonic	fond of music

The word *prefix* is made up of the Latin prefix *prae*, which means "before," and the root word *fix*, which means "firmly placed." It takes a prefix to describe *prefix*!

3. Prefixes Are Different Lengths.

Prefixes can be as short as one letter or as long as six letters. The following chart shows some examples:

Number of Letters	Prefix	Sample Words	Meaning
One-Letter Prefix	a-	amoral	not moral
Two-Letter Prefix	co-	cohabit	live together
Three-Letter Prefix	pre-	premature	before becoming mature
Four-Letter Prefix	para-	paragraph	subsection of a writing
Five-Letter Prefix	tract-	tractile	ductile; able to be drawn out
Six-Letter Prefix	circum-	circumlocution	a roundabout way of speaking

4. Prefixes Can Have More Than One Meaning.

For example, the Latin prefix *in-* can mean "in" (as in *inhabit*), but it can also mean "not" (as in *inhuman*). As a result, knowing a prefix will take you only so far in defining test-worthy words. You'll also have to use context clues to check meaning.

Here are some examples of Latin prefixes that have more than one meaning:

Prefix	Meaning	Examples
in-	in, into	inhabit
in-	not	inflexible
il-	in, into	illuminate
il-	not	illiterate
im-	in, into	import
im-	not	immodest
ir-	in, into	irradiate
ir-	not	irregular

5. Prefixes Can Have More Than One Spelling.

For instance, the prefix for "together" can be spelled *syn-* or *sym-*. The prefix for "apart" can be spelled *dis-*, *di-*, and *dif-*. Ignore these minor variations because the prefix still has the same meaning.

Time for Fun: Word-Find Puzzle

Time for a break. There are fifteen words hidden in this word-find puzzle. (See the word list below.) Ten words have already been covered in this chapter, but five are new. To complete the puzzle, locate and circle all the words. The words may be written forward, backward, or upside down. The answers appear on page 53. Good luck!

```
r  e  a  b  s  o  r  b  x  b  i  g  d  n
e  c  t  n  e  t  n  o  c  l  a  m  e  g
a  m  o  r  a  l  l  d  i  c  u  l  m  i
c  o  h  a  b  i  t  r  a  b  i  d  e  l
q  c  o  l  l  o  q  u  i  a  l  d  n  a
u  q  r  e  t  n  i  s  i  d  o  l  t  m
a  b  t  i  d  e  r  c  s  i  d  l  i  q
i  n  t  r  a  c  t  a  b  l  e  z  a  l
n  g  i  m  r  o  f  i  t  l  u  m  q  q
t  r  a  c  t  i  l  e  d  e  l  u  d  e
```

Word List

1. **multiform:** having many different forms
2. **cohabit:** live together
3. **intractable:** hard to handle; unmanageable
4. **disinter:** to unearth
5. **reacquaint:** meet again
6. **malcontent:** a dissatisfied person
7. **amoral:** not moral
8. **tractile:** ductile; able to be drawn out
9. **reabsorb:** absorb again
10. **discredit:** to cause to be doubted
11. **colloquial:** informal, as in conversation or writing
12. **lucid:** clear; bright
13. **delude:** to deceive
14. **malign:** to speak badly of another with the intent to harm
15. **dementia:** a loss of mental abilities or powers

Learn Test-worthy Words with Greek Prefixes

Ten Useful Greek Prefixes

Many important test-worthy words have Greek prefixes. Knowing these prefixes can help you decode and define many important words. Below are ten Greek prefixes that can help you do your best on standardized tests.

Prefix	Meaning	Examples	Definition
a-	not, without	atypical	not typical
		asymmetrical	not even
anthrop-	human	anthropology	study of humans
		anthropoid	resembling humans
anti-	against	antipathy	hatred
		antisocial	unfriendly; misanthropic
aster-/astro-	star	asteroid (*as*-ter-oid)	star-like body
		astrology	study of influence of stars on people
auto-	self	autocracy	government by absolute monarch
		automate	operate without people
biblio-	book	bibliophile (*bib*-lee-oh-file)	book lover
		bibliography (bib-lee-*ah*-graf-ee)	list of books
bio-	life	biography	person's life story
		biofeedback	controlling bodily functions
chrom-	color	chromophil	staining readily with dyes
		chromatics	the science of colors
chron-	time	chronological	time order
		chronicle	history
cosmo-	universe; world	cosmology	study of the physical universe
		cosmonaut	a Russian astronaut

It's Your Turn: Ten Useful Greek Prefixes

Take a break and test yourself by completing the following chart. For each word, first write the prefix and its meaning. Then, use what you learned about prefixes to define each word. Feel free to look back at the ten prefixes you just learned. The answers appear on page 53.

Word	Prefix	Meaning	Word Meaning
1. anemia	_____	_____	_____
2. anthropoid	_____	_____	_____
3. antidote	_____	_____	_____
4. asterisk	_____	_____	_____
5. astronaut	_____	_____	_____
6. autonomous	_____	_____	_____
7. autonomy	_____	_____	_____
8. automation	_____	_____	_____
9. autopsy	_____	_____	_____
10. bibliophile	_____	_____	_____
11. biodegradable	_____	_____	_____
12. biopsy	_____	_____	_____
13. chronometer	_____	_____	_____
14. cosmos	_____	_____	_____
15. chronograph	_____	_____	_____

Ten More Greek Prefixes

Below are ten more prefixes that have made their way from ancient Greek to modern English. Read through the prefixes, meanings, and examples. Pause after each row to see how many other words you can brainstorm that start with the same prefix.

Prefix	Meaning	Examples	Definition
dem-	people	epidemic (eh-pih-*dem*-ik)	among the people
eu-	good	eulogize (*yoo*-low-jize)	speak well of someone (funeral speech)
gee-, geo-	earth	geography	writing about Earth
hydro-	water	hydrophobia (hi-dro-*fo*-bee-uh)	fear of water
hyper-	over	hypercritical	overly critical
hypo-	under	hypodermic	under the skin
micro-	small	microscope	tool for looking at small objects
mis-	hate	misanthropy (mis-*an*-throw-pee)	hatred of people
mono-	one	monotone	one tone
neo-	new, recent	neonatal	relating to first few weeks of a baby's life

It's Your Turn: Ten More Greek Prefixes

Remember what you learned on Day 3: one of the most effective ways to remember words is to review them often. To help you remember the prefixes you just learned, fill out the following chart. First identify the prefix, then define it, and finally use what you learned to define the word. Refer to the previous chart if you need a quick review. The answers appear on page 54.

Word	Prefix	Meaning	Word Meaning
1. euphonious	_____	_____	_____
2. graphic	_____	_____	_____
3. microfilm	_____	_____	_____
4. neophyte	_____	_____	_____
5. monotheism	_____	_____	_____
6. geology	_____	_____	_____
7. cryptogram	_____	_____	_____
8. euphemism	_____	_____	_____
9. demagogue	_____	_____	_____
10. euphoria	_____	_____	_____

Even More Greek Prefixes!

It's plain from the number of Greek prefixes in this chapter that these are very important word parts. Study the following ten additional Greek prefixes. As you read each one, look up and repeat the information to yourself. Then, write some of the least familiar words on cards, as you learned in Day 3. Refer to these cards often to help you lock these test-worthy words in your consciousness.

Prefix	Meaning	Examples	Definition
pan-	all	panacea	cure-all
peri-	around	perimeter	outer measurement
phil-	love	philanthropy	love of humanity
phon-	sound; voice	phonology	science of speech sounds
poly-	many	polyphonic	many sounds
pseudo-	false	pseudoscience	false science
psycho-	mind	psychology	study of the mind
syn-, sym-	together	synthesis	putting together
tele-	distance	telephone	phone
theo-	God	theology	study of God or religion

It's Your Turn: Even More Greek Prefixes!

Identify the prefix, define it, and then define the word. Feel free to look back at the chart if you need to refresh your memory. Remember: practice makes perfect. The words aren't going to help you unless you remember them on test day! The answers appear on page 54.

Word	Prefix	Meaning	Word Meaning
1. synopsis	_____	_____	_____
2. telecommunication	_____	_____	_____
3. pandemic	_____	_____	_____
4. polynomial	_____	_____	_____
5. symmetrical	_____	_____	_____
6. Pan-American	_____	_____	_____
7. polyglot	_____	_____	_____
8. symbiosis	_____	_____	_____
9. telepathy	_____	_____	_____
10. phonograph	_____	_____	_____

The Greek Prefix Archi-

An *architect* is a person who designs and oversees the construction of buildings. The Greeks called their architects *architekton*s, or master builders. The word comes from the Greek prefix *archi-* (chief) and the root *tekton* (workman).

The Greek prefix *archi-* and the verb from which it is derived—*archein* (to be the first, to rule)—appear in many English words. The prefix is generally defined as "chief." The following chart shows some of these "arch" words that you are likely to find especially useful on standardized tests.

Prefix	Example	Definition
arch-	archaic (ar-*kay*-ic)	public record
arch-	archangel	a chief angel
arch-	archbishop	chief of the church province
arch-	archconservative	an extreme conservative
arch-	archduke	a sovereign prince
arch-	archenemy	a principal enemy
arche-	archetype (*ar*-keh-typ)	prototype
arch-	archrival	a principal rival
arch-	archive (*ar*-kyv)	public record

The Greek Prefix Cata-

Also from the Greeks comes the prefix *katarasso,* meaning "down rushing," as in rain or a river. The earliest evidence of this prefix in English can be found in the Bible, where *cataracts* were the floodgates of heaven to keep back the rain. Today, we use the word *cataract* to mean a waterfall or a deluge. As a medical term, a *cataract* is an opacity that blocks light from entering the lens of the eye. From these examples, it's clear that the word retains its sense of being a floodgate as well as a flood. The prefix *cata-* is defined as "down, against, or wholly."

Here are some test-worthy words that come from this Greek prefix. Use the techniques you learned on Day 3 to make these words part of your permanent vocabulary.

Prefix	Example	Definition
cata-	cataclysm (*kat*-uh-kliz-um)	calamity
cata-	catalyst (*kat*-uh-list)	reactant
cata-	catapult (*kat*-uh-pult)	throw, hurl
cata-	catastrophe (kah-*tas*-troh-fee)	disaster
cata-	catechism (*cat*-uh-kiz-um)	manual for instruction
cata-	category (*kat*-uh-gor-ee)	division
cata-	cathode (*kath*-ohd)	vacuum tube
cata-	catholic (*kath*-lik or *kath*-eh-lik)	universal, general

Learn Test-worthy Words with Latin Prefixes

Not to be outdone by Greek, Latin has given us some extremely useful prefixes. The Latin prefix *circum-* is a case in point. *Circum-*, which means "around," can be used to form heaps of useful everyday words. Here are twelve such examples:

The Latin Prefix Circum-

Word	Definition
circumjacent	surrounding
circumambulate	walk around
circumference	the boundary line of a circle
circumfluent	flowing around
circumfuse	envelop
circumlocution	a roundabout way of speaking
circumnavigate	to sail around
circumpolar	around the North or South Pole
circumrotate	to rotate like a wheel
circumscribe	restrict
circumspect	cautious, prudent
circumvent	to get around

Ten Test-worthy Latin Prefixes

Study these ten Latin prefixes, their meanings, and examples.

Prefix	Meaning	Examples
a-	to, toward	ascribe
act-, ag-	do, act	action
ad-	to, toward	adverb
ante-	before	anteroom
aud-	to hear	audiology
bene-	good	beneficial
bi-	two	bicycle
capt-, cept-	take	capture
circum-	around	circumference
co-, com-	with, together	coworker, commotion
con-, col-	with, together	conduct, collaborate
contra-	against, opposite	contraband
cur-	run	current

Give It a Try: Word Scramble

Time for fun! First unscramble each of the ten test-worthy words so that it matches its definition. All but two of the words begin with prefixes. Then, use the words to fill the appropriate spaces on the corresponding line. When you have completed the entire puzzle, another test-worthy word will read vertically in the column with circles. The answers appear on page 54.

Scramble	Definition
elltaabrcoo	work together
seolobte	old-fashioned
vionec	beginner
yethpatle	communicating through transference
uqialyref	qualify again
oegape	farthest point from Earth in satellite's orbit
rnestdii	unearth
aeactltrbin	hard to handle; unmanageable
ariidactntnoce	against indications
etyghool	study of God or religion

Seventh-Inning Stretch: Multiple Choice

Use what you've learned so far about Latin prefixes to figure out the meanings of the following ten words in boldface. Write the letter of your choice in the space provided. The answers appear on page 54.

_____ 1. **cursive**

    (A) cruel
    (B) foul language
    (C) commonplace
    (D) criminal
    (E) flowing handwriting

_____ 2. **agitate**

    (A) clean
    (B) tap your foot
    (C) tranquilize
    (D) stir up
    (E) annoy

_____ 3. **adjoin**

    (A) separate
    (B) listen closely
    (C) touch
    (D) disunite
    (E) admonish

_____ 4. **cohabit**

    (A) nun's garb
    (B) dependent
    (C) change
    (D) live together
    (E) mortify

_____ 5. concede
- (A) yield
- (B) build
- (C) augment
- (D) curtail
- (E) remunerate

_____ 6. depress
- (A) elevate
- (B) upraise
- (C) invigorate
- (D) annotate
- (E) bring down

_____ 7. adjudicate
- (A) subjoin
- (B) deduct
- (C) lessen
- (D) arbitrate
- (E) annex

_____ 8. affix
- (A) withhold
- (B) repair
- (C) fasten
- (D) injure
- (E) disparage

_____ 9. confederation
- (A) Southerners
- (B) antagonism
- (C) alliance
- (D) aversion
- (E) panorama

_____ 10. collateral
- (A) security
- (B) far away
- (C) considerably
- (D) dependent
- (E) peer

Ten More Test-worthy Latin Prefixes

Here are ten more Latin prefixes for your examination. Remember: the more prefixes you learn, the more words you can decode. Knowing just one prefix can help you figure out five or even more words. As a result, consider how many words you can define when you know ten, twenty, or thirty prefixes!

Prefix	Meaning	Example	Definition
de-	down	demolish	tear down
e-	out	elongate	stretch out
ex-	out	exchange	replace
inter-	between	intercom	two-way radio
infra-	under	infrared	rays under red
mal-	bad	malodor	bad odor
male-	evil	maledict	curse
ob-	toward	obedient	respectful
per-	through	perambulate	walk through
post-	after	postpone	do after

It's Your Turn: Ten More Latin Prefixes

Now, apply what you learned to define the following ten words. Each one uses a prefix you just covered. Choose the best definition from the words in the box. You will have definitions left over. The answers appear on page 55.

flowing forth	teach	awkward
criminal	attractive	odd
vulgar	restless	comely
write on	dig out	invocation
compatriot	a fellow countryman	expedient
berate	compendium	pendant
to scold harshly	an abridged form of a work	principles
sound waves with a frequency below the audible range		

1. excavate _____
2. infrasonic _____
3. impart _____
4. maladroit _____
5. malefactor _____
6. eccentric _____
7. impatient _____
8. effluent _____
9. inscribe _____
10. indecent _____

Prefixes for Numbers

The symbols we use for numbers—1, 2, 3, 4, etc.—come from the Arabs, the first great mathematicians. The words we use to speak or write these symbols—one, two, three, four, etc.—are from the Anglo-Saxons.

How many sides does the Pentagon have? How many tentacles does an octopus have? If you know your number prefixes, these questions are a snap to answer. The envelope, please: The *Pentagon* has <u>five</u> sides (penta = five). An *octopus* has <u>eight</u> tentacles (octo = eight).

As you can see, when we want to combine a number and a word to form another word, such as a synonym for a "five-sided figure," we use the Greek or Roman word for the number, pentameter.

Here are ten Greek and Latin prefixes that show the numbers one to ten.

Number	Prefix	Example	Definition
1	uni-	unicycle	cycle with one wheel
2	bi-	bicycle	cycle with two wheels
3	tri-	tripod	three-legged stand
4	quad-	quadrangle	four-sided enclosure, especially when surrounded by buildings
5	penta-	Pentateuch	first five books of Jewish and Christian Scriptures
6	hexa-	hexagon	six-sided figure
7	hepta-	heptameter	a line of verses consisting of seven metrical feet
8	oct-	octet	a group of eight, usually singers
9	nov-	novena	Roman Catholic prayers or services conducted on nine consecutive days
10	deca-	decathlon	ten-event athletic contest

Anglo-Saxon Prefixes

Below are the five most common Anglo-Saxon prefixes and their variations. Read through the chart and examples. To help you remember the prefixes, complete the activities that follow.

Prefix	Meaning	Examples	Definition
a-	on, to, at, by	ablaze	on fire
be-	around, over	besiege	attack
mis-	wrong, badly	mistake	error
over-	above, beyond	overreach	reach too high
un-	not	unambiguous	clear

Give It a Try: Anglo-Saxon Prefixes

Based on the meaning of its prefix, define each of the following words. The answers appear on page 55.

1. accord _____

2. irradiate _____

3. predestination _____

4. reincarnation _____

5. convolute _____

6. invoke _____

7. irrelevant _____

8. excommunicate _____

Seventh-Inning Stretch: More Anglo-Saxon Prefixes

Define each of the following underlined words, based on the way it is used in the phrase. Write the letter of your choice in the space provided. The answers appear on page 55.

_____ 1. miscarriage of justice

    (A) benediction
    (B) detail
    (C) villain
    (D) example
    (E) failure

_____ 2. beseech emotionally

    (A) implore
    (B) deny
    (C) shriek
    (D) pursue
    (E) debase

_____ 3. something strange is afoot

    (A) underneath
    (B) going on
    (C) clandestine
    (D) covert
    (E) epigram

_____ 4. unethical behavior

    (A) judicial
    (B) impartial
    (C) unprincipled
    (D) competent
    (E) impeccable

_____ 5. an overwrought child

    (A) heavy
    (B) unmannerly
    (C) placid
    (D) distraught
    (E) innocuous

It's Your Turn: Even More Anglo-Saxon Prefixes

Each of the following words starts with a prefix. Use what you learned about prefixes to see how many of these words you can define. Select the correct meaning for each of the following boldfaced words. Circle your choice. The answers appear on page 55.

1. **accede**

    go very fast   agree   excessive   debate

2. **hypocrisy**

    overpriced   false virtue   sweet natured   injection

3. **subsistence**

    wealth   existing   under water   farming

4. **aggregate**

    complete   annoy   marbles   clot

5. **ultramarine**

    fashionable   weird   deep blue   famous

6. **hyperactivity**

    illness   medicine   excessive activity   slow

7. **catacomb**

   comb for cats   dessert   underground room   crooked

8. **amoral**

   very moral   not moral   story lesson   high spirits

9. **compress**

   squeeze   heal   measurement tool   pat

10. **supercilious**

    arrogant   high achieving   very silly   long hairs

Answers and Explanations

Word-Find Puzzle (page 40)

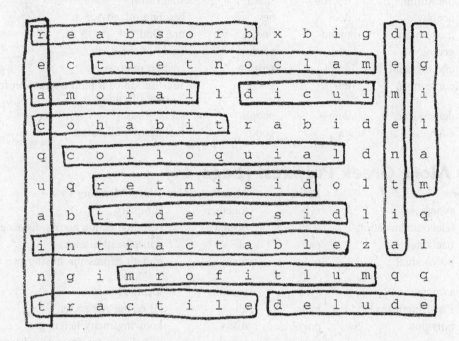

Ten Useful Greek Prefixes (page 42)

Word	Prefix	Meaning	Word Meaning
1. anemia	a-	not	blood deficiency
2. anthropoid	anthro-	man	resembling man
3. antidote	anti-	against	remedy against poison
4. asterisk	aster-	star	star-shaped mark
5. astronaut	astro-	star	"star sailor"
6. autonomous	auto-	self	self-governing
7. autonomy	auto-	self	self-government
8. automation	auto-	self	robot
9. autopsy	auto-	self	inspection and dissection of a body after death
10. bibliophile	biblio-	books	someone who values books
11. biodegradable	bio-	life	decays and is absorbed into the environment
12. biopsy	bio-	life	excision and study of a piece of bodily tissue
13. chronometer	chron-	time	timepiece; watch
14. cosmos	cosmo-	world	universe
15. chronograph	chron-	time	instrument for measuring and recording time intervals

Ten More Greek Prefixes (page 43)

Word	Prefix	Meaning	Word Meaning
1. euphonious	eu-	good	pleasing sound
2. graphic	graph-	write	written
3. microfilm	micro-	small	small film
4. neophyte	neo-	new	beginner or novice
5. monotheism	mono-	one	one God
6. geology	geo-	earth	study of the earth
7. cryptogram	gram-	writing	written in code
8. euphemism	eu-	good	substitution of a mild expression for one that may offend
9. demagogue	dem-	people	rabble-rouser
10. euphoria	eu-	good	feeling of well-being

Even More Greek Prefixes! (page 44)

Word	Pefix	Meaning	Word Meaning
1. synopsis	syn-	together	summary
2. telecommunication	tele-	distance	communication across distances
3. pandemic	pan-	all	widespread disease
4. polynomial	poly-	many	a math expression having two or more terms
5. symmetrical	sym-	together	identical parts
6. Pan-American	pan-	all	all of the Americas
7. polyglot	poly-	many	knowing many languages
8. symbiosis	sym-	together	two dissimilar organisms living together in a mutually beneficial relationship
9. telepathy	tele-	distance	through transference
10. phonograph	phono-	sound	instrument for reproducing sounds

Word Scramble (page 47)

collaborate
obsolete
novice
telepathy
requalify
apogee
disinter
intractable
contraindicate
theology

Reading down: **contradict**

Multiple Choice (page 47)

1. E	6. E
2. D	7. D
3. C	8. C
4. D	9. C
5. A	10. A

Ten More Latin Prefixes (page 49)

1. dig out
2. sound waves with a frequency below the audible range
3. teach
4. awkward
5. criminal
6. odd
7. restless
8. flowing forth
9. write on
10. vulgar

Anglo-Saxon Prefixes (page 50)

1. agreement
2. illuminate
3. fate
4. rebirth
5. twist up
6. request
7. not pertinent
8. exclude from communion

More Anglo-Saxon Prefixes (page 51)

1. E   2. A   3. B   4. C   5. D

Even More Anglo-Saxon Prefixes (pages 51–52)

1. agree
2. false virtue
3. existing
4. complete
5. deep blue
6. excessive activity
7. underground room
8. not moral
9. squeeze
10. arrogant

Day 5

Branch Out with Word Roots

There are no shortcuts in test preparation. . .or are there? You *will* have to memorize lists of words; after all, some test-worthy words can only be learned through memorization. But you can also acquire heaps of test-worthy words by mastering only a handful of roots. This is a great shortcut: it's fun, it's easy, and, best of all, it works!

A *root* is a stem or base form for many words. It has been estimated that 90 percent of all English words can be traced back to classical Greek and Latin roots.

How Roots Work

1. Prefixes and Suffixes Are Added to Roots to Create Many Words.

For example, the root *vor* means "to eat." If you are a *voracious* (voh-*ray*-shus) eater, you eat a lot of food. In the following examples, the root "vor(e)" is combined with prefixes and suffixes to describe types of eaters in the plant and animal kingdoms.

Cover the last column and see how many of these words you can figure out by just knowing the meaning of the root "vor."

Word	Prefix	Meaning	Root	Meaning	Word Definition
carnivore	carni-	meat	vor	eat	meat eater
insectivore	insect-	bug	vor	eat	bug eater
herbivore	herb-	plants	vor	eat	plant eater
granivore	gran-	grain	vor	eat	grain eater
frugivore	frug-	fruit	vor	eat	fruit eater
graminivore	gram-	grass	vor	eat	grass eater
nectarivore	nectar-	juice	vor	eat	nectar (juice) eater
omnivore	omni-	everything	vor	eat	eats everything

Knowing how the words were created can help you figure out many words you encounter on standardized tests. In addition, you can use these decoding skills to figure out the meaning of all the new words that are created every day. (You'll learn more about suffixes in Day 6.)

Here's the basic drill:

Adding a prefix to a root	Adding a suffix to a root
de + hydrate = dehydrate	zoo + *ology* = zoology
hydro + power = hydropower	bronch + *itis* = bronchitis

The following chart shows additional examples of how words are put together. Knowing this process can help you take them apart to define them. Remember, words are like people: it's easy to figure them out . . . once you know their parts.

Prefix	+	Root	+	Suffix	=	New Word	Meaning
re-	+	fer	+	-al	=	referral	connection
de-	+	ter	+	-ent	=	deterrent	impediment
re-	+	pul	+	-sion	=	repulsion	send back
dis-	+	pel	+	-ed	=	dispelled	dissipated
re-	+	tract	+	-able	=	retractable	draw back
im-	+	peril	+	-ed	=	imperiled	put in danger
dis-	+	credit	+	-ed	=	discredited	compromise
ab-	+	duct	+	-ed	=	abducted	kidnapped

Whenever you come upon an unfamiliar word, first check to see if it has a recognizable root. Even if you can't define a word exactly, recognizing the root will give you a general idea of the word's meaning. For example, if you read the word *geocentric*, knowing the root *geo* would help you figure out that *geocentric* has to do with the center ("centric") of the Earth or Earth as the center.

2. A Word Can Contain More Than One Root.

For example, the word *matrilineal* contains the roots *matri* (mother) and *lineal* (line). Putting it together, you can deduce that matrilineal means "determining ancestry through the female line."

3. Some Roots Are Words Themselves.

For example, the root *term* also means "name or length of time." In a similar way, the root *vent* also means "an opening that allows air to enter." Even though these roots are words, they can still function as roots, as the following chart shows:

Root	Meaning	Suffix	New Word	Meaning
term	name	-ology	terminology	wording
term	name	-agant	termagant	shrewish woman
term	end limit	-inal	terminal	end of a series
term	end limit	-less	termless	not limited

4. Some Roots Must Be Combined with Other Word Elements to Form Words.

Take a look at the examples on the following chart:

Root	Meaning	Suffix	New Word	Meaning	Pronunciation
aud	heard	-ible	audible	able to be heard	*aw*-dih-bul
capit	head	-al	capital	most important	*cap*-ih-tul
carn	flesh	-al	carnal	of the flesh	*car*-nal

5. When It Comes to Building Words from Roots, Placement Matters.

Some roots can also function as prefixes, depending on their placement in a word. For example, *graphy* means "writing."

used as a root   *calligraphy*

used as a prefix   *graphology*

Time for Fun: Word-Find Puzzle

Time for a break. There are fifteen words hidden in this word-find puzzle. (See the word list below.) Every word begins with "a." To complete the puzzle, locate and circle all the words. The words may be written forward, backward, or upside down. The answers appear on page 68. Good luck!

```
a  a  a  a  s  s  i  d  u  o  u  s  y  a
q  a  b  h  o  r  k  k  q  q  a  a  r  m
a  b  r  o  g  a  t  e  z  q  s  p  o  p
b  w  d  n  o  c  s  b  a  v  y  o  t  h
l  x  a  d  m  o  n  i  s  h  l  s  a  i
u  a  a  a  a  a  a  a  a  a  a  u  t  a  b
t  n  e  l  a  v  i  b  m  a  m  l  l  i
i  z  e  t  o  d  i  t  n  a  m  e  u  o
o  z  a  n  t  i  p  a  t  h  y  e  b  u
n  v  a  p  p  e  a  s  e  z  z  x  m  s
a  g  g  r  a  n  d  i  z  e  x  x  a  s
h  e  y  a  n  t  i  t  h  e  s  i  s  x
```

Word List:

1. **abhor:** to turn away from; loathe

2. **ablution:** washing away; cleansing

3. **abrogate:** to repeal; do away with

4. **abscond:** to steal away and hide

5. **admonish:** to strongly urge or caution

6. **aggrandize:** to make more powerful, important, or wealthier

7. **ambivalent:** having conflicting emotions

8. **amphibious:** capable of living both on land and in water

9. **antidote:** a remedy against a poison

10. **antipathy:** a strong feeling of dislike; hostility; aversion

11. **antithesis:** a contrast of ideas

12. **apostle:** a person sent away to deliver a message

13. **appease:** to pacify; bring toward peace

14. **assiduous:** diligent; industrious

15. **asylum:** a place of security or retreat

Learn Test-worthy Words with Greek Roots

Many of the words we use every day come from Greek roots. This is especially true of the language of scientific words, because much of the language of science was created primarily from Greek roots. Scientific words often appear on standardized tests.

Greek Roots for Measurement

You'll notice that some of the roots have more than one spelling. For example, *macro* and *mega* both mean "large." Read the following chart several times, and you'll soon get accustomed to the slight variations in spelling.

Root	Meaning	Example	Definition
acr	topmost	acrophobia (ak-roh-*foh*-bee-uh)	fear of high places
arch/prot	first	archbishop prototype	highest bishop first of its kind
chron	time	chronicle (*krah*-nih-kul)	historical record
ger/paleo	old	geriatric (jer-ee-*at*-trik) paleogeology (pay-lee-oh-jee-*ol*-oh-jee)	relating to old age the science of Earth's history
horo	hour	horoscope (*hor*-oh-scope)	signs of the zodiac
macro/mega	large	macroscopic megalith	seen with the naked eye huge stone
meter	measure	altimeter (*al*-tih-mee-ter or al-*tih*-meh-ter)	device to measure altitude
micro	small	microbe (*my*-krob)	tiny organism
morph	form	metamorphosis (meh-tah-*mor*-foh-sis)	change of form
neo	new	neophyte (*nee*-oh-fyt)	beginner
pan	all	panacea (pan-eh-*see*-uh)	a cure-all
ped	foot	pedometer (peh-*dahm*-eh-ter)	device for measuring steps
poly	many	polyglot (*pah*-lee-glot)	speaking several languages
tele	far off	telescope	device for seeing distant objects

Words with the Hydro/Hydra Root

Many useful words are formed from the *hydro/hydra* root. The following chart shows some of the most important ones that often appear on standardized tests:

Word	Definition	Pronunciation
hydrostat	electrical device for detecting water	*hi*-droh-stat
dehydrate	dry out	dee-*hi*-drate
hydrophobia	fear of water	hi-droh-*foh*-bee-uh
hydroplane	boat that travels on water	*hi*-droh-playn
hydroponics	growing plants in water	*hi*-droh-pon-iks
hydropower	power generated from water	*hi*-droh-pow-ur
hydrate	combine with water	*hi*-drate
hydrangea	flower (that needs much water)	hi-*drayn*-jah
hydrotherapy	water therapy	hi-droh-*ther*-uh-pee
hydrosphere	water on Earth	*hi*-droh-sfeer

Words About the Natural World

While we're on the topic of water, below are some Greek roots and words formed from them that concern the natural world. You'll find these words quite test-worthy.

Root	Meaning	Example	Definition
anthrop	human	anthropology (an-throh-*pol*-oh-jee)	study of humankind
bio	life	biology	the study of life
dem	people	democracy	rule by the people
gen	race	genetics (jen-*eh*-tiks)	study of heredity
		eugenics (yoo-*jen*-iks)	improving offspring
helio	sun	heliotrope (*hee*-lee-uh-trop)	sunflower
ichthy	fish	ichthyology (ik-thee-*ol*-oh-jee)	study of fish
ornith	bird	ornithology (or-neh-*thol*-oh-jee)	study of birds
ped	foot	pedometer (peh-*dah*-meh-ter)	instrument that measures footsteps
phyt	plant	phytology (fy-*tuhl*-oh-jee)	study of plants
polit	citizen	cosmopolitan	citizen of the world
pyr	fire	pyrogenic (py-roh-*jen*-ik)	producing heat
soma	body	somatic (soh-*mah*-tik)	physical
thermo	heat	thermostat	device for regulating heat
zoo	animal	zoology	study of animals

Give It a Try: Word Scramble

Time for fun! First unscramble each of the seven test-worthy words so that it matches its definition. Then, use the words to fill the appropriate spaces on the corresponding line. When you have completed the entire puzzle, another test-worthy word will read vertically in the column with circles. The answers appear on pages 68–69.

Scramble	Definition
tryooppet	first of its kind
bldiuae	able to be heard
hpyteeon	beginner
iahobroacp	fear of high places
leronichc	historical record
scnieegu	improving offspring
ophbichars	highest bishop

Greek Roots for Beliefs and Ideas

The Greek roots form many test-worthy words that describe beliefs and ideas as well. How many of the following words do you know? Test yourself by covering the fourth column and trying to define each word.

Root	Meaning	Example	Definition
archy/cracy	rule by	monarchy (*mon*-ar-kee)	rule by inherited leader
biblio	book	bibliophile (*bib*-lee-oh-fy-uhl)	book lover, book collector
dox	belief	orthodox (*or*-thoh-dahx)	conforming to approved beliefs
gam	marriage	polygamy (poh-*lih*-guh-mee)	multiple spouses
graph	writing	graphology (graf-*ahl*-oh-jee)	study of handwriting
ideo	idea	ideology (eye-dee-*ahl*-oh-jee)	body of knowledge
logy	study of	anthropology (an-throh-*pol*-oh-jee)	study of humanity
nom	rule	autonomy (aw-*ton*-oh-mee)	self-rule
onym	name	pseudonym (*soo*-do-nim)	pen name
orama	view	panorama (pan-oh-*ram*-mah)	complete view
path	feeling	sympathy (*sim*-pah-thee)	compassion
psycho	mind	psychology (sy-*kahl*-oh-jee)	study of the mind
theo	god	theology (thee-*ahl*-oh-jee)	study of god
soph	deceptive	sophistry (*sof*-es-tree)	tricky reasoning

It's Your Turn: Roots and Their Meanings

Assess what you've learned so far by completing the following chart. For each word, first write the root and its meaning. Then, use what you've learned about roots to define each word. Don't hesitate to look back at what you just learned—or to use a dictionary. The answers appear on pages 68–69.

Word	Root	Meaning	Word Meaning
1. pyrotechnics			
2. thermometer			
3. gene			
4. android			
5. zoological			
6. thermodynamics			
7. politician			
8. pyrography			
9. engender			
10. heliocentric			
11. polity			
12. zoometry			
13. gynarchy			
14. ichthyoid			
15. ornithopod			

Learn Test-worthy Words with Latin Roots

If you think we've borrowed a lot of roots from the Greeks, wait until you see what we've recycled from Latin! For example, the Latin root *plac* means "pleasure." Words formed from this root include *placid, complacent, implacable, complaisant,* and *placate.*

The Latin root *nomin/nomen* (name) has given us a great many words, including these half-dozen:

Word	Meaning	Pronunciation
ignominious	disgracing one's name	ig-noh-*min*-ee-us
misnomer	wrong name	mis-*noh*-mer
nomenclature	system of naming	*noh*-men-clay-cher
nominal	so-called	*nah*-muh-nil
nominate	name someone for an office	*nom*-in-ayt
nominee	candidate	nom-in-*ee*

Latin Roots for Size and Amount

Below are fifteen Latin roots that describe size and amount. Study the roots, examples, and definitions. As you read, use some of the techniques you learned in Day 3 to help you learn and recall the words. For example, say the words aloud to help you remember them for standardized tests.

Root	Meaning	Example	Definition
alt	high	altitude	height above surface
ann	year	biennial (bi-*en*-ee-al)	happening every two years
brev	short	brevity	being brief
centr	center	centrist	moderate viewpoint
dors	back	dorsal	back fin
fin/term	final	finale (fi-*nal*-ee) terminal	the last piece of music end
magni	large	magniloquent (mag-*nil*-uh-kwent)	pompous speaking style
med	middle	median (*mee*-dee-an)	in the middle
multi	many	multifarious (mul-te-*far*-e-us)	numerous and varied
nihil	nothing	annihilate (ann-*ni*-ah-late)	kill
omni	all	omniscient (om-*nish*-ehnt)	all-knowing
pend	weigh	pendulous	hanging
sed/sess	sit	sedate (seh-*date*)	quiet
ten/tin	hold	tenet (*tehn*-ent)	belief held as true
vid, vis	see	visual (*vih*-shu-al)	seen

Seventh-Inning Stretch: Word-Definition Match

Match the word to its definition. You may wish to underline the Latin root in each word as you do so. Then, write your answers in the space provided. The answers appear on page 69.

_____ 1. abdication   a. overpass

_____ 2. diversification   b. guess

_____ 3. repulsion   c. variety

_____ 4. benediction   d. decree; order

_____ 5. edict   e. renounce a throne

_____ 6. misconduct   f. assembly; caucus

_____ 7. viaduct   g. questionable

_____ 8. Congress   h. aversion

_____ 9. conjecture   i. wrongdoing

_____ 10. objectionable   j. blessing

Latin Roots for "Kill or Cut"

The Latin root *cide* means "kill or cut." As you read the following chart, cover the fifth column. See how many words you can decode using what you know about the root and its meaning.

Word	Prefix	Meaning	Root	Word Meaning
insecticide	insect-	bug	cide	killing bugs
genocide	gen-	people	cide	killing a race of people
homicide	homo-	mankind	cide	a person killing a person
matricide	matr-	mother	cide	killing one's mother
patricide	patr-	father	cide	killing one's father
fratricide	frat-	brother	cide	killing one's brother
sororicide	soro-	sister	cide	killing one's sister
suicide	sui-	self	cide	killing yourself
infanticide	infant-	baby	cide	killing one's baby
ceticide	cet-	whales	cide	killing whales

Time for Fun: Latin Roots—True or False

In the space provided, write **T** if the definition is true and **F** if it is false. Use what you learned about Latin roots to help you figure out what each test-worthy word means. The answers appear on page 69.

_____ 1. unification   union

_____ 2. degradation   encouragement

_____ 3. induce   influence

_____ 4. jettison   bring on board

_____ 5. addiction   habit; fixation

_____ 6. gentrification   growing old

_____ 7. scribe   writer

_____ 8. malediction   good luck

_____ 9. dejected   depressed

_____ 10. propellant   meddler

_____ 11. contradict   dissent; deny

_____ 12. gradient   flat surface

_____ 13. inscribe   write on

_____ 14. traduce   praise

_____ 15. abduct   kidnap

Give It a Try: Definitions

Define each word, using its root to help you. Write your definition on the line provided. The answers appear on page 69.

1. compendium _____
2. biennial _____
3. continence _____
4. append _____
5. omniscient _____
6. supersede _____
7. pendulous _____
8. invidious _____
9. secede _____
10. omnivorous _____

Answers and Explanations

Word-Find Puzzle (page 60)

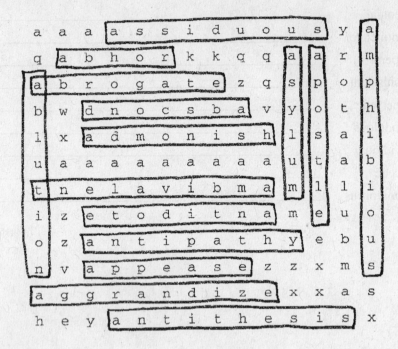

Word Scramble (page 63)

prototype
audible
neophyte
acrophobia
chronicle
eugenics
archbishop

Reading down: **panacea**

Roots and Their Meanings (page 64)

Word	Root	Meaning	Word Meaning
1. pyrotechnics	pyro	fire	fireworks
2. thermometer	thermo	heat	device for measuring heat
3. gene	gen	race	unit of heredity
4. android	andr	man	man-shaped robot
5. zoological	zoo	animal	about animals
6. thermodynamics	thermo	heat	using heat
7. politician	polit	citizen	officeholder
8. pyrography	pyro	fire	burning designs on wood, etc.
9. engender	gen	race	to produce
10. heliocentric	helio	sun	relating to the sun as center

11. polity	polit	citizen	form of government
12. zoometry	zoo	animal	measuring animals
13. gynarchy	gyn	women	government by women
14. ichthyoid	ichthy	fish	fish-like
15. ornithopod	ornith	bird	bird-like dinosaur

Word-Definition Match (page 65)

1. e	6. i
2. c	7. a
3. h	8. f
4. j	9. b
5. d	10. g

Latin Roots—True or False (page 66)

1. T	6. F	11. T
2. F	7. T	12. F
3. T	8. F	13. T
4. F	9. T	14. F
5. T	10. F	15. T

Definitions (page 67)

1. digest; synopsis
2. happening every two years
3. self-control
4. add
5. perceiving all things
6. go beyond; replace
7. hanging
8. causing resentment
9. withdraw; resign
10. eating all kinds of foods

Day 6

Master Suffixes

A *suffix* is a letter or group of letters added to the end of a word or root to change the word's meaning. Suffixes determine a word's part of speech—whether it is used as a noun, verb, adjective, or adverb.

How Suffixes Work

1. Suffixes Are Added to the End of Roots to Create Many Words.

In the same way that prefixes are placed at the beginning of a word to change its meaning, suffixes are placed at the *end* to change a word's meaning. Here are some examples:

Word +	Suffix =	Word	Definition
allege	-ation	allegation	assertion, claim
recognize	-ation	recognition	identification
alienate	-ation	alienation	estrangement, cut off from
peril	-ous	perilous	dangerous
hazard	-ous	hazardous	dangerous
capacity	-ous	capacious	large, roomy
tonsils	-itis	tonsillitis	inflammation of the tonsils
bronchi	-itis	bronchitis	inflammation of the bronchia
appendix	-itis	appendicitis	inflammation of the appendix

2. Suffixes Are Always Attached to Words Without a Break.

Even though you may have seen the suffix written with a hyphen (as in *-eous, -ion, -ment*), the suffix is attached without a hyphen. The following chart shows some examples:

Word +	Suffix =	New Word	Definition
combust	-ible	combustible	flammable
pasture	-al	pastoral	country-like
palace	-ial	palatial	like a palace
abstain	-ious	abstemious	moderate, sober
wasp	-ish	waspish	irritable, crabby
fellow	-ship	fellowship	sociability

3. Suffixes Are Different Lengths.

As with prefixes, suffixes can be as short as one letter or far longer. The following chart shows some examples:

Number of Letters	Suffix	Word	Pronunciation	Meaning
One-Letter Suffix	-d	promulgated	*prom*-mul-gay-ted	published or disseminated widely
Two-Letter Suffix	-ed	besmirched	bee-*smirch*-d	to soil; make filthy
Three-Letter Suffix	-ity	instability		not stable
Four-Letter Suffix	-ment	inducement	in-*doos*-ment	incentive
Five-Letter Suffix	-ation	vacillation	vah-sih-*lay*-shun	indecision

4. Suffixes Can Affect How a Word Functions in a Sentence.

Unlike prefixes, suffixes can create a word's part of speech. For example, adding a suffix can change a word from a verb to an adjective, as in *risk* to *risky*.

Adjective

The following suffixes show that a word is an *adjective* (word that describes):

    -ful   -less   -able/-ible   -y

Noun

The following suffixes show that a word is a *noun* (person, place, or thing):

    -ance/-ence   -ful   -ment   -sion/-tion   -age   -ity

Verb

The following suffixes show that a word is a *verb* (action or state of being):

    -ate   -en   -ite   -ize

If you know a word's part of speech, you can figure out how it is being used—even if you don't know its meaning. Study the following examples:

Word	Suffix	Part of Speech	Meaning
bountiful	-ful	adjective	plentiful
boundless	-less	adjective	infinite
perdurable	-able	adjective	permanent; everlasting
frangible	-ible	adjective	easily broken
fallible	-ible	adjective	makes mistakes
decadence	-ence	noun	deterioration, esp. in morality
mouthful	-ful	noun	morsel
excrement	-ment	noun	matter expelled or ejected; waste
perdition	-tion	noun	entire loss; utter destruction; ruin
premonition	-tion	noun	a forewarning
posterity	-ity	noun	those who come after
abdicate	-ate	verb	to formally relinquish or renounce an office or right
mutate	-ate	verb	change
extradite	-ite	verb	to deliver (give up) a suspect from one state or nation to another
demonize	-ize	verb	make a demon

5. Suffixes Can Change a Word's Tense (or Time).

For instance, adding *-d* or *-ed* makes a present-tense verb into a past-tense verb, as the following chart shows:

Present tense	Past tense	Meaning
denude	denuded	to strip bare
depose	deposed	to remove from a position
exacerbate	exacerbated	to make worse
expunge	expunged	to rub out; obliterate
embalm	embalmed	to inject a preservative into a corpse
embark	embarked	to board a ship or train for a trip
embellish	embellished	to decorate or make beautiful
envelop	enveloped	to assimilate (bring in as part of)
enswath	enswathed	to enfold or enclose with or as if with a covering
extrapolate	extrapolated	to deduce an unknown from a known

6. Adding a Suffix to the End of a Word Changes the Word's Meaning.

For example: *kitchen* becomes *kitchenette*, the diminutive.

Just as knowing a small number of prefixes and roots can help you figure out many unfamiliar words, so knowing a few everyday suffixes can help you decode many test-worthy words.

Time for Fun: Word-Find Puzzle

Remember what you learned on Day 3 about using mnemonics and puzzles to help you make new test-worthy words part of your everyday vocabulary? Time to practice what you learned! There are fifteen words hidden in this word-find puzzle. (See the word list below.) Some of the words have already been covered in this chapter, but others are new. To complete the puzzle, locate and circle all the words. The words may be written forward, backward, or upside down. The answers appear on page 84. Good luck!

```
c a t a r a c t e d u n e d m a
a l l e g a t i o n n o w s i d
p c n o i t a l l i c a v x s e
a b s t e m i o u s b i g x n g
c a b b e s m i r c h e d m o n
i z z d e t a g l u m o r p m u
o q u e p i t h e t w i g e e p
u z e x a c e r b a t e d q r x
s x d e t i d a r t x e a a a e
e h s i l l e b m e p r o l i x
```

Word List

1. **capacious:** large, roomy

2. **cataract:** a waterfall

3. **epithet:** a word or phrase describing a person; a derogatory word or phrase used to show contempt

4. **besmirched:** to soil; make filthy

5. **exacerbated:** to make worse

6. **denude:** to strip bare

7. **misnomer:** a wrong name or designation

8. **embellish:** to decorate or make beautiful

9. **prolix:** needlessly prolonged or drawn out

10. **expunged:** to rub out; obliterate

11. **extradited:** to give up a suspect from one state or nation to another

12. **vacillation:** indecision

13. **promulgated:** publish or disseminate widely

14. **abstemious:** moderate, sober

15. **allegation:** assertion, claim

Understand Suffixes That Describe State of Being

Below are twelve suffixes that describe a state of being. How many more words can you think of that end with these suffixes that describe a state of being?

Suffix	Example
-ance	appearance
-ant	deviant
-cy	infancy
-dom	freedom
-ence	independence
-ent	corpulent
-hood	neighborhood
-mony	matrimony
-ness	lightness
-sis	thesis
-tic	gigantic
-ty	novelty

It's Your Turn: Suffixes and Meanings

Assess what you've learned about suffixes that describe a state of being by completing the following chart. For each word, first write the suffix and its meaning. Then, use what you've learned about suffixes to define each word. Don't hesitate to look back at what you just learned or to use a dictionary. The answers appear on page 84.

Word	Suffix	Meaning	Word Meaning
1. goodness	_____	_____	_____
2. anxiety	_____	_____	_____
3. brilliance	_____	_____	_____
4. despondence	_____	_____	_____
5. catharsis	_____	_____	_____
6. effulgent	_____	_____	_____
7. hypothesis	_____	_____	_____
8. resilient	_____	_____	_____
9. repellent	_____	_____	_____
10. officialdom	_____	_____	_____
11. thrifty	_____	_____	_____
12. bibliomancy	_____	_____	_____
13. truculent	_____	_____	_____
14. brotherhood	_____	_____	_____
15. convalescence	_____	_____	_____
16. adamant	_____	_____	_____
17. diligent	_____	_____	_____
18. parity	_____	_____	_____
19. disenchant	_____	_____	_____
20. ambivalent	_____	_____	_____

Explore Suffixes That Indicate Occupations

A *lawyer* is someone who deals with the law; a *buyer* is someone who buys items. Below are ten suffixes that indicate a person who is something, does something, or deals with something.

Suffix	Example
-ar	scholar
-ard	dullard
-ary	revolutionary
-er	conjurer (magician)
-ian	historian
-ier	furrier
-ist	psychologist
-ite	socialite
-or	bettor
-ship	craftsmanship

Get the Gist of *-ist*

Many useful words have been formed with the suffix *-ist*. Often, these words describe hobbies or careers. The following chart shows the most test-worthy of these words:

Word	Definition	Pronunciation
aborist	deals with tree care	*ahr*-bur-ist
entomologist	deals with insects	en-tuh-*mahl*-uh-jist
geneticist	deals with heredity	juh-*net*-uh-sist
meteorologist	deals with the weather	meet-ee-uh-*ral*-uh-jist
numismatist	deals with coins	noo-*miz*-muh-tist
philatelist	deals with stamps	fuh-*lat*-uh-list
psychologist	deals with people's problems	sy-*kahl*-uh-jist

Seventh-Inning Stretch: Word-Definition Match #1

Match the word to its definition. If you wish, underline the suffix in each word to help you remember how they are used. Write your answers in the space provided. The answers appear on page 85.

_____	1. functionary	a. philosopher, scholar
_____	2. editor	b. person who sits
_____	3. taxidermist	c. person who edits
_____	4. comedian	d. mediator
_____	5. arbitrator	e. an official
_____	6. pedestrian	f. opponent
_____	7. theorist	g. handwriting
_____	8. adversary	h. person who stuffs animals
_____	9. sedentary	i. person who walks
_____	10. penmanship	j. humorist

Study Suffixes That Show Resemblance

Below are twelve suffixes that all mean "resembling, like, or of." Study them and the examples. Then, complete the activity that follows to help you incorporate these words and suffixes into your daily vocabulary.

Suffix	Example	Definition
-ac	cardiac	having to do with the heart
-al	natural	having to do with nature
-an	suburban	having to do with the suburbs
-esque	statuesque	curvaceous, shapely
-ile	infantile	like a child
-ine	masculine	manly
-ish	foolish	asinine
-ly	yearly	occurring every year
-ory	advisory	helping out
-oid	android	human-like
-some	worrisome	distressing, disconcerting
-wise	likewise	in the same way

Time for Fun: True or False

In the space provided, write **T** if the definition is true and **F** if it is false. Use what you learned about suffixes that mean "resembling, like, or of" to help you figure out what each word means. The answers appear on page 85.

_____ 1. devilish   like a devil
_____ 2. cuboid   like a cube
_____ 3. puerile   mature
_____ 4. saturnine   sluggish, gloomy
_____ 5. fulsome   shortage
_____ 6. sensory   pertaining to the senses
_____ 7. Romanesque   like the Romans
_____ 8. pastoral   wild, untamed
_____ 9. ovoid   like an egg
_____ 10. dollarwise   pertaining to money
_____ 11. fictional   factual
_____ 12. churlish   polite

Seventh-Inning Stretch: Multiple-Choice #1

How good are you at using suffixes to decipher words? Find out by completing the following self-test. Each of the following words ends with a suffix. Use what you already know about suffixes to see how many of these words you can decode. Select the correct meaning for each of the following boldfaced words. Write the letter of your choice in the space provided. The answers appear on page 85.

_____ 1. **culinary**

    (A) cute; attractive
    (B) picky
    (C) dealing with cooking
    (D) dealing with cue balls
    (E) obdurate

_____ 2. **insignificance**

    (A) momentous
    (B) sign; insignia
    (C) consequential
    (D) unimportant
    (E) officiousness

_____ 3. **palatial**

    (A) luxurious
    (B) incomplete
    (C) roof of the mouth
    (D) paradigm
    (E) precocious

_____ 4. **seditious**

    (A) rebellious
    (B) cooperative
    (C) mutual
    (D) perspicacious
    (E) polygamous

_____ 5. **intransigent**

    (A) not traveling
    (B) insolvent
    (C) close-minded
    (D) prolific
    (E) surfeited

_____ 6. **erudite**

    (A) ruddy-skinned
    (B) pencil lead
    (C) synergistic
    (D) intransigent
    (E) learned

_____ 7. apothecary

(A) pharmacist
(B) quack
(C) heavy burden
(D) demagogue
(E) misanthrope

_____ 8. partisan

(A) windmill
(B) section
(C) supporter
(D) cadaver
(E) demigod

_____ 9. preponderance

(A) minority
(B) immaturity
(C) overweight
(D) valediction
(E) majority

_____ 10. mercenary

(A) generous
(B) avaricious
(C) docile
(D) dogmatic
(E) perfunctory

Discover Suffixes That Show Amount

Below are ten suffixes that show quantity. Some of these suffixes were discussed earlier in this chapter in different context. This was done on purpose because repetition makes it easier for you to remember crucial test-worthy words and concepts.

Suffix	Meaning	Example	Pronunciation	Definition
-aceous	having	curvaceous	cur-_vay_-shush	having curves
-ed	characterized by	cultured	_kul_-cherd	civilized
-lent	inclined to be	prevalent	_preh_-vah-lent	common
-ose	full of	morose	more-_ose_	gloomy
-ous	full of	perilous	_per_-ih-lus	dangerous
-ious	having	vicious	_vish_-ush	vile
-less	without	guiltless	_gihlt_-lehs	innocent
-ling	minor	yearling	_yeer_-leeng	year-old horse
-fold	increased by	tenfold	_tehn_-fohld	ten times
-ful	full	healthful	_helth_-fuhl	nutritious

Master Twelve Useful Suffixes

Let's finish with some important suffixes that crop up in many of the test-worthy words you will encounter in your academic career.

Suffix	Meaning	Example	Pronunciation	Definition
-erly	to, directly	easterly	*ees*-ter-lee	go east
-escent	beginning	opalescent	oh-pah-*less*-ent	shiny
-eum	place for	museum	mew-*zee*-uhm	storehouse of exhibits
-ferous	carrying, bearing	odoriferous	oh-dur-*if*-ur-us	stinky
-fy	marked by	magnify	*mag*-nih-fy	make larger
-ia	condition	anorexia	an-uh-*reks*-ee-uh	eating disorder
-ical	having to do with	musical	*mew*-sih-kul	lyric
-id	inclined to be	florid	*flor*-id	gaudy
-ive	inclined to be	festive	*fes*-tive	joyful
-ism	practice/quality	baptism	*bap*-tiz-um	religious ceremony
-tude	condition	rectitude	*rek*-tuh-tood	virtue
-ure	means, quality	rapture	*rap*-chur	bliss

Seventh-Inning Stretch: Word-Definition Match #2

Match each word in the first column to its definition in the second column. If you wish, underline the suffix in each word to help you remember how it is used. Write your answers in the space provided. The answers appear on page 85.

_____ 1. bursitis	a.	eager
_____ 2. discernment	b.	to suggest
_____ 3. nihilism	c.	surrender
_____ 4. adolescent	d.	inflammation of the bursa
_____ 5. expenditure		(area between the bone and a tendon)
_____ 6. abandonment	e.	open-air theater
_____ 7. heroism	f.	judgment
_____ 8. inducement	g.	reversion; throwback
_____ 9. intensify	h.	enhance
_____ 10. signify	i.	expenses
_____ 11. coliseum	j.	bravery
_____ 12. obsolescence	k.	teen years
_____ 13. fervid	l.	used up
_____ 14. sinusitis	m.	repudiation
_____ 15. atavism	n.	inflammation of sinuses
	o.	motive

Seventh-Inning Stretch: Multiple-Choice #2

How about one final activity to tie it together? Select the correct meaning for each of the following boldfaced words. Use what you learned about suffixes as well as all the other vocabulary techniques you have mastered so far. Circle your choice. The answers appear on page 85.

1. The murder scene can only be described as a **carnage**.

   (A) confusion
   (B) cluttered area
   (C) holy area
   (D) epigram
   (E) massacre

2. The drunk's **clownish** actions embarrassed his family.

   (A) amusing
   (B) admirable
   (C) foolish
   (D) humorous
   (E) long-winded

3. The lawyer functioned as an **intermediary** between the warring couple.

   (A) junta
   (B) friend
   (C) confidant
   (D) mediator
   (E) jetsam

4. Some people think that acne is **chromosomal**.

   (A) genetic
   (B) judicious
   (C) conjugal
   (D) abnormal
   (E) contagious

5. The new college president kicked off his appointment with a big **convocation**.

   (A) speech
   (B) gathering
   (C) rejoinder
   (D) lexicon
   (E) levee

6. The preacher had an annoying habit of **proselytizing** at inappropriate moments.

   (A) eating
   (B) attempting to convert people to his way of thinking
   (C) trying to sleep
   (D) elucidating
   (E) malingering

7. Children hate to be **castigated** in front of their friends.

   (A) praised
   (B) rebuked
   (C) out in a cast
   (D) mercurial
   (E) morbid

8. There was no doubt who was **culpable** for the mistake.

   (A) able to cope
   (B) out of control
   (C) impenitent
   (D) implacable
   (E) liable

9. The florist placed flowers, moss, and stones in the **terrarium**.

   (A) a shallow pool
   (B) case
   (C) an environment for plants and land animals
   (D) an environment for extinct creatures
   (E) back room

10. After treatment, the former alcoholic was happy to be **abstinent**.

(A) conical
(B) stubborn
(C) intoxicated
(D) sober
(E) lachrymose

Answers and Explanations

Word-Find Puzzle (page 74)

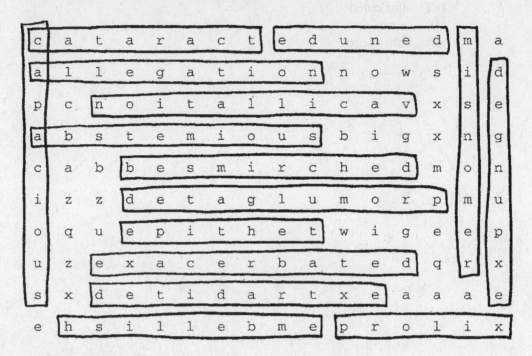

Suffixes and Meanings (page 76)

Word	Suffix	Meaning	Word Meaning
1. goodness	-ness	state of being	being good
2. anxiety	-ty	state of being	nervousness
3. brilliance	-ance	state of being	brightness
4. despondence	-ence	state of being	sadness
5. catharsis	-sis	state of being	purging
6. effulgent	-ent	state of being	flowing
7. hypothesis	-sis	state of being	guess
8. resilient	-ent	state of being	elastic
9. repellent	-ent	state of being	offensive
10. officialdom	-dom	state of being	authoritative
11. thrifty	-ty	state of being	frugal
12. bibliomancy	-cy	state of being	Biblical books
13. truculent	-ent	state of being	harsh
14. brotherhood	-hood	state of being	friendship
15. convalescence	-ence	state of being	recovering
16. adamant	-ant	state of being	definite
17. diligent	-ent	state of being	hard-working
18. parity	-ty	state of being	equality
19. disenchant	-ant	state of being	disillusion
20. ambivalent	-ent	state of being	unsure

Word-Definition Match #1 (page 78)

1. e
2. c
3. h
4. j
5. d
6. i
7. a
8. f
9. b
10. g

True or False (page 79)

1. T
2. T
3. F
4. T
5. F
6. T
7. T
8. F
9. T
10. T
11. F
12. F

Multiple-Choice #1 (page 79)

1. C
2. D
3. A
4. A
5. C
6. E
7. A
8. C
9. E
10. B

Word-Definition Match #2 (page 81)

1. d
2. f
3. m
4. k
5. i
6. c
7. j
8. o
9. h
10. b
11. e
12. l
13. a
14. n
15. g

Multiple-Choice #2 (pages 82–83)

1. E
2. C
3. D
4. A
5. B
6. B
7. B
8. E
9. C
10. D

Part III

Build Your Word Bank

Day 7:
Discuss Useful Words About Speaking

Day 8:
Explore Test-worthy Words About the Law and Making Judgments

Day 9:
Acquire Some Test-worthy Words About the Human Condition

Day 7

Discuss Useful Words About Speaking

Many words that relate to speaking appear on standardized tests. That's because these words are useful in daily life. Further, grouping words by a common theme makes them easier to remember as you study. Today, you'll learn some of the words you're most likely to encounter on the GED, PSAT/NMSQT, SAT, ACT, and TOEFL and other important standardized tests.

Learn Ten Words About Talking

Below are ten useful words that all deal with speech and speaking. As you read each word, say it aloud, using the pronunciation as a guide. Then link the word to a mnemonic, such as a place, person, or color, to help you remember it. (Look back to Day 3 for help with creating mnemonics.)

Word	Pronunciation	Meaning
assertion	uh-*sur*-shun	statement
allegation	al-lih-*gay*-shun	claim
clarity	*klair*-uh-tee	clearness of expression
explicit	ex-*plih*-sit	outspoken, specific
circumlocution	sir-kum-loh-*kyu*-shun	talk that is not to the point
discourse	*dis*-kors	conversation
dialectic	dy-uh-*lehk*-tik	argument through critical discussion
diatribe	*dy*-uh-tribe	a long, usually abusive, argument
effervescent	*eff*-er-ves-ent	bubbling; lively
effusive	eh-*fyoo*-sive	pouring forth freely; gushing

Here's how the words would be used in sentences. You'll recall that standardized tests often assess how well you can figure out words used in context. You'll get a sentence and have to define the words based on the surrounding words and phrases. Context clues are especially important when it comes to reading comprehension passages, too.

For example:

1. John made a strong **assertion** during the debate about immigration.

2. The plaintiff's **allegation** of innocence was clearly ridiculous.

3. Due to the **clarity** of his speech, the teacher was easily understood by one and all.

4. The prostitutes were so **explicit** that their speech was censored by the networks!

5. After the professor gave a speech characterized by **circumlocution**, the students were left scratching their heads in confusion.

6. The politicians welcomed the chance to have some serious **discourse**.

7. Socrates and Plato engaged in a famous **dialectic**.

8. The teenager was late, but did he deserve his mother's violent 3-hour **diatribe**?

9. The **effervescent** speaker held the audience's attention through her bubbly personality.

10. You want a partner to share his or her feelings, but do they have to be **effusive** and let it all hang out?

Speak with the Root *Loq*

On Day 5, you learned that knowing just a handful of roots can help you decode scads of unfamiliar words. The root *loq* means "speak." As you read the following words with the "loq" root, cover the last column and try to guess the meaning of each word.

Word	Part of Speech	Pronunciation	Meaning
colloquy	noun	*kol*-uh-kwee	dialogue
elocution	noun	el-oh-*cue*-shun	art of public speaking
locution	noun	loh-*kue*-shun	style of speech
loquacious	adjective	low-*quay*-shus	talkative
eloquent	adjective	*el*-oh-kwent	articulate
obloquy	noun	*ob*-luh-kwee	abusive language
soliloquy	noun	so-*lil*-oh-kwee	point in a drama when a character reveals his or her thoughts to the audience

Seventh-Inning Stretch: Multiple-Choice #1

Select the correct meaning for each of the following boldfaced words. Circle your choice. The answers appear on page 101.

1. **allegation**
   - (A) lively
   - (B) locution
   - (C) talk that is not to the point
   - (D) claim
   - (E) long, usually abusive, argument

2. **soliloquy**
   - (A) abusive language
   - (B) locution
   - (C) clearness of expression
   - (D) point in a drama when a character reveals his or her thoughts to the audience
   - (E) loquacious

3. **effervescent**
   - (A) bubbling; lively
   - (B) talk that is not to the point
   - (C) eloquent
   - (D) dialogue
   - (E) art of public speaking

4. **circumlocution**
   - (A) lively
   - (B) soliloquy
   - (C) talk that is not to the point
   - (D) loquacious
   - (E) clearness of expression

5. **diatribe**
   - (A) clearness of expression
   - (B) lively
   - (C) talkative
   - (D) abusive language
   - (E) long, usually abusive, argument

6. **locution**
   - (A) eloquent
   - (B) claim
   - (C) talkative
   - (D) colloquy
   - (E) style of speech

7. **explicit**
   - (A) outspoken, specific
   - (B) soliloquy
   - (C) obloquy
   - (D) a long, usually abusive, argument
   - (E) claim

8. **eloquent**
   - (A) art of public speaking
   - (B) articulate
   - (C) outspoken, specific
   - (D) talk that is not to the point
   - (E) conversation

9. **clarity**
   - (A) soliloquy
   - (B) lively
   - (C) clearness of expression
   - (D) colloquy
   - (E) art of public speaking

10. **assertion**
    - (A) a long, usually abusive, argument
    - (B) statement
    - (C) conversation
    - (D) outspoken, specific
    - (E) argument through critical discussion

11. **effusive**
    - (A) pouring forth freely; gushing
    - (B) art of public speaking
    - (C) conversation
    - (D) colloquy
    - (E) claim

12. **loquacious**

   (A) talkative
   (B) clearness of expression
   (C) a long, usually abusive, argument
   (D) gushing
   (E) outspoken, specific

13. **elocution**

   (A) claim
   (B) gushing
   (C) conversation
   (D) argument through critical discussion
   (E) art of public speaking

14. **dialectic**

   (A) clearness of expression
   (B) outspoken, specific
   (C) obloquy
   (D) soliloquy
   (E) argument through critical discussion

15. **discourse**

   (A) abusive language
   (B) obloquy
   (C) argument through critical discussion
   (D) gushing
   (E) conversation

Word-Find Puzzle

Time for a break. There are fifteen words hidden in this word-find puzzle. (See the word list below.) Ten words have already been covered in this chapter, but five are new. To complete the puzzle, locate and circle all the words. The words may be written forward, backward, or upside down. The answers appear on page 101. Good luck!

```
e  c  l  a  r  i  t  y  x  e  v  l  a  s  e  e
l  o  o  b  l  o  q  u  y  n  i  c  e  r  x  b
o  l  o  q  u  a  c  i  o  u  s  i  n  t  p  i
q  l  o  c  u  t  i  o  n  x  c  o  y  a  l  r
u  o  q  n  o  i  t  r  e  s  s  a  t  a  i  t
e  q  x  n  o  i  t  u  c  o  l  e  t  a  c  a
n  u  i  x  p  u  g  i  l  i  s  m  n  e  i  i
t  y  t  n  e  c  s  e  v  r  e  f  f  e  t  d
c  i  r  c  u  m  l  o  c  u  t  i  o  n  e  y
```

Word List

1. **colloquy:** dialogue
2. **clarity:** clearness of expression
3. **obloquy:** abusive language
4. **locution:** style of speech
5. **loquacious:** talkative
6. **assertion:** statement
7. **elocution:** art of public speaking
8. **effervescent:** bubbling; lively
9. **pugilism:** the art of hand-to-hand fighting; boxing
10. **eloquent:** articulate
11. **coy:** pretending to be shy
12. **salve:** to soothe; to make better
13. **explicit:** outspoken, specific
14. **diatribe:** a long, usually abusive, argument
15. **circumlocution:** talk that is not to the point

Discover Words Everyone's Talking About

Of the many words that have entered English from the Bible, few are more common than *Babel.* Now spelled *babble,* it means a "confusion of sound; senseless speech."

If you look for the word *Babel* in the Bible, you'll discover that it's a proper noun. (That's why it's capitalized.) It refers to the city of Babylon. The Book of Genesis tells the story of the people of Babel who tried to build a tower to heaven. To block them, the Lord decided "to confound their language, that they may not understand one another's speech." From that *din* (racket) emerged many languages.

Knowing a word's history is another way to enrich your vocabulary. Unfortunately, not all words have memorable pasts. Below are ten useful words about speech that have prosaic, pedestrian pasts. Nonetheless, they are often tested on standardized assessments because they are useful in professional discourse.

Word	Pronunciation	Meaning
cogent	*ko*-jent	convincing; compelling
confabulate	con-*fab*-yoo-layt	to talk together; prattle
didactic	dy-*dak*-tik	intended to teach
eloquence	*eh*-low-kwens	the ability to speak persuasively
epigram	*eh*-pih-gram	clever, pithy saying; aphorism
epithet	*eh*-pih-thet	nasty word or phrase used to show contempt
eulogy	*yoo*-low-gee	words of praise, especially for a deceased person
euphemism	*yoo*-fah-miz-um	a pleasant or complimentary word or phrase instead of one that is harsh
hyperbole	hy-*per*-boh-lee	exaggeration used to make a point
magniloquent	mag-*nil*-uh-kwent	bombastic, pompous, or grandiose speech

Master the Important *Dic/Dict* Root

The following words all include the root *dic/dict,* which means "say, claim." Read the list and see how many of these words you already know. Try to memorize the new ones now.

Word	Part of Speech	Pronunciation	Meaning
abdicate	verb	*ab*-dah-kate	to formally renounce an office or right
interdict	verb	*in*-ter-dict	to prohibit with authority
maledictory	adjective	mal-uh-*dik*-tor-ee	speaking evil of someone
predicate	noun	*preh*-dah-kit	statement contingent on something else
valediction	noun	val-ah-*dik*-shun	farewell speech or utterance
vindicate	verb	*vin*-dah-kayt	to clear from accusation, blame, or suspicion

Word-Definition Match

Match each numbered word in the left column with its lettered definition in the right column. Write your answer in the space provided. The answers appear on page 101.

_____ 1. abdicate	a. a pleasant or complimentary word or phrase instead of one that is harsh
_____ 2. predicate	
_____ 3. vindicate	b. convincing; compelling
_____ 4. valediction	c. exaggeration used to make a point
_____ 5. interdict	d. to clear from accusation, blame, or suspicion
_____ 6. epithet	
_____ 7. eloquence	e. nasty word or phrase used to show contempt
_____ 8. didactic	
_____ 9. hyperbole	f. words of praise, especially for a deceased person
_____ 10. eulogy	
_____ 11. cogent	g. to formally renounce an office or right
_____ 12. magniloquent	h. to prohibit with authority
_____ 13. epigram	i. to talk together; prattle
_____ 14. euphemism	j. bombastic, pompous, or grandiose speech
_____ 15. confabulate	
	k. statement contingent on something else
	l. intended to teach
	m. farewell speech or utterance
	n. clever, pithy saying; aphorism
	o. the ability to speak persuasively

Seventh-Inning Stretch: Multiple-Choice #2

Select the word that best completes each sentence. Then, write the letter of the word in the space. The answers appear on page 101.

1. In 1936, the Duke of Windsor _____ the throne so he could marry the woman he loved; as a result, he gave up all rights to becoming King of England.

(A) procured
(B) seized
(C) embraced
(D) abdicated
(E) salved

2. The DNA test completely _____ the accused and cleared him from blame.

(A) vindicated
(B) sanctified
(C) assimilated
(D) predicated
(E) abdicated

3. The teenager made a logical and _____ argument, but she was still grounded for a month because she chose to stay out all night.

   (A) cogent
   (B) asinine
   (C) fallacious
   (D) fraudulent
   (E) insolvent

4. The retiring president of the company delivered a _____ at the last meeting.

   (A) specter
   (B) valediction
   (C) stanchion
   (D) torque
   (E) colloquy

5. A person who is _____ is most likely academic and preachy.

   (A) placid
   (B) irrational
   (C) didactic
   (D) obtrusive
   (E) perturbed

6. A(n) _____ person is often long-winded and bombastic.

   (A) vindicated
   (B) illustrious
   (C) intrusive
   (D) magniloquent
   (E) eminent

7. "Early to bed and early to rise makes a man healthy, wealthy, and wise" is an example of a(n) _____.

   (A) epithet
   (B) epigram
   (C) eulogy
   (D) epitaph
   (E) euphemism

8. People with _____ speak smoothly and persuasively.

   (A) verbiage
   (B) eloquence
   (C) turbulence
   (D) effervescence
   (E) malevolence

9. Saying "passed on" instead of "died" is an example of a(n) _____.

   (A) epithet
   (B) epigram
   (C) epitaph
   (D) eulogy
   (E) euphemism

10. A(n) _____ is delivered at a funeral.

    (A) revulsion
    (B) convulsion
    (C) artifice
    (D) epigram
    (E) eulogy

11. Saying "My sister is as big as an elephant" is an example of _____.

    (A) hyperbole
    (B) valediction
    (C) sedition
    (D) mutiny
    (E) eczema

12. The success of the project was _____ on the company obtaining sufficient funds to proceed.

    (A) expunged
    (B) vindicated
    (C) predicated
    (D) exacerbated
    (E) embellished

Keep Up the Conversation: Twenty More Words About Speaking

A *kibitzer* is an onlooker who offers a great deal of advice—mostly unwanted. Originally, the word referred to a person who offered advice at a card game. Today, however, the word has been expanded to mean anyone who meddles in someone else's business. The word comes from Yiddish, a German-Jewish language.

Now, you don't need to meddle in another person's affairs, but you do need to know the words you need to speak about speaking. These words will also help you excel on standardized tests that involve English.

Word	Pronunciation	Meaning
articulation	ar-*tik*-you-lay-shun	speaking clearly, saying each word clearly
brusque	brusk	abrupt, impatient
candor	*kan*-dor	open, sincere
cant	cant	jargon used by a particular group or profession
caustic	*kaw*-stick	biting, sarcastic, or bitter
cogitate	*coh*-jih-tayt	to think or meditate
demagogue	*dem*-a-gog	charismatic leader (especially a politician) who stirs up negative emotions in others
dogmatic	dog-*mah*-tik	asserted without proof, usually arrogantly
emphasize	*em*-fah-syz	to stress
fluid	*floo*-id	flows easily
frank	fraynk	open, sincere
implication	im-pli-*kay*-shun	inference
ineffable	in-*eff*-ah-bul	inexpressible; overwhelming
insolent	*in*-suh-lent	insulting speech or mannerisms
neologism	nee-*al*-a-*jiz*-em	newly coined word
paraphrase	*par*-uh-frayz	to restate
polyglot	*pah*-lee-glaht	speaker of several languages
pundit	*pun*-dit	expert
recant	re-*cant*	to formally renounce one's previous beliefs or statements
reiterate	ree-*it*-er-ayt	to repeat

Root for *Clam!*

The following words about speech all contain the root *clam* (or *claim*), which refers to speech. (By the way, *to clam up* is a slang expression that means "to stop speaking.")

Word	Part of Speech	Pronunciation	Meaning
acclaim	verb	a-*claym*	to shout approval
clamorous	adjective	*klam*-o-rus	loud; noisy
declamation	noun	deh-clah-*may*-shun	speech
exclaim	verb	ex-*claym*	to cry out abruptly
proclaim	verb	pro-*claym*	to announce to the public

Seventh-Inning Stretch: Multiple-Choice #3

Select the correct meaning for each of the following boldfaced words. Circle your choice. The answers appear on page 102.

1. **articulation**

   (A) speaking quietly
   (B) keeping secrets
   (C) delivering a criminal from one state or nation to another
   (D) deducing an unknown (e.g., a quantity) from something that is known
   (E) speaking clearly

2. **neologism**

   (A) newly created word
   (B) newly born person
   (C) violent speech
   (D) sedition
   (E) praise

3. **acclaim**

   (A) to close out or block out
   (B) to shout approval
   (C) to cry out abruptly
   (D) to announce privately
   (E) to filter (liquid) through a membrane

4. **reiterate**

   (A) withhold
   (B) rhetoric
   (C) repeat
   (D) recant
   (E) revise

5. **ineffable**

   (A) limpid
   (B) clear
   (C) unequivocal
   (D) inexpressible
   (E) manifest

6. **insolent**

   (A) rude
   (B) chivalrous
   (C) decorous
   (D) polished
   (E) polite

7. **pundit**

   (A) expert
   (B) dilettante
   (C) novice
   (D) dabbler
   (E) bluestocking

8. **brusque**

   (A) meek
   (B) docile
   (C) submissive
   (D) dumb
   (E) abrupt, impatient

9. **frank**

   (A) disingenuous
   (B) taciturn
   (C) reticent
   (D) secretive
   (E) open, sincere

10. **cogitate**

   (A) to speak
   (B) to think
   (C) to dream
   (D) to wish
   (E) to write

11. **caustic**

   (A) sweet
   (B) luscious
   (C) sarcastic
   (D) melodious
   (E) effulgent

12. **candor**

   (A) withholding necessary facts
   (B) using jargon
   (C) eating candy
   (D) being open, sincere
   (E) traveling on foot through the countryside

13. **emphasize**

   (A) ignore
   (B) downplay
   (C) stress
   (D) overhaul
   (E) correct

14. **cant**

   (A) jargon
   (B) unable to complete a task
   (C) slow gallop
   (D) slander
   (E) edge; boundary; outer region

15. **dogmatic**

   (A) dog-like
   (B) asserted without proof, usually arrogantly
   (C) loyal
   (D) abrupt, impatient
   (E) flows easily

Give It a Try: Word Scramble

To complete the following acrostic, first unscramble each of the vocabulary words so that it matches its definition. Then, use the words to fill in the appropriate spaces on the corresponding lines. When you have completed the entire puzzle, another vocabulary word will read vertically in the circles. The answers appear on page 102.

bfiaenfle	inexpressible; overwhelming	
osloeginm	newly coined word	
oliyloqsu	point in a drama when a character reveals his or her thoughts to the audience	
bqyloou	abusive language	
daceerlat	jagged; torn	
ffeteecrvesn	bubbling; lively	
vnaal	pertaining to ships	
yroansittr	temporary	

Answers and Explanations

Word-Find Puzzle (page 93)

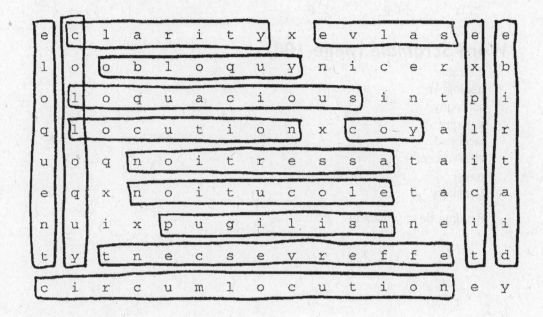

Multiple-Choice #1 (page 91)

1. D	6. E	11. A
2. D	7. A	12. A
3. A	8. B	13. E
4. C	9. C	14. E
5. E	10. B	15. E

Word-Definition Match (page 95)

1. g	6. e	11. b
2. k	7. o	12. j
3. d	8. l	13. n
4. m	9. c	14. a
5. h	10. f	15. i

Multiple-Choice #2 (pages 95–96)

1. D	4. B	7. B	10. E
2. A	5. C	8. B	11. A
3. A	6. D	9. E	12. C

Multiple-Choice #3 (page 98)

1. E	6. A	11. C
2. A	7. A	12. D
3. B	8. E	13. C
4. C	9. E	14. A
5. D	10. B	15. B

Word Scramble (page 100)

ineffable
neologism
soliloquy
obloquy
lacerated
effervescent
naval
transitory

Reading down: **insolent**

Day 8

Explore Test-worthy Words About the Law and Making Judgments

Bylaws (also spelled *by-laws*) are not laws adopted on the by-and-by. Neither are they casual or secondary laws. As used today, the word *bylaws* refers to the rules governing the internal affairs of an organization. When the word was first created, however, it had a very different meaning. The word *bylaws* comes from the Old Norse word *bylog*, and it referred to the laws of a village. In Middle English, the word came to mean the local law as distinguished from the general laws of the realm.

Knowing the history of the word *bylaws* can help you remember it for test-taking time as well as general usage. In this chapter, you'll learn a series of words that all have to do with laws and making judgments.

Be a Legal Beagle

Here are twelve words that concern judgments and the law. All these words are likely to crop up on standardized tests.

Word	Pronunciation	Meaning
accuse	a-*kyooz*	to charge with a crime
acquit	a-*kwit*	to free from blame
arbiter	*ahr*-bih-ter	a judge who decides a disputed issue
biased	*bye*-ist	prejudiced
collusion	coh-*loo*-shun	conspiracy; a secret agreement for fraudulent purposes
exculpate	*ek*-skul-payt	free from guilt
extradite	*ek*-strah-dyt	to give up a fugitive to another nation or authority

Be a Legal Beagle—continued

Word	Pronunciation	Meaning
fraud	*frawd*	deceit or trickery to gain an unfair advantage
jurisprudence	jer-is-*proo*-dence	the science of law
larceny	*lar*-sen-ee	theft; robbery
libel	*ly*-bul	false and malicious written statements
vindicated	*vin*-duh-kayt-id	freed from blame

Time for Fun: Word-Find Puzzle

There are ten words hidden in this word-find puzzle. Many of the words have already been introduced in this chapter, but a few are new. To complete the puzzle, locate and circle all the words. (See the word list below.) The words may be written forward, backward, or upside down. The answers appear on page 115. Good luck!

```
a  c  q  u  i  t  l  a  w  l  r
c  o  l  l  u  s  i  o  n  i  e
c  x  d  u  a  r  f  a  x  b  t
u  s  d  e  s  a  i  b  a  e  i
s  z  y  n  e  c  r  a  l  l  b
e  x  t  r  a  d  i  t  e  s  r
d  e  t  a  c  i  d  n  i  v  a
```

Word List

1. **accuse:** to charge with a crime

2. **acquit:** to free from blame

3. **collusion:** conspiracy; a secret agreement for fraudulent purposes

4. **fraud:** deceit or trickery to gain an unfair advantage

5. **extradite:** to give up a fugitive to another nation or authority

6. **biased:** prejudiced

7. **larceny:** theft; robbery

8. **libel:** false and malicious written statements

9. **vindicated:** freed from blame

10. **arbiter:** a judge who decides a disputed issue

It's Your Turn: Synonyms and Antonyms

This time, write the synonym and antonym for each word. (Remember that a *synonym* means the same; an *antonym* means the opposite.) You may wish to say the word aloud as you look for the match. Remember: saying the words will help you remember them! Then write your answers in the space provided. The answers appear on page 115.

Word	Synonym	Antonym
1. accuse	_____	_____
2. acquit	_____	_____
3. biased	_____	_____
4. collusion	_____	_____
5. extradite	_____	_____
6. exculpate	_____	_____
7. fraud	_____	_____
8. larceny	_____	_____
9. libel	_____	_____
10. vindicated	_____	_____

Explore Ten Test-worthy Words About Legal Matters

Following are some important words about legal matters, especially crimes and criminals. All of these words are likely to appear on standardized tests. As you read these words, cover the right column and see if you can guess the definitions of the words.

Word	Pronunciation	Definition
assault	a-*salt*	attempt or threaten to harm someone
battery	*bah*-ter-ee	an unlawful attack on another person by touching, beating, etc.
manslaughter	*man*-slaw-ter	murder
misdemeanor	miss-dih-*mee*-nor	a criminal offense, less serious than a felony
perjury	*per*-joor-ee	uttering false statements while under oath in court
swindle	*swin*-del	to cheat
terrorism	*terr*-or-ism	a violent act to force a government or people to support a specific political or social agenda
treason	*tree*-zon	the actions of a citizen to help a foreign government or entity overthrow or harm the government to which the citizen owes allegiance

Explore Ten Test-worthy Words About Legal Matters—*continued*

Word	Pronunciation	Definition
vagrancy	*vay*-gren-see	wandering idly without any means of support
vandalism	*van*-dal-ism	destroying or damaging property

Words About Criminals

The following five words all have to do with criminals and unlawful acts:

1. **alias** (*ay*-lee-us)

   any name used for an official purpose that is different from a person's legal name

2. **culprit** (*kul*-prit)

   a person arrested for an offense

3. **subpoena** (suh-*pee*-nuh)

   written order commanding a person to testify in court

4. **warrant** (*war*-ent)

   in criminal proceedings, any of a number of writs issued by a judicial officer that direct a law enforcement officer to perform a specified act

5. **writ** (riht)

   a document issued by a judicial officer ordering or forbidding the performance of a specified act

Myth: People dislike serving on juries.

Fact: A National Center for State Courts survey revealed that 81 percent of those who served on juries had a favorable attitude toward jury service.

Words Formed from "Judge"

It's not surprising that the word "judge" is part of many useful words about the law. Below are five of these "judge" words. Many appear on the GED, SAT, ACT, TOEFL, and other standardized tests.

1. **judge** (*juhdj*)

   noun: a public officer authorized to hear and determine cases in a court of law

   verb: to form an opinion

2. **adjudicator** (a-joo-dih-*kay*-tor)

   a person who acts as a judge and sits in judgment

3. **judicial**   (joo-*dish*-el)

pertaining to the justice system

4. **jurisdiction**   (joor-is-*dik*-shun)

legal power to hear and decide cases

5. **jurist**   (*joor*-ist)

someone who is part of a jury

Seventh-Inning Stretch: Multiple-Choice #1

Select the word that best completes each sentence. Then, write the letter of the word in the space. The answers appear on page 115.

1. The criminal was caught because his _____ was so close to his real name; in fact, he even used the same initials!

(A) swindle
(B) battery
(C) assault
(D) alias
(E) felony

2. The _____ who stole the canoe was apprehended when he returned for the oars.

(A) culprit
(B) swindle
(C) arbiter
(D) perquisite
(E) libel

3. Although it was clear that his testimony was _____, the accused swore that he was telling the truth.

(A) perjury
(B) authentic
(C) bona fide
(D) sacrosanct
(E) salubrious

4. When the accused ignored the _____ to appear in court, she was arrested by a police officer and hauled off to jail.

(A) battery
(B) subpoena
(C) assault
(D) prospectus
(E) insignia

5. After being convicted of a _____, the teenager had his license revoked.

(A) jurist
(B) warrant
(C) misdemeanor
(D) subpoena
(E) specter

6. The court's _____ was extensive—stretching across the entire state—giving it great legal power.

(A) collusion
(B) stanchion
(C) terrorism
(D) jurisdiction
(E) contagion

7. The driver was convicted of _____, a type of murder, because he deliberately ran over his neighbor.

   (A) subpoena
   (B) manslaughter
   (C) writ
   (D) arbiter
   (E) temperance

8. The _____ was so clever that it took the victim weeks to realize that she had been cheated.

   (A) verbiage
   (B) swindle
   (C) subpoena
   (D) writ
   (E) tenet

9. The _____ was furious about being called to serve on a jury for two weeks.

   (A) convoy
   (B) jurisdiction
   (C) writ
   (D) subpoena
   (E) jurist

10. The revolutionary was convicted of _____ for trying to help a foreign government overthrow or harm the United States.

    (A) inclemency
    (B) amiability
    (C) jurisdiction
    (D) philanthropy
    (E) treason

11. Smashing someone over the head with a stick is a clear-cut case of _____.

    (A) battery
    (B) terrorism
    (C) vagrancy
    (D) vandalism
    (E) benevolence

12. The jurists were guilty of _____ because they made a secret agreement to vote to acquit the accused.

    (A) jurisdiction
    (B) subpoena
    (C) collusion
    (D) culprit
    (E) warrant

Word-Definition Match

Match each word to its definition. Write the letter of your answer in the space provided. The answers appear on page 115.

_____ 1. manslaughter
_____ 2. misdemeanor
_____ 3. swindle
_____ 4. vagrancy
_____ 5. battery
_____ 6. perjury
_____ 7. culprit
_____ 8. jurisdiction
_____ 9. alias
_____ 10. subpoena
_____ 11. judicial
_____ 12. terrorism

a. use of violence as a means of coercion
b. legal power to hear and decide cases
c. uttering false statements while under oath in court
d. murder
e. written order commanding a person to testify in court
f. to cheat
g. a criminal offense, less serious than a felony
h. an unlawful attack on a person
i. pertaining to the justice system
j. fake name
k. wandering idly without any means of support
l. accused of a crime

Myth: America has too many lawyers—more than any other country.

Fact: The United States has 9.4 percent of the world's lawyers and ranks 35th in number of lawyers on a per capita basis. Among those ranked ahead of us are Japan, France, and Italy.

Investigate Twelve More Words About the Law

Below are twelve test-worthy words about testimony, the courts, and legal matters. As you study these words, try to use each one in a sentence.

Word	Pronunciation	Definition
bailiff	*bay*-liff	the court officer who keeps order in the courtroom and takes care of the jury
defendant	de-*fen*-dent	the person being accused or sued
deposition	dep-oh-*zish*-un	testimony taken down in writing under oath
hearsay	*heer*-say	evidence based on someone else's statements
impartial	im-*par*-shul	unbiased; not supporting either side
indict	in-*dite*	accuse or charge with a crime
integrity	in-*teg*-rit-ee	trustworthiness
litigation	lit-i-*gay*-shun	act of carrying out a lawsuit
objectivity	ob-jek-*tiv*-ity	impartiality
penitent	*pen*-uh-tent	expressing remorse for your mistakes
plaintiff	*plane*-tiff	the person who brings the lawsuit
venue	*ven*-yu	the area in which a court may hear or try a case

Present the Body!

The Latin root *corp* means "body." Several important legal words come from this root, including the phrase *writ of habeas corpus*. Literally, the phrase means "produce the body." A writ of habeas is used in some criminal proceedings to direct the court officer to bring the prisoner to court to determine the lawfulness of the imprisonment. Therefore, a *writ of habeas corpus* safeguards individuals from being unlawfully taken into custody. You can also figure out the term *corpus delict* by knowing that the root *corp* means "body." Literally, the phrase means "body of the crime." It is used to refer to facts that show a crime has taken place.

Words from the Root Appeal

An *appeal* is a request that a court review the decision of a lower court. Knowing what *appeal* means can help you decode related words. For instance, an *appellant* makes the appeal or is the person on whose behalf the appeal is made. The *appellate court* reviews the judgments of other courts. As you would expect, the appellate court has *appellate jurisdiction,* the legal authority to review a decision made by a lower court. Many other legal terms are built on similar roots, so knowing just a handful of legal words can help you figure out many more.

Seventh-Inning Stretch: Multiple-Choice #2

For each item, circle the word that is closest in meaning to the word in boldface. The answers appear on page 116.

1. **litigation**

    (A) lawsuit
    (B) loose
    (C) credible
    (D) view from a distance

2. **hearsay**

    (A) something overheard
    (B) gossip
    (C) the grapevine
    (D) evidence based on someone else's statements

3. **integrity**

    (A) infidelity
    (B) dishonesty
    (C) trustworthiness
    (D) neutrality

4. **venue**

    (A) bailiff
    (B) the area in which a court tries a case
    (C) sold
    (D) vivacious

5. **objectivity**

    (A) bias
    (B) impartiality
    (C) proclivity
    (D) inclination

6. **indict**

    (A) charge with a crime
    (B) provoke
    (C) exonerate from guilt
    (D) divulge

7. **deposition**

    (A) bailiff
    (B) divulge
    (C) oral testimony
    (D) written testimony

8. **penitent**

    (A) defiant
    (B) mutinous
    (C) expressing remorse for your mistakes
    (D) brave

9. **impartial**

    (A) dogmatic
    (B) unbiased
    (C) racist
    (D) humorous

10. **defendant**

    (A) plaintiff
    (B) jurist
    (C) bailiff
    (D) the person being accused or sued

Campaign for Political Terms with Multiple Meanings

"Pork barrel" is an odd term. In the grocery, it might refer to a barrel of sausage, but when applied to politics, "pork barrel" refers to spending that is primarily for the benefit of particular local interests.

Below are four words with multiple meanings. One meaning of each word can be applied to legal issues. Don't be fooled if you encounter these words on standardized tests. Be sure to use context to help you figure out the correct meaning in each particular situation.

Word	General Meaning	Political Meaning
cabinet	dresser; bureau	group of key presidential advisers
lobby	foyer; entryway	to attempt to persuade members of Congress to support or oppose particular policies or pieces of legislation
rider	person who rides	an attachment to a piece of legislation that is generally unrelated to the rest of the bill
whip	lash; rod	political party official in a legislative body charged with the duty of encouraging party members to vote with their parties on crucial legislation

Learn Words About Government

"E" is such a small letter that it couldn't have much impact on your legal rights . . . or could it? Actually, that little "e" matters a whole lot when it comes to cases and cakes. To a lawyer, a *tort* (tort) is a civil wrong for which the injured party is entitled to compensation. To a baker, a *torte* (tort) is a rich cake, especially one that contains little or no flour. As you can tell, both words are pronounced the same way. The only change is that itty-bitty "e." Small, but powerful.

Word	Pronunciation	Definition
bipartisanship	by-*par*-tis-en-ship	cooperation between Republicans and Democrats
caucus	*kaw*-kiss	a group of legislators unified by common goals or characteristics
census	*sen*-sus	an official counting of the U.S. population conducted by the government every ten years
deficit	*def*-eh-sit	amount by which spending exceeds funds during a fiscal year
delegate	*del*-uh-git	a representative who bases his or her votes on the majority opinions of the people he or she represents
filibuster	*fil*-eh-buss-ter	tactic employed to block legislation by speaking and refusing to stop
initiative	ih-*nish*-uh-tiv	a public policy question started by the people
laissez faire	*lay*-zay fahr	a "hands-off" approach to the economy characterized by minimal governmental interference
patronage	*pah*-troh-nij	awarding government jobs to political allies after winning election
subsidy	*sub*-sih-dee	economic benefit given by the government to a person or business to help a larger group
surplus	*sur*-plus	amount by which available funds exceed spending
veto	*vee*-toh	to reject a bill; Latin for "I forbid."

Seventh-Inning Stretch: Multiple-Choice #3

Select the correct meaning for each of the following boldfaced words. Circle your choice. The answers appear on page 116.

1. **surplus**

   (A) objective
   (B) shortage
   (C) extra
   (D) fatuous
   (E) catastrophe

2. **subsidy**

   (A) tariff
   (B) levy
   (C) endowment
   (D) assessment
   (E) penalty

3. **patronage**

   (A) reproof
   (B) castigation
   (C) reward
   (D) penalty
   (E) long-lasting friendship

4. **deficit**

   (A) shortfall
   (B) insult
   (C) auxiliary
   (D) character flaw
   (E) indignity

5. **laissez faire**

   (A) French food
   (B) foreign forms of leadership
   (C) government by fiat
   (D) "hands-off" approach to the economy
   (E) circuitous

6. **veto**

   (A) support a bill
   (B) victory
   (C) debacle
   (D) triumph
   (E) reject a bill

7. **collusion**

   (A) accident
   (B) conspiracy
   (C) detriment
   (D) mischief
   (E) magnate

8. **delegate**

   (A) a demotion
   (B) a slur
   (C) a triumph
   (D) a foe
   (E) a representative

9. **vindicated**

   (A) freed from blame
   (B) censured
   (C) denounced
   (D) reproached
   (E) violated

10. **filibuster**

    (A) type of nut
    (B) legal defense
    (C) long-winded oratory
    (D) type of judge
    (E) form of punishment

11. **integrity**

   (A) fraud
   (B) trustworthiness
   (C) misrepresentation
   (D) type of crime
   (E) innocence

12. **caucus**

   (A) boisterous
   (B) strident
   (C) serene
   (D) gathering
   (E) swift justice

Answers and Explanations

Word-Find Puzzle (page 104)

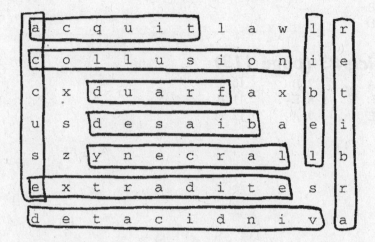

Synonyms and Antonyms (page 105)

(Possible answers)

Word	Synonym	Antonym
1. accuse	charge	vindicate
2. acquit	pardon	condemn
3. biased	prejudiced	impartial
4. collusion	conspiracy	independence
5. extradite	give up	imprison
6. exculpate	free	convict
7. fraud	deceit	honesty
8. larceny	theft	charity
9. libel	slander	praise
10. vindicated	freed	imprisoned

Multiple-Choice #1 (page 107)

1. D	4. B	7. B	10. E
2. A	5. C	8. B	11. A
3. A	6. D	9. E	12. C

Word-Definition Match (page 108)

1. d	4. k	7. l	10. e
2. g	5. h	8. b	11. i
3. f	6. c	9. j	12. a

Multiple-Choice #2 (page 110)

1. A	6. A		
2. D	7. D		
3. C	8. C		
4. B	9. B		
5. B	10. D		

Multiple-Choice #3 (page 113)

1. C	4. A	7. B	10. C
2. C	5. D	8. E	11. B
3. C	6. E	9. A	12. D

Day 9

Acquire Test-worthy Words About the Human Condition

The word *narcissism* refers to excessive self-admiration and vanity. It comes from the Greek myth of Narcissus. According to one version of the legend, the handsome Narcissus fell in love with his own image reflected in a pool of water. Because he was unable to embrace his image, he died from unrequited love.

The words in this chapter concern what it's like being human. Some of the words describe our faults; others, our strengths. Many of the words come from the fields of psychology, religion, and sociology. There are also a lot of games to make learning fun—as well as help you remember the words by using them in different ways.

Learn Ten Words About Vanity and Pride

The following ten test-worthy words all concern human faults: in this case, excessive pride. As you read the chart, use each word in a sentence to help you fix it in your mind.

Word	Pronunciation	Definition
arrogant	*ar*-oh-gant	conceited
condescending	kon-de-*send*-ing	patronizing, smug
contemptuous	kun-*temp*-choo-us	scornful
dictatorial	dik-tuh-*tor*-ee-ul	domineering
haughty	*haw*-tee	vain and egotistical

Learn Ten Words About Vanity and Pride—continued

Word	Pronunciation	Definition
imperious	im-*peer*-ee-us	overbearing
indolent	*in*-duh-lunt	lazy
insipid	in-*sip*-id	dull; unchallenging
patronizing	*pay*-truh-ny-zing	to treat someone in a condescending way
torpor	*tor*-per	dullness; inactivity

It's Your Turn: Synonyms and Antonyms

Write a *synonym* (word that means the same) and *antonym* (word that means the opposite) for each of the following words. The answers appear on page 126.

Word	Synonym	Antonym
arrogant		
condescending		
contemptuous		
dictatorial		
haughty		
imperious		
indolent		
insipid		
patronizing		
torpor		

Give It a Try: The Blame Game

Each of the following words concerns disapproval, criticism, and punishment. Determine which of the following four phrases best describes each word in the list that follows. Write the number of your answer choice on the line to the left of each entry. The answers appear on page 126.

> 1. to free from blame
> 2. to disapprove, criticize, or blame
> 3. to criticize or condemn abusively
> 4. to punish or discipline

___ absolve	___ exculpate	___ ostracize
___ acquit	___ execrate	___ reprimand
___ castigate	___ exonerate	___ reproach
___ censure	___ fulminate	___ reprove
___ chastise	___ indict	___ vindicate
___ deprecate	___ inveigh	___ vituperate
___ excoriate		

Time for Fun: I Cogitate (Think), Therefore I Am

Determine which of the following four words or phrases best describes each word in the list that follows. Write the number of your answer choice on the line to the left of each entry. The answers appear on page 127.

> 1. existing
> 2. newly existing
> 3. enduring or everlasting
> 4. temporary; not lasting

___ evanescent	___ neonate	___ tangible
___ extant	___ perdurable	___ temporal
___ inchoate	___ perennial	___ transient
___ incipient	___ protracted	___ transitory

Analyze Test-worthy Words from Psychology

The word *quixotic* is used to describe lofty but impractical sentiments like those of its namesake, Don Quixote. In 1605, the Spanish writer Miguel Cervantes created the novel's tragicomic hero, nobleman Don Quixote, and his stout servant, Sancho Panza, to parody valiant knights and faithful servants created by previous writers. The elderly Don was the purest embodiment of chivalry; unfortunately, he was also pitifully unaware of his false dreams.

The following ten words are all psychological terms that often appear on standardized tests. Try to vocalize as you learn. Remember that saying the words several times aloud can help fix them in your mind.

1. **angst** (*angst*) noun, anxiety

2. **catharsis** (kuh-*thar*-sis) noun, a discharge of strong emotions

3. **empathy** *(em*-puh-thee) noun, the ability to participate in another person's feelings and experiences and to understand them

4. **euphoria** (yoo-*for*-ee-uh) noun, a feeling of well-being or happiness

5. **gestalt** (*guh*-shtawlt) noun, a unified whole

6. **libido** (lih-*bee*-doh) noun, sexual energy

7. **misogynist** (mih-*sah*-juh-nist) noun, a person who hates women

8. **neurosis** (nore-*oh*-sis) noun, mild emotional disorder

9. **subliminal** (suh-*blim*-uh-nul) adjective, beneath the threshold of consciousness

10. **vicarious** (vy-*kayr*-ee-us) adjective, experienced indirectly through observation

Give It a Try: Word Scramble

To complete the following acrostic, first unscramble each of the vocabulary words so that it matches its definition. Then, use the words to fill in the appropriate spaces on the corresponding lines. When you have completed the entire puzzle, another vocabulary word will read vertically in the circles. The answers appear on page 127.

paeuorih	a feeling of well-being or happiness
tiyssnomgi	a woman-hater
aptrzgoniin	condescending
ntsag	anxiety
orrtpo	dullness; inactivity
yahtugh	egotistical
elloyw	a pale lemon color

It's Your Turn: A Love-Hate Relationship

For each word below, determine whether the word is closer in meaning to love (like) or hate (dislike). Indicate your choice by writing "L" for "love" or "H" for "hate" on the line to the left of each word. The answers appear on pages 127–128.

> L = love (like)
> H = hate (dislike)

___ abhor	___ delectation	___ pique
___ abominate	___ infatuation	___ predilection
___ amity	___ loathe	___ repugnant
___ antipathy	___ odium	___ umbrage
___ captivate	___ penchant	

Give It a Try: For Richer, for Poorer

Divide the following words into seven pairs of synonyms. The answers appear on page 128.

dowry	penurious	profligate	specie	wastrel
parsimonious	mercenary	largess	philanthropic	penury
impecunious	munificent	lucre	venal	

_____ = _____   _____ = _____
_____ = _____   _____ = _____
_____ = _____   _____ = _____
_____ = _____

Get the Test Writers' Favorite Test Words About Religion

Below are some important words about religion that are sure to appear on the next standardized test you take. The words are arranged in alphabetical order for ease of use. As you study, rearrange the words into other groupings that help you learn them.

Word	Pronunciation	Part of Speech	Meaning
apostle	uh-*pah*-sul	noun	disciple
benediction	ben-uh-*dik*-shun	noun	blessing, prayer
canon	*kan*-un	noun	religious doctrine
cherub	*chayr*-ub	noun	angel, represented as a child
cleric	*kler*-ik	noun	member of the clergy
creed	*kreed*	noun	statement of religious beliefs
ecclesiastical	eh-klee-zee-*as*-tih-kul	adjective	pertaining to the church

Get the Test Writers' Favorite Test Words About Religion—*continued*

Word	Pronunciation	Part of Speech	Meaning
ecumenical	ek-yoo-*men*-ih-kul	adjective	universal; worldwide
laity	*lay*-uh-tee	noun	non-clergy
liturgy	*lih*-ter-jee	noun	religious ceremonies
martyr	*mar*-ter	noun	one who suffers death as a penalty of refusing to renounce religious beliefs
orthodox	*or*-thuh-dahks	adjective	conventional; traditional
penance	*pen*-uns	noun	act of repentance
sect	*sekt*	noun	a breakaway religious group

Seventh-Inning Stretch: Multiple Choice

Select the correct meaning for each of the following boldfaced words. Circle your choice. The answers appear on page 128.

1. **orthodox**

   (A) liturgy
   (B) ecumenical
   (C) religious ceremonies
   (D) conventional; traditional
   (E) radical

2. **ecclesiastical**

   (A) pertaining to dissenters
   (B) pertaining to pain
   (C) pertaining to the church
   (D) pertaining to fidelity
   (E) pertaining to religious doubt

3. **laity**

   (A) liturgy
   (B) slothful
   (C) canon
   (D) clergy
   (E) non-clergy

4. **penance**

   (A) heartache
   (B) anguish
   (C) liturgy
   (D) benediction
   (E) act of repentance

5. **cherub**

   (A) angel, represented as a child
   (B) canon
   (C) liturgy
   (D) religious ceremonies
   (E) benediction

6. **apostle**

   (A) disciple
   (B) benediction
   (C) blessing
   (D) curse
   (E) heretic

7. **canon**

   (A) martyr
   (B) religious doctrine
   (C) criterion
   (D) religious test
   (E) spiritual journey

8. **liturgy**

   (A) martyr
   (B) religious ceremonies
   (C) sect
   (D) breakaway religious group
   (E) cleric

9. **benediction**

   (A) denunciation
   (B) canon
   (C) blessing, prayer
   (D) affliction
   (E) small, poor religious meeting place

10. **creed**

   (A) cruel
   (B) martyr
   (C) statement of religious doubt
   (D) cream of the crop
   (E) statement of religious beliefs

It's Your Turn: Good versus Evil

Each of the following words concerns morality. For each word below, determine whether the word is closer in meaning to righteous or depraved. Indicate your choice by writing "R" for "righteous" or "D" for "depraved" on the line to the left of each word. The answers appear on pages 128–129.

> R = righteous
> D = depraved

____ altruistic ____ infamous ____ opprobrious

____ beneficent ____ licentious ____ pious

____ benevolent ____ magnanimous ____ reprobate

____ heinous ____ nefarious ____ vile

____ ignominious ____ odious

Explore Test-worthy Words from Sociology

The following eight words come from the field of sociology, so they all describe aspects of the human condition. How many of these words do you already know?

1. **anomie** (*an*-uh-mee) noun, weakened social norms

2. **caste** (*kast*) noun, a hierarchical social system

3. **ethnocentric** (eth-noh-*sen*-trik) adjective, evaluating others according to your own ethnic group

4. **guild** (*gild*) noun, an association for the promotion of common goals

5. **more** (*mor*-ay) noun, a custom

6. **stigma** (*stig*-muh) noun, negative trait

7. **taboo** (tab-*oo*) adjective, forbidden action

8. **yeoman** (*yoh*-man) noun, farmer

Time for Fun: Word-Find Puzzle

There are twelve words hidden in this word-find puzzle. Many of the words have already been introduced in this chapter, but a few are new. To complete the puzzle, locate and circle all the words. (See the word list below.) The words may be written forward, backward, or upside down. The answers appear on page 129. Good luck!

```
s  a  t  l  a  t  s  e  g  o  l  a
t  a  b  o  o  m  o  r  e  d  i  n
i  e  n  a  m  o  e  y  e  i  b  o
g  u  i  l  d  e  l  i  v  o  i  n
m  a  e  t  s  a  c  i  o  u  d  a
a  n  o  m  i  e  a  n  a  s  o  c
```

Word List

1. **stigma:** negative trait
2. **anomie:** social instability caused by a breakdown in standards and values
3. **taboo:** forbidden action
4. **guild:** workers' cooperative
5. **caste:** a hierarchical social system
6. **yeoman:** farmer
7. **gestalt:** a unified whole
8. **more:** a custom
9. **odious:** disgusting
10. **vile:** hateful
11. **libido:** sexual energy
12. **canon:** religious doctrine

Give It a Try: Relatively Speaking

Each of the following words concerns family relationships. To play this game, match each word in the left column below to the word or phrase in the right column that best describes it. Write the matching letter on the line to the left of each entry in the left column. The answers appear on page 129.

_____	1. affinity	a. ancestor
_____	2. consanguineous	b. produce offspring
_____	3. fecund	c. kinship
_____	4. kin	d. father
_____	5. patriarch	e. brother or sister
_____	6. procreate	f. fertile
_____	7. progeny	g. descendants
_____	8. sibling	h. related by blood
_____	9. posterity	i. a relative
_____	10. progenitor	j. future generations

It's Your Turn: In the Mood

The following words describe moods and temperaments—your personality. To play this game, determine which of the following three words or phrases best describes each word in the list that follows. Write the number of your answer choice on the line to the left of each entry. The answers appear on page 130.

1. cheerful
2. irritable
3. somber or gloomy

___ acrimonious	___ despondent	___ peevish
___ bilious	___ irascible	___ pensive
___ buoyant	___ jocular	___ petulant
___ choleric	___ jocund	___ querulous
___ demure	___ lugubrious	___ saturnine

Answers and Explanations

Synonyms and Antonyms (page 118)

(Possible answers)

Word	Synonym	Antonym
arrogant	conceited	modest
condescending	smug	humble
contemptuous	scornful	kind
dictatorial	domineering	considerate
haughty	egotistical	modest
imperious	overbearing	obsequious
indolent	lazy	hard-working
insipid	dull	exciting
patronizing	condescending	solicitous
torpor	inactivity	activity

The Blame Game (page 119)

1. **to free from blame**

   absolve: to free from blame
   acquit: to clear from blame
   exculpate: to free from blame
   exonerate: to clear from blame
   vindicate: to clear from blame

2. **to disapprove, criticize, or blame**

   censure: to criticize severely
   deprecate: to express disapproval of
   indict: to charge with a crime
   reprimand: to scold
   reproach: to scold
   reprove: to blame

3. **to criticize or condemn abusively**

   excoriate: to denounce severely
   execrate: to denounce
   fulminate: to denounce
   inveigh: to denounce
   vituperate: to censure harshly

4. **to punish or discipline**

   castigate: to punish
   chastise: to discipline
   ostracize: to banish

I Cogitate (Think), Therefore I Am (page 119)

1. **existing**

   extant: outstanding
   tangible: real

2. **newly existing**

   inchoate: new
   incipient: initial
   neonate: newborn

3. **enduring or everlasting**

   perdurable: permanent
   perennial: lasting for a long time
   protracted: prolonged

4. **temporary; not lasting**

   evanescent: temporary
   temporal: pertaining the present life
   transient: of short duration
   transitory: existing only for a time

Word Scramble (page 120)

euphoria
misogynist
patronizing
angst
torpor
haughty
yellow

Reading down: **empathy**

A Love-Hate Relationship (page 121)

Love (like)

amity: friendship
captivate: to attract
delectation: delight
infatuation: foolish love
penchant: bias
predilection: a predisposition to prefer

Hate (dislike)

> *abhor:* to detest
> *abominate:* to hate
> *antipathy:* strong dislike
> *loathe:* to detest
> *odium:* hatred
> *pique:* fit of displeasure
> *repugnant:* repulsive
> *umbrage:* offense

For Richer, for Poorer (page 121)

dowry: money or property given by the bride's family to the bridegroom at marriage
largess: a generous bestowal of gifts

impecunious: penniless
penury: poverty

lucre: money
specie: coins

mercenary: available for hire
venal: mercenary

munificent: very generous
philanthropic: giving to charity

parsimonious: stingy
penurious: stingy

profligate: extravagant
wastrel: wasteful, especially with money

Multiple Choice (page 122)

1. D	6. A
2. C	7. B
3. E	8. B
4. E	9. C
5. A	10. E

Good versus Evil (page 123)

Righteous

> *altruistic:* generous
> *beneficent:* kind-hearted
> *benevolent:* generous
> *magnanimous:* generous
> *pious:* devout

Depraved

heinous: abominable
ignominious: shameful
infamous: notorious
licentious: immoral
nefarious: wicked
odious: disgusting
opprobrious: disgraceful
reprobate: depraved
vile: evil

Word-Find Puzzle (page 124)

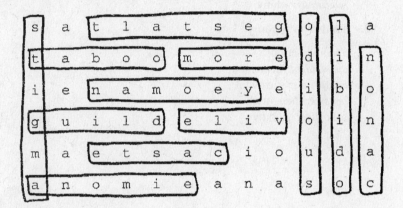

Relatively Speaking (page 125)

1. c   6. b
2. h   7. g
3. f   8. e
4. i   9. j
5. d   10. a

In the Mood (page 125)

1. **cheerful**

   buoyant: light-hearted; vivacious; cheerful
   jocular: joking
   jocund: merry; cheerful

2. **irritable**

   acrimonious: caustic; bitter
   bilious: ill-tempered
   choleric: angry
   irascible: easily provoked to anger
   peevish: ill-tempered
   petulant: cranky
   querulous: whiny

3. **somber or gloomy**

   demure: serious
   despondent: depressed
   lugubrious: sorrowful
   pensive: thoughtful
   saturnine: gloomy

Part IV

Unlock Key Words

Dissect Test-worthy Words About Medicine and Anatomy

A surprising number of medical terms appear on standardized tests. That's because these words are useful in daily life. Test makers know that everyday medical terminology will be helpful for you in the future, so they test it now.

Play Doctor with Fifteen Words About Body Parts

As you learned earlier in this book, mastering prefixes, roots, and suffixes is the easiest way to decode many unfamiliar words. Don't be put off by the length and seeming difficulty of the following words. Many medical and anatomical words come from Greek and Latin roots, which makes them relatively easy to figure out—if you stay cool and remember what you learned in Part II about affixes and roots. Use that knowledge now to decode the following words that concern body parts.

Root	Mean-ing	Example	Pronunciation	Meaning
arteri	artery	artery	*ar*-ter-ree	blood vessel
arthr	joint	arthritis	ar-*thri*-tus	inflammation of the joints
bronch	throat	bronchitis	bron-*ky*-tus	inflammation of the bronchial tubes
cardio	heart	cardiovascular	kar-dee-oh-*vas*-quoo-lar	dealing with the heart, blood vessels
chiro	hand	chiropractic	ky-roh-*prak*-tik	spinal column manipulation to cure illness
cranio	skull	cranium	*kray*-nee-um	skull
derm	skin	epidermis	eh-pih-*der*-mis	skin

Play Doctor with Fifteen Words About Body Parts—*continued*

Root	Meaning	Example	Pronunciation	Meaning
digit	finger, toe	digital	*dij*-ih-tal	pertaining to a digit
gastr	stomach	gastrology	gas-*strol*-oh-jee	stomach complaints
hem	blood	hematology	hee-mah-*tol*-oh-jee	pertaining to blood
laryn	larynx	larynx	*lar*-inks	structure in the throat
neur	nerve	neurology	nuh-*rah*-loh-jee	pertaining to the nervous system
pneum	lung	pneumonia	noo-*mohn*-ya	illness of the lungs
pulmo	lung	pulmonary	*puhl*-moh-nair-ee	pertaining to the lungs
sarc	flesh; connective tissue	sarcoma	sar-*koh*-mah	malignant tumor arising in tissue

Uncover Test-worthy Words About Medical Procedures

The following twelve words crop up often on standardized tests. They're also useful in everyday life, so they're twice as worthy of your time. Read each word and the pronunciation. Then, cover the last column and try to guess the definition using what you learned about word parts.

Word	Pronunciation	Meaning
anesthetized	ah-*nes*-tha-tized	deaden to pain
antibiotic	an-tih-by-*ah*-tik	bacteria-killing substances
antidote	*an*-tih-doht	remedy that acts against poison
antiseptic	an-tih-*sep*-tik	substance that kills germs
asymptomatic	ay-sim-toh-*mah*-tik	not showing any symptoms of disease
benign	bih-*nyn*	not life-threatening; harmless
coagulate	ko-*ag*-yu-layt	thicken or clot (as in blood)
convalescence	kahn-vah-*less*-ence	gradual recovery; period of recovery
diagnosis	dy-ag-*noh*-sis	identification of an illness
remission	ree-*mih*-shun	disappearance of disease symptoms
sutured	*soo*-chured	closed with stitches
therapy	*ther*-uh-pee	treatment of disease

Time for Fun: Word-Find Puzzle

There are fifteen words hidden in this word-find puzzle. Many of the words have already been introduced in this chapter, but a few are new. To complete the puzzle, locate and circle all the words. (See the word list below.) The words may be written forward, backward, or upside down. The answers appear on page 147. Good luck!

```
s  c  a  r  d  i  o  v  a  s  c  u  l  a  r  a  a
i  o  s  a  r  c  o  m  a  n  t  s  i  c  k  l  y
s  a  r  t  e  r  y  i  l  l  e  c  i  p  s  o  h
o  g  n  o  b  e  a  x  y  g  o  l  o  h  t  a  p
n  u  a  e  a  s  y  m  p  t  o  m  a  t  i  c  d
g  l  a  t  a  n  h  e  k  l  o  x  n  y  r  a  l
o  a  q  q  i  l  l  n  y  t  i  d  i  b  r  o  m
r  t  h  e  r  a  p  y  x  a  x  n  g  i  n  e  b
p  e  p  i  d  e  r  m  i  s  l  a  t  i  g  i  d
```

Word List

1. **cardiovascular:** dealing with the heart, blood vessels

2. **coagulate:** thicken or clot

3. **artery:** blood vessel

4. **therapy:** treatment of disease

5. **epidermis:** skin

6. **natal** (*nay*-tul): pertaining to birth

7. **pathology** (path-*ahl*-uh-jee): the study of the processes and causes of disease

8. **morbidity** (mor-*bid*-ih-tee): the incidence or prevalence of disease or death

9. **sarcoma:** malignant tumor in tissue

10. **larynx:** structure in the throat

11. **asymptomatic:** not showing any symptoms of disease

12. **hospice** (*hah*-spis): a caregiving environment for the terminally ill

13. **benign:** harmless

14. **digital:** pertaining to fingers and toes

15. **prognosis** (prahg-*noh*-sis): a medical forecast of the course of an illness and chances of recovery

Seventh-Inning Stretch: Multiple-Choice #1

Select the correct meaning for each of the following boldfaced words. Circle your choice. The answers appear on page 147.

1. **cranium**

    (A) chest cavity
    (B) nose
    (C) fingers
    (D) bones
    (E) skull

2. **epidermis**

    (A) sensitive
    (B) depilatory
    (C) skin
    (D) blood vessels
    (E) serious illness

3. **arthritis**

    (A) inflammation of the liver
    (B) inflammation of the spleen
    (C) inflammation of the joints
    (D) inflammation of the bronchial tubes
    (E) type of microscopic surgery

4. **antiseptic**

    (A) a substance that kills germs
    (B) deaden to pain
    (C) not showing any symptoms of disease
    (D) asymptomatic
    (E) remedy that acts against poison

5. **benign**

    (A) cancerous
    (B) not life-threatening; harmless
    (C) dangerous
    (D) beneficial
    (E) one of nine

6. **coagulate**

    (A) type of chiropractic
    (B) attenuate
    (C) thin
    (D) thicken
    (E) convalescence

7. **diagnosis**

    (A) type of surgery
    (B) pertaining to the lungs
    (C) forecast
    (D) identification of an illness
    (E) estimate

8. **anesthetize**

    (A) deaden to pain
    (B) anecdote
    (C) pertaining to the blood vessels
    (D) type of permanent cure
    (E) informed consent

9. **antibiotic**

    (A) type of health food
    (B) poison
    (C) closed with stitches
    (D) sacrament
    (E) bacteria-killing substances; medicine a doctor prescribes

10. **remission**

    (A) renege
    (B) relapse
    (C) readmitted to the hospital
    (D) disappearance of disease symptoms
    (E) reinvent

Explore Types of Medical Conditions

The following medical terms describe illnesses or injuries. They are all words you are likely to see on standardized tests, so why not meet them now? As you read the list, say each word aloud. Then, use each word in a sentence to help you remember it.

Word	Pronunciation	Meaning
aneurysm	*an*-yoor-is-um	abnormal blood-filled part of an artery
carcinogenic	car-sin-oh-*jen*-ik	cancer-producing
comatose	*koh*-mah-tose	unconscious; in a coma
concussion	kuhn-*kush*-un	brain injury
hematoma	hee-mah-*toh*-mah	swelling
incision	in-*sih*-shun	cut, as in surgery
lacerated	*lah*-sir-ray-ted	torn, as in a wound
lesion	*lee*-shun	injury
melanoma	meh-lah-*no*-mah	cancerous skin cell
migraine	*my*-grayn	intense headache
toxic	*tahx*-ik	poisonous
ulcer	*ul*-sur	an open sore

Give It a Try: Word Scramble

To complete the following acrostic, first unscramble each of the vocabulary words so that it matches its definition. Then, use the words to fill in the appropriate spaces on the corresponding lines. When you have completed the entire puzzle, another vocabulary word will read vertically in the circles. The answers appear on page 147.

rgneaiim	intense headache
demiperis	skin
arlceeatd	torn, as in a wound
rytera	blood vessel
atnal	pertaining to birth
rpmttosoeit	eyecare provider who tests vision and prescribes eyeglasses and contact lenses
ybidormit	the incidence or prevalence of disease (or death)
enursmya	abnormal blood-filled part of an artery

Learn More Words About Medicine

The suffix *-itis* means "inflammation." For example, *dermatitis* is a skin inflammation, *gastritis* is a stomach inflammation, *gingivitis* is a gum inflammation, *meningitis* is an inflammation of the lining of the brain, and *phlebitis* is an inflammation of a vein.

Below are some test-worthy words that describe medical conditions. You're likely to see these words on the SAT, GED, ACT, PSAT/NMSQT, or TOEFL.

Word	Pronunciation	Meaning
alopecia	al-oh-*pee*-shuh	hair loss
anorexia nervosa	ahn-uh-*rex*-ee-uh nur-*voh*-suh	extreme aversion to food
asthma	*as*-mah	disease marked by recurrent attacks of distressed breathing
bulimia	buh-*leem*-ee-uh	abnormal food craving followed by purging
cirrhosis	sir-*roh*-sus	disease of the liver
congenital	kun-*jen*-ih-tul	condition originating before birth
diabetes	dy-uh-*bee*-tees	insulin deficiency disease
insomnia	in-*som*-nee-uh	inability to sleep
lymph nodes	*limf nodes*	lymphoid organs
plasma	*plas*-muh	fluid portion of the blood
schizophrenia	skitz-oh-*fren*-ee-uh	type of psychosis
tumor	*too*-mer	abnormal mass of tissue that grows rapidly

Seventh-Inning Stretch: Word-Definition Match #1

This time, match the word to its definition. You may wish to say the word aloud as you look for the match. Remember: saying the words will help you remember them. Then, write the letter of your answer in the space provided. The answers appear on page 148.

_____	1. schizophrenia	a.	hair loss
_____	2. diabetes	b.	poisonous
_____	3. tumor	c.	ritual
_____	4. congenital	d.	type of psychosis
_____	5. insomnia	e.	lymphoid organs
_____	6. anorexia nervosa	f.	inability to sleep
_____	7. toxic	g.	portion of the blood
_____	8. cirrhosis	h.	torn, as a wound
_____	9. lacerated	i.	abnormal mass of tissue that grows too fast
_____	10. sacrament	j.	extreme aversion to food
_____	11. lymph nodes	k.	disease marked by recurrent attacks of distressed breathing
_____	12. bulimia	l.	insulin deficiency disease
_____	13. plasma	m.	abnormal food craving and purging
_____	14. asthma	n.	condition originating before birth
_____	15. alopecia	o.	disease of the liver

Master Words About Fears

The root *mania* means a "compulsion" or "preoccupation with." *Phobia* means "fear." Many of these words are likely to appear on standardized tests.

Word	Fear of	Pronunciation
acrophobia	heights	ak-kroh-*foh*-bee-uh
chronophobia	time	krahn-oh-*foh*-bee-uh
demophobia	people	deh-moh-*foh*-bee-uh
entomophobia	insects	en-toh-moh-*foh*-bee-uh
ergophobia	work	er-goh-*foh*-bee-uh
gerontophobia	old people	jer-ahn-toh-*foh*-bee-uh
hematophobia	blood	hee-mat-toh-*foh*-bee-uh
necrophobia	corpses	nek-roh-*foh*-bee-uh
nyctophobia	night	nick-toh-*foh*-bee-uh
pedophobia	children	ped-doh-*foh*-bee-uh
theophobia	God	thee-oh-*foh*-bee-uh
thermophobia	heat	therm-oh-*foh*-bee-uh

Discover Words About Obsessions

Along with fears come our fixations. The following words describe these conditions. The words are long and seemingly difficult so they are ideal for standardized tests. However, if you take them apart and look at the prefixes, roots, and suffixes, you'll discover that these words are all relatively easy to decode.

Word	Preoccupation with	Pronunciation
gamomania	marriage	gah-moh-*may*-nee-uh
kleptomania	stealing	klep-toh-*may*-nee-uh
megalomania	self-greatness	meh-ga-loh-*may*-nee-uh
mythomania	lies	mith-oh-*may*-nee-uh
phagomania	eating	fag-oh-*may*-nee-uh
plutomania	wealth	ploo-toh-*may*-nee-uh
pyromania	fire	py-roh-*may*-nee-uh
xenomania	foreigners	zen-no-*may*-nee-uh
zoomania	animals	zoo-*may*-nee-uh

Time for Fun: True or False

In the space provided, write **T** if the definition of each word is true and **F** if it is false. Try to use what you learned in this lesson. The answers appear on page 148.

_____ 1. entomophobia   fear of insects
_____ 2. mythomania   fear of lies
_____ 3. plutomania   obsession with the planet Pluto
_____ 4. necrophobia   fear of corpses
_____ 5. pyromania   obsession with fire
_____ 6. megalomania   obsession with eating
_____ 7. acrophobia   fear of heights
_____ 8. nyctophobia   fear of night
_____ 9. kleptomania   obsession with stealing
_____ 10. xenomania   obsession with work

Seventh-Inning Stretch: Multiple-Choice #2

Select the correct meaning for each of the following boldfaced words. Circle your choice. The answers appear on page 148.

1. After he was booked in the police station, the **kleptomaniac** admitted that he had a long-standing problem with _____.

   (A) foreigners
   (B) fire
   (C) stealing
   (D) night terrors
   (E) alienation

2. The CEO can only be described as a **megalomaniac**, because she was obsessed with _____.

   (A) corpses
   (B) eating
   (C) heights
   (D) lies
   (E) self-greatness

3. A **pyromaniac** might gravitate toward a job as a _____.

   (A) mortician
   (B) firefighter
   (C) teacher
   (D) weather forecaster
   (E) chef

4. **Xenophobics** are likely to sponsor a law to keep out _____.

   (A) land developments
   (B) foreigners
   (C) the elderly
   (D) organized religion
   (E) children

5. People who suffer from **zoomania** are most likely to be found visiting _____.

   (A) wildlife preserves
   (B) extended-care residential facilities
   (C) hospitals
   (D) funeral homes
   (E) observatories

6. A person with **necrophobia** would be best off avoiding _____.

   (A) fires
   (B) infants and young children
   (C) the elderly
   (D) dead bodies
   (E) large insects

7. My friend with **nyctophobia** always slept with a light on because she was afraid of _____.

   (A) insects
   (B) the dark
   (C) fire
   (D) noises
   (E) insomnia

8. Although fearless as a child, Carlos developed **acrophobia** in his late teens and had to abandon his dream of becoming a _____.

   (A) lion tamer
   (B) rodeo cowboy
   (C) racecar driver
   (D) submarine sailor
   (E) tight-rope walker

9. The **chronophobiac** never wore a watch because she had a fear of _____.

   (A) tight bindings
   (B) leather
   (C) chrome
   (D) losing precious things
   (E) time

10. The **entomophobiac** hiker stayed out of the woods because she had a fear of _____.

   (A) big trees
   (B) avalanches
   (C) falling down
   (D) insects
   (E) bears

Dissect More Medical Words

The following medical terms are all in general use, which makes them not only likely to appear on a standardized test but also important for educated people to know. Select the words you find most difficult and write them on note cards, as you learned on Day 3.

1. **astringent** (uh-*strin*-junt): a harsh, biting substance

2. **chronic** (*krah*-nik): continuous; constant

3. **congenital** (kun-*jen*-ih-tul): inborn; innate

4. **emetic** (uh-*meh*-tik): any substance used to induce vomiting

5. **febrile** (*feh*-bryl): feverish

6. **geriatric** (jayr-ee-*at*-rik): relating to medical care and treatment of the elderly

7. **morbidity** (mor-*bid*-ih-tee): the incidence or prevalence of disease or death

8. **prognosis** (prahg-*noh*-sis): a medical prediction or forecast of the course of an illness and chances of recovery

9. **prosthesis** (prahs-*thee*-sis): an artificial device to replace a missing part of the body

10. **quarantine** (*kwor*-un-teen): isolation of a person to prevent spread of disease (also used as a verb)

11. **senescent** (suh-*nes*-unt): growing old; aging

12. **vertigo** (*ver*-tih-goh): dizziness and the sensation of head-spinning

Seventh-Inning Stretch: Word-Definition Match #2

Match each numbered word in the left column with its lettered definition in the right column. Then, write the letter of your answer in the space provided. The answers appear on page 148.

_____ 1. febrile	a.	dizziness
_____ 2. congenital	b.	isolation of a person to prevent spread of disease
_____ 3. astringent	c.	relating to medical care and treatment of the elderly
_____ 4. emetic	d.	feverish
_____ 5. geriatric	e.	aging
_____ 6. morbidity	f.	substance used to induce vomiting
_____ 7. prosthesis	g.	the incidence or prevalence of disease or death
_____ 8. quarantine	h.	harsh, biting substance
_____ 9. senescent	i.	an artificial limb
_____ 10. vertigo	j.	innate

Prescribe Words for Special Doctors

The following chart shows the terms for specialists. These are often used in analogies involving a person and his or her occupation.

Doctor	Specialty
allergist (*a*-ler-jist)	doctor who treats sensitivity to pollen, food, pets, and so on
anesthesiologist (ah-nis-thee-zee-*ahl*-oh-jist)	doctor who reduces pain and renders patients unconscious
audiologist (aw-dee-*ah*-loh-jist)	hearing specialist
cardiologist (car-dee-*ah*-loh-jist)	doctor who specializes in heart diseases
dermatologist (der-mah-*tahl*-loh-jist)	doctor who specializes in skin conditions
endocrinologist (en-doh-crin-*nol*-oh-jist)	doctor who specializes in glands and metabolic disorders
epidemiologist (eh-pih-dee-mee-*ol*-oh-jist)	doctor who specializes in infectious diseases
gastroenterologist (gas-trow-en-ter-*rah*-lo-jist)	doctor who specializes in diseases of the digestive organs
gerontologist (jeh-rahn-*tahl*-oh-jist)	health-care professional who specializes in the study of aging and the problems of older adults
hematologist (hee-mah-*tah*-loh-jist)	doctor who specializes in diseases of the blood
immunologist (im-yu-*nahl*-oh-jist)	doctor who specializes in the phenomena and causes of immunity and immune responses
internist (*in*-turn-ist)	doctor who specializes in internal medicine
neonatologist (nee-oh-nay-*tahl*-oh-jist)	doctor who specializes in very young infants, usually birth to ten days
nephrologist (neh-*frah*-loh-jist)	doctor who specializes in diseases of the kidneys and related organs
neurologist (noo-*rahl*-oh-jist)	doctor who deals with the nervous system
obstetrician (ahb-stah-*trih*-shun)	doctor who delivers babies All obstetricians are gynecologists, but not all gynecologists are obstetricians because they may choose not to deliver babies.
oncologist (ohn-*col*-oh-jist)	doctor who treats cancer
ophthalmologist (ohf-tho-*mahl*-oh-jist)	doctor who treats diseases of the eye and tests vision These are the doctors to see if you want or need eye surgery.
optometrist (ahp-*tahm*-uh-trist)	eye-care provider who tests vision and prescribes eyeglasses and contact lenses
orthopedist (or-thoh-*pee*-dist)	doctor who fixes broken bones

Words for Special Doctors—*continued*

Doctor	Specialty
osteopath (*ahs*-tee-oh-path)	doctor who treats illness through the skeleton and muscle systems These doctors often function as general practitioners.
otolaryngologist (oh-toh-lahr-en-*gahl*-oh-jist)	doctor who treats conditions of the ear, nose, and throat Often called "ENT" (ear, nose, and throat) specialists, for short.
pathologist (path-*ahl*-oh-jist)	doctor who identifies diseases by studying cells and tissues under a microscope Your doctor will send slides of growths and masses to these doctors for analysis.
pediatrician (pee-dee-uh-*trish*-un)	doctor who treats children See these doctors if your child is ill with a virus, ear infection, and so on.
periodontist (per-ee-oh-*dahn*-tist)	doctor who treats gum diseases
plastic surgeon	doctor who repairs and remakes the body See these doctors to correct certain types of birth defects or for cosmetic surgery.
podiatrist (poh-*dy*-uh-trist)	doctor who deals with foot problems
psychiatrist (sy-*ky*-uh-trist)	physician (M.D.) who specializes in the prevention, diagnosis, and treatment of mental illness See these doctors for extended therapy and medication to deal with mental illness or trauma.
psychologist (sy-*kahl*-oh-jist)	social scientist who studies behavior and mental processes in a research or clinical setting Psychologists can only use talk therapy as treatment; you must see a psychiatrist or other medical doctor to be treated with medication.

Psychology, the science of the mind, gets its name from Psyche, a beautiful woman in Greek mythology who was desired by Eros, the god of love. He forbade her to look at him because he was a god. When she disobeyed him by lighting a lamp in the dark, he abandoned her. Eventually she was reunited with Eros and joined the immortals. She was worshipped as the personification of the human soul.

Words for Special Doctors—continued

Doctor	Specialty
pulmonologist (pul-mah-*nahl*-oh-jist)	doctor who deals with the lungs and related diseases See these doctors if you have a disease of the respiratory system, such as asthma.
radiologist (ray-dee-*ahl*-oh-jist)	medical doctor who specializes in the reading and interpretation of X-rays and other medical images
rheumatologist (roo-mah-*tahl*-oh-jist)	doctor who deals with inflammation and pain in muscles and joints
urologist (yoo-*rahl*-oh-jist)	doctor who specializes in the diagnosis and treatment of diseases of the urinary tract and urogenital system

Seventh-Inning Stretch: Multiple-Choice #3

Select the word that best completes each sentence. Then, write the letter of the word in the space. The answers appear on page 148.

1. Consult an _____ if you have hay fever or a severe reaction to any kind of food.

    (A) allergist
    (B) anesthesiologist
    (C) obstetrician
    (D) oncologist
    (E) osteopath

2. An _____ would be present during surgery to handle the patient's pain.

    (A) epidemiologist
    (B) anesthesiologist
    (C) allergist
    (D) obstetrician
    (E) otolaryngologist

3. A(n) _____ usually does research and tracks outbreaks of major contagious diseases.

    (A) hematologist
    (B) nephrologist
    (C) neurologist
    (D) epidemiologist
    (E) urologist

4. See a _____ if you suspect you have an ulcer or trouble with your stomach.

    (A) periodontist
    (B) dermatologist
    (C) hematologist
    (D) gastroenterologist
    (E) surgeon

5. A(n) _____ specializes in the needs and issues of older individuals.

    (A) gastroenterologist
    (B) osteopath
    (C) gerontologist
    (D) surgeon
    (E) oncologist

6. Consult a(n) _____ if you suspect you have difficulty hearing.

    (A) audiologist
    (B) hematologist
    (C) pediatrician
    (D) psychologist
    (E) dermatologist

7. See a _____ if you suspect you had a heart attack.

    (A) urologist
    (B) surgeon
    (C) podiatrist
    (D) periodontist
    (E) cardiologist

8. A _____ would be consulted if an infant were in distress.

    (A) psychologist
    (B) neurologist
    (C) neonatologist
    (D) plastic surgeon
    (E) radiologist

9. Consult a(n) _____ if you have a kidney infection.

    (A) otolaryngologist
    (B) psychologist
    (C) podiatrist
    (D) nephrologist
    (E) urologist

10. See a _____ if you have a burn, acne, or suspicious moles.

    (A) dermatologist
    (B) neonatologist
    (C) plastic surgeon
    (D) pediatrician
    (E) radiologist

Answers and Explanations

Word-Find Puzzle (page 135)

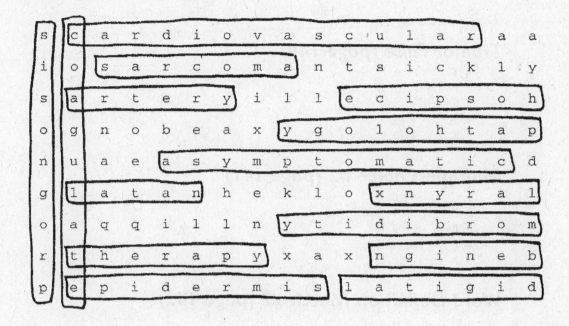

Multiple-Choice #1 (page 136)

1. E	6. D
2. C	7. D
3. C	8. A
4. A	9. E
5. B	10. D

Word Scramble (page 137)

migraine
epidermis
lacerated
artery
natal
optometrist
morbidity
aneurysm

Reading down: **melanoma**

Word-Definition Match #1 (page 139)

1. d	6. j	11. e
2. l	7. b	12. m
3. i	8. o	13. g
4. n	9. h	14. k
5. f	10. c	15. a

True or False (page 140)

1. T	6. F
2. F	7. T
3. F	8. T
4. T	9. T
5. T	10. F

Multiple-Choice #2 (page 141)

1. C	6. D
2. E	7. B
3. B	8. E
4. B	9. E
5. A	10. D

Word-Definition Match #2 (page 142)

1. d	6. g
2. j	7. i
3. h	8. b
4. f	9. e
5. c	10. a

Multiple-Choice #3 (pages 145–146)

1. A	6. A
2. B	7. E
3. D	8. C
4. D	9. D
5. C	10. A

Day 11

Master Test-worthy Words About Learning

Everyone has a weak, unguarded spot. We use the term "Achilles' heel" to refer to this weak point. The term comes from Homer's epic poem the *Iliad.* According to legend, Achilles' mother, Thetis, plunged her infant son into the river Styx to make him invulnerable. Since she held him by the heel, it stayed dry—and vulnerable. Many years later, during the siege of Troy, Paris shot an arrow into Achilles' heel, fatally wounding him.

This chapter will help make sure that words about learning aren't *your* Achilles' heel on standardized tests! As you work through this chapter, use all the techniques you learned on Day 3 to help you remember the words.

Distinguish Between Words with Multiple Meanings

Many words in English have a dual meaning, depending on their part of speech. No wonder the English language is so difficult to learn! Study the following examples:

- We must polish the Polish furniture.
- He could lead if he would get the lead out.
- The farm was used to produce produce.
- The dump was so full that it had to refuse more refuse.
- The soldier decided to desert in the desert.
- This was a good time to present the present. (And this last word could mean "gift" or "era of time.")
- A bass was painted on the head of the bass drum.
- When shot at, the dove dove into the bushes.
- I did not object to the object.
- The insurance was invalid for the invalid.
- The bandage was wound around the wound.
- There was a row among the oarsmen about how to row.

- They were too <u>close</u> to the door to <u>close</u> it.
- They sent a <u>sewer</u> down to stitch the tear in the <u>sewer</u> line.
- To help with planting, the farmer taught his <u>sow</u> to <u>sow</u>.
- The <u>wind</u> was too strong to <u>wind</u> the sail.
- Upon seeing the <u>tear</u> in my clothes, I shed a <u>tear</u>.
- I had to <u>subject</u> the <u>subject</u> to a series of tests.
- How can I <u>intimate</u> this to my most <u>intimate</u> friend?

The moral of the story? Even supposedly "easy" words can stump unwary test takers because they are being used in unfamiliar ways. Therefore, it's not enough to know the words; you also have to know how they are used. Apply this lesson today (and as you work through this book) by using each word in a sentence as you learn it.

Today, you'll learn more words about learning. These test-worthy words will serve you in good stead on standardized tests. But first, a game. After all, learning words should be fun, not boring.

Time for Fun: Indefinite Definitions

The following twenty-one common words have uncommon meanings. Match each word in the left column to the word or phrase in the right column that best describes it. Write the letter of your answer on the line. The answers appear on page 161.

_____ 1. ape	a. postpone
_____ 2. appropriate	b. lessen vibration
_____ 3. crop	c. tear
_____ 4. damp	d. criticize
_____ 5. fault	e. rind
_____ 6. fell	f. dock
_____ 7. graft	g. make harmless
_____ 8. list	h. acquire
_____ 9. more	i. ill-gotten gain
_____ 10. pan	j. bare hill
_____ 11. rake	k. custom
_____ 12. relief	l. tilt
_____ 13. rent	m. make suitable
_____ 14. scotch	n. cut off
_____ 15. slip	o. womanizer
_____ 16. spit	p. raised
_____ 17. table	q. straddle
_____ 18. tack	r. mimic
_____ 19. temper	s. skewer
_____ 20. waffle	t. direction
_____ 21. zest	u. fracture

Study Ten Test-worthy Words About Learning

Every subject area has its special words, and learning is no exception. Below are ten words that test makers like to include on their standardized assessments. As you read each of the following words, try to visualize it in your mind. Then, "tag" each word to an object or a place to help it stick in your mind. Finally, say the word again.

Word	Pronunciation	Meaning
abstract	ab-*strakt*	theoretical; hypothetical
acquire	ak-*wy*-er	learn
conception	kun-*sep*-shun	the ability to understand an idea
conviction	kun-*vik*-shun	a strong belief
dogmatic	dawg-*mat*-ik	stubbornness
enlighten	en-*lyt*-un	educate; inform
impression	im-*preh*-shun	understanding something you've experienced
intuition	in-too-*ish*-un	perception; insight
misconception	mis-kun-*sep*-shun	mistaken idea
paradigm	*pair*-a-dym	model; example

Master Five More Words About Learning

In the *Odyssey*, Mentor is Odysseus' friend. He also tutors Odysseus' son, Telemachus. Today, the term *mentor* has come to mean a "trusted teacher or guide." The following five words also concern scholarship and knowledge, though none has as interesting a history as *mentor*!

Read each word and its sentence. Then, try to create sentences of your own using these words.

1. **perception** (per-*sep*-shun) insight
Lucia had a new perception about consumerism from reading *The Great Gatsby*.

2. **perspective** (per-*spek*-tiv) vantage point
From his perspective, the car appeared to be a total loss.

3. **profound** (pro-*found*) very serious or deep
With a profound sigh, Jack turned back to the profound discussion of life and death.

4. **rational** (*rash*-un-ul) logical
Wanda made a rational decision when she opted to study physics instead of underwater fire prevention.

_____

5. **theoretical** (thee-oh-*ret*-ih-kul) speculative; hypothetical
Theoretical physics is concerned with particles far too small to be seen by the naked eye.

_____

Look into Six "Learning" Words with the Same Root

Study the following six words. Notice that they all contain the roots *cogn* or *gno*, "to know or learn." How can knowing this root help you remember these words?

1. **agnostic:** noun, a person who holds the view that any ultimate reality (as God) is unknown and probably unknowable

2. **cognizant:** adjective, involving conscious intellectual activity (as thinking, reasoning, or remembering)

3. **cognizant:** adjective, knowledgeable of something especially through personal experience

4. **incognito:** adjective, with one's identity concealed

5. **prognosis:** noun, a prediction of the probable course and outcome of a disease

6. **recognize:** verb, to know something that has been perceived before

Seventh-Inning Stretch: Multiple Choice

Select the word that best completes each sentence. Write the letter of the word in the space. The answers appear on page 161.

1. Some people dismiss _____, but subtle clues in our environment often help us recognize these sudden and unexplained insights.

   (A) sedition
   (B) agnostics
   (C) conviction
   (D) intuition
   (E) vacillation

2. A few lucky people _____ new skills easily, while others have to work hard to learn new ideas and concepts.

   (A) reconnoiter
   (B) bedaub
   (C) acquire
   (D) berate
   (E) extradite

3. The student's _____ and stubborn adherence to outmoded theories made it difficult for her to accept new ideas.

   (A) abstract
   (B) incognito
   (C) agnostic
   (D) pliant
   (E) dogmatic

4. Due to a _____, the chemistry student mixed the wrong chemicals and nearly blew up the lab! Fortunately, the mistake was easily rectified.

   (A) conviction
   (B) reconnoiter
   (C) preamble
   (D) subpoena
   (E) misconception

5. Sometimes, hands-on experience can help _____ students more than old-fashioned lecturing can.

   (A) enlighten
   (B) abstract
   (C) reconnoiter
   (D) obliterate
   (E) nullify

6. Even on the first day, Nikki got the _____ that her teacher was determined to help her students learn how to write. This feeling was reinforced as the days went on.

   (A) impression
   (B) abstract
   (C) subterfuge
   (D) alibi
   (E) precept

7. E. B. White's writing style is often held up as a _____ of clear, concise, and elegant prose.

   (A) conviction
   (B) paradigm
   (C) reconnoiter
   (D) sedition
   (E) cordial

8. The experiment made previously _____ ideas far more specific and concrete.

   (A) incognito
   (B) abstract
   (C) agnostic
   (D) reconnoiter
   (E) explicit

9. From Sam's _____, the island appeared to be a wasteland. Only upon a closer look was he able to see that there was indeed vegetation.

   (A) reconnoiter
   (B) incognito
   (C) perspective
   (D) concord
   (E) increment

10. Bill is a _____ of the finer things in life: classic novels, cars, and chocolates. As an expert, he knows just which items are the best.

    (A) greenhorn
    (B) novice
    (C) amateur
    (D) reconnoiter
    (E) connoisseur

Give It a Try: Word Scramble

To complete the following acrostic, first unscramble each of the vocabulary words so that it matches its definition. Then, use the words to fill in the appropriate spaces on the corresponding lines. When you have completed the entire puzzle, another vocabulary word will read vertically in the circles. The answers appear on page 161.

pea	copy	⬭⬜⬜
titerlb	fragile	⬭⬜⬜⬜⬜⬜
tpis	skewer	⬭⬜⬜⬜
itacohterel	speculative; hypothetical	⬭⬜⬜⬜⬜⬜⬜⬜⬜⬜
aerk	womanizer	⬭⬜⬜⬜
cauirqe	learn	⬭⬜⬜⬜⬜⬜
nviocticon	a strong belief	⬭⬜⬜⬜⬜⬜⬜⬜⬜
aeltb	postpone	⬭⬜⬜⬜⬜

Explore Words About Linguistics

The following ten words all concern linguistics, the branch of learning that deals with words and how they are used. Write the especially challenging words on cards, as described on Day 3. Refer to the cards in your spare moments. Practice *does* make perfect!

Word	Pronunciation	Part of Speech	Meaning
alliteration	uh-lih-ter-*ay*-shun	noun	repeating the same sound at the beginning of words
anachronism	uh-*nak*-ruh-nih-zum	noun	from another time
anagram	*an*-uh-gram	noun	word game
aphasia	uh-*fay*-zhyuh	noun	loss of the ability to speak
assonance	*as*-uh-nens	noun	repeating the same vowel sounds
cadence	*kay*-dins	noun	meter or beat in speech
colloquial	kuh-*loh*-kwee-ul	adjective	informal speech or writing
connote	kuh-*noht*	verb	understood meaning
dialect	*dy*-uh-lekt	noun	regional language
elocution	el-uh-*kyoo*-shun	noun	public speaking

Discover More Words About Linguistics

A person who speaks or writes in several languages is called a *polyglot* (*pah*-lee-glaht). Fortunately, to do well on most standardized tests, you need only know English. Below are twelve more words that often appear on these tests. Knowing these words can make it easier for you to earn a high score.

1. **evocative** (ih-*vahk*-uh-tiv) causing an emotional reaction

2. **expletive** (*eks*-pluh-tiv) word used as a filler

3. **idiom** (*id*-ee-um) a phrase that has a nonliteral meaning, such as "It's raining cats and dogs."

4. **intonation** (in-toh-*nay*-shun) pitch

5. **lexicon** (*lek*-sih-kahn) a dictionary

6. **mnemonic** (nee-*mah*-nik) memory aid

7. **pejorative** (puh-*jor*-uh-tiv) negative connotation

8. **phonetic** (fuh-*net*-ik) of or relating to spoken language or speech sounds

9. **pidgin** (*pih*-jun) a mixture of different languages

10. **rebus** (*ree*-bus) showing a word by pictures or symbols

11. **rhetoric** (*ret*-uh-rik) persuasion through argument

12. **syntax** (*sin*-taks) arrangement of words in a sentence

Time for Fun: Word-Find Puzzle

Time for a break. There are fifteen words hidden in this word-find puzzle. Ten words have already been covered in this chapter, but five are new. To complete the puzzle, locate and circle all the words. (See the word list below.) The words may be written forward, backward, or upside down. The answers appear on page 162. Good luck!

```
a  g  n  o  s  t  i  c  m  o  i  d  i  c  e  l
n  o  i  t  a  r  e  t  i  l  l  a  x  a  t  e
a  p  h  a  s  i  a  x  s  u  b  e  r  d  o  x
g  x  i  n  c  o  g  n  i  t  o  s  a  e  n  i
r  u  e  s  s  i  o  n  n  o  c  a  n  n  n  c
a  s  s  o  n  a  n  c  e  o  r  d  x  c  o  o
m  s  r  e  t  i  o  n  n  o  c  e  r  e  c  n
l  e  x  o  c  o  n  o  c  x  p  i  d  g  i  n
v  m  s  i  n  o  r  h  c  a  n  a  s  p  l  w
```

Word List

1. **anagram:** word game
2. **agnostic:** a person who doubts the existence of a Supreme Being
3. **aphasia:** loss of the ability to speak
4. **anachronism:** from another time
5. **connoisseur:** an expert in the arts
6. **alliteration:** repeating the same sound at the beginning of words
7. **incognito:** under an assumed name
8. **assonance:** repeating the same vowel sounds
9. **rebus:** showing a word by pictures or symbols
10. **idiom:** a phrase that has non-literal meaning
11. **cadence:** meter or beat in speech
12. **connote:** understood meaning
13. **lexicon:** dictionary
14. **reconnoiter:** to survey an area for information (about an enemy's position)
15. **pidgin:** a mixture of different languages

Seventh-Inning Stretch: Word-Definition Match #1

Match each numbered word in the left column with its lettered definition in the right column. Write the letter of your answer in the space provided. The answers appear on page 162.

_____	1. incognito	a. persuasion through argument
_____	2. aphasia	b. negative connotation
_____	3. anachronism	c. memory aid
_____	4. colloquial	d. with one's identity concealed
_____	5. mnemonic	e. arrangement of words in a sentence
_____	6. pejorative	f. from another time
_____	7. expletive	g. word used as a filler
_____	8. anagram	h. loss of the ability to speak
_____	9. rhetoric	i. informal speech or writing
_____	10. syntax	j. word game

Read Words About Learning Literature

The following ten words all concern the study of books. Use each word in a sentence to help you fix it in your mind.

1. **allegory** (*al*-uh-gor-ee) noun, a story with a lesson

   _____

2. **allusion** (uh-*loo*-zhun) noun, a reference to a famous person, event, place, or literary passage

   _____

3. **anthology** (an-*thah*-luh-jee) noun, a collection of writings

   _____

4. **apocryphal** (uh-*pahk*-rih-ful) adjective, of doubtful authenticity

   _____

5. **ballad** (*bal*-id) noun, a narrative poem

   _____

6. **denouement** (day-noo-*mahn*) noun, the plot resolution

   _____

7. **doggerel** (*daw*-guh-rul) noun, poetic verse of generally poor quality

   _____

8. **elegy** (*el*-uh-jee) noun, a lament

   _____

9. **epic** (*ep*-ik) noun, a literary work recounting the travels and deeds of a hero

10. **lampoon** (lam-*poon*) noun, satire

Explore Eight More Literary Words

A few of our most test-worthy words come from literature. For example, in 1726, Irish writer Jonathan Swift created the word "Lilliput" for the imaginary country he described in his famous satire *Gulliver's Travels*. The inhabitants of Lilliput were no more than six inches tall. To them, Lemuel Gulliver looked like a giant. Today, we use the noun "lilliput" or the adjective "lilliputian" to describe a small person or a person of little importance.

Below are eight more words associated with literature and books. Write the new words on note cards to study in your spare moments.

Word	Pronunciation	Part of Speech	Meaning
motif	moh-*teef*	noun	repeated element
parody	*payr*-uh-dee	noun	humorous imitation of a literary selection
pseudonym	*soo*-duh-nim	noun	pen name
satire	*sah*-ty-er	noun	sarcastic literary work
tome	*tohm*	noun	very large or scholarly work
treatise	*tree*-tis	noun	scholarly study
vignette	vin-*yet*	noun	short, sketchy story
vita	*vee*-tuh	noun	scholarly résumé

It's Your Turn: Fill-in-the-Blank

Complete the following story with words from the box. You will have words left over. The answers appear on page 162.

satire	ballad	denouement	apocryphal
lampooned	doggerel	pseudonym	parody
allusion	motif	vita	anthology

Sally Student wrote a _____ that _____ all the people in the school. The verse was low-quality _____ , it's true, but it was funny bad poetry. The long poem was such a strong _____ that Sally decided to protect her reputation by circulating the poem under a _____ so no one could guess her identity. Soon, everyone had a copy of the _____ , and people were actually reciting lines! There's a rumor that the poem was put into an _____ of poetry, but we all know that story is surely _____ .

In the poem, she made an _____ to the principal and mocked his funny way of walking and talking. Sally used the _____ or repeated element of the school bell to unify her poem. It was a funny joke, but Sally knew she'd never put the poem on her résumé or _____ .

Seventh-Inning Stretch: Word-Definition Match #2

Match each numbered word in the left column with its lettered definition in the right column. Some of the eighteen words have already been covered in this chapter, but others are new. The answers appear on page 162.

_____ 1. amnesty   a. ancient commentator of classic texts
_____ 2. anachronism   b. conclusion of a speech
_____ 3. analects   c. dictionary
_____ 4. apocryphal   d. effective public speaking
_____ 5. colloquial   e. emblems of office
_____ 6. colophon   f. general pardon for past offenses
_____ 7. despot   g. informal expression
_____ 8. elegy   h. selected literary fragments or passages
_____ 9. elocution   i. of doubtful authenticity
_____ 10. junta   j. official or formal letter
_____ 11. lexicon   k. persuasion through argument
_____ 12. missive   l. poem or song of mourning
_____ 13. peroration   m. publisher's emblem
_____ 14. regalia   n. seemingly from another time
_____ 15. rhetoric   o. slavery
_____ 16. scholiast   p. small military group ruling a country
_____ 17. secede   q. to separate from a governmental body
_____ 18. thralldom   r. tyrant or dictator

Calculate Test-worthy Words from Mathematics

The following words all concern mathematics. These are especially important words for test takers because many of them are used in other fields as well. For example, the word **congruent** (kahn-*groo*-ent) is an adjective that means "equivalent" when applied to math. However, we also use this word to show that other objects have exactly the same size and shape.

A **matrix** (*may*-triks) is a series of numbers arranged in columns and rows. The word **ordinal** (*or*-duh-nul), an adjective, indicates the order, position, or rank of an item among others in a group or set. We distinguish the *ordinal numbers* (first, second, third, fourth, etc.) from the *cardinal numbers* (1, 2, 3, 4, etc.). The noun **permutation** (per-myoo-*tay*-shun) refers to changing a set of numbers. We also use the word **permutation** to refer to any change.

It's Your Turn: Less Is More . . . More or Less

The following words all have to do with adding, reducing, or completeness. Determine which of the following two phrases better describes each word in the list that follows. Write the number of your answer choice on the line to the left of each entry. The answers appear on page 163.

> 1. to fill or complete
> 2. to lessen or reduce

____ abate   ____ augment

____ aggrandize   ____ consummate

____ append   ____ mitigate

____ attenuate   ____ sate

Answers and Explanations

Indefinite Definitions (page 150)

1. r	8. l	15. f
2. h	9. k	16. s
3. n	10. d	17. a
4. b	11. o	18. t
5. u	12. p	19. m
6. j	13. c	20. q
7. i	14. g	21. e

Multiple Choice #1 (pages 152–153)

1. D	6. A
2. C	7. B
3. E	8. B
4. E	9. C
5. A	10. E

Word Scramble (page 154)

ape

brittle

spit

theoretical

rake

acquire

conviction

table

Reading down: **abstract**

Word-Find Puzzle (page 156)

Word-Definition Match #1 (page 157)

1. d	6. b
2. h	7. g
3. f	8. j
4. i	9. a
5. c	10. e

Fill-in-the-Blank (page 159)

Sally Student wrote a **ballad** that **lampooned** all the people in the school. The verse was low-quality **doggerel,** it's true, but it was funny bad poetry. The long poem was such a strong **satire** that Sally decided to protect her reputation by circulating the poem under a **pseudonym** so no one could guess her identity. Soon, everyone had a copy of the **parody,** and people were actually reciting lines! There's a rumor that the poem was put into an **anthology** of poetry, but we all know that story is surely **apocryphal.**

In the poem, she made an **allusion** to the principal and mocked his funny way of walking and talking. Sally used the **motif** or repeated element of the school bell to unify her poem. It was a funny joke, but Sally knew she'd never put the poem on her résumé or **vita.**

Word-Definition Match #2 (page 159)

1. f	7. r	13. b
2. n	8. l	14. e
3. h	9. d	15. k
4. i	10. p	16. a
5. g	11. c	17. q
6. m	12. j	18. o

Less Is More . . . More or Less (page 160)

1. **to fill or complete**

   aggrandize: to make greater
   append: to add
   augment: to add to
   consummate: to complete
   sate: to satisfy

2. **to lessen or reduce**

   abate: to diminish
   attenuate: to weaken
   mitigate: to lessen

Day 12

Tune into Test-worthy Words About the Arts

As you've learned in this book, arranging words into related groups is an effective way to learn new vocabulary. Giving the words a common frame of reference makes them easier to memorize, recall, and use correctly—especially in a high-stakes pressurized test situation.

The words in this chapter are grouped around the common theme of "the arts" to help them stick in your mind. So hum a happy tune, and get to work learning these words!

Learn Ten Words About the Artistic Culture

A *dilettante* (*dih*-luh-tahnt) is someone who only dabbles in a field. As a result, a dilettante has only a superficial knowledge of the area, such as painting, sculpture, or opera. When you finish this chapter, however, you'll have the words you need to be an expert—on standardized tests, that is!

The following words all describe the general culture of the arts:

Word	Pronunciation	Definition
aesthetic	es-*thet*-ik	the appreciation of beauty
contemporary	kun-*tem*-por-rare-ee	modern; current; up-to-date
eclectic	eh-*klek*-tik	made up of a variety of sources and styles
excerpt	*ek*-serpt	a selected portion of a passage or scene
genre	*zhahn*-ruh	a category of artistic achievement (novel, poem, short story, etc.)
medley	*med*-lee	an assortment, especially musical pieces
mural	*myur*-ul	a large painting applied directly to a wall
parody	*pair*-uh-dee	travesty; satire
realism	*ree*-uh-liz-um	true-to-life artistic representation
virtuoso	ver-choo-*oh*-so	a very skilled artist

It's Your Turn: Find the Right Definition

Write the definition for each word in boldface. The definitions are found in the boxes. You will have boxed words left over. The answers appear on page 176.

short choral song	travesty; satire
the appreciation of beauty	repetition of a musical phrase
true-to-life artistic representation	large painting applied directly to a wall
hymn sung to a melody	modern; current; up-to-date
a category of artistic achievement	made up of a variety of sources and styles
an assortment	highest singing voice
selected portion of a passage	a very skilled artist

1. **genre** _____
2. **realism** _____
3. **virtuoso** _____
4. **medley** _____
5. **parody** _____
6. **eclectic** _____
7. **mural** _____
8. **contemporary** _____
9. **excerpt** _____
10. **aesthetic** _____

Give It a Try: Synonyms and Antonyms

Complete the chart below by writing a synonym and antonym for each of the following words. The answers appear on page 176.

Word	Synonym	Antonym
contemporary	_____	_____
excerpt	_____	_____
eclectic	_____	_____
parody	_____	_____
realism	_____	_____
virtuoso	_____	_____
mural	_____	_____

Tune Up the Band to Master Fifteen Words About Music

The Italian phrase *prima donna* (literally "first woman") refers to the principal female singer in an opera or concert company. Prima donnas are notorious for their unwillingness to share the stage, and so the term *prima donna* is often used to describe a temperamental show-off. The term is used whether or not the person is in the arts.

The following fifteen test-worthy words all concern music. Study them carefully because test writers often include them on standardized tests.

Word	Pronunciation	Meaning
anthem	*an*-thum	a short, serious song
aria	*ahr*-ee-uh	song in an opera
ballad	*bal*-ud	song whose words tell a story
baroque	buh-*rohk*	ornate, elaborate
cadence	*kay*-duns	beat
canon	*kan*-un	musical round (repeated verse)
chorale	koh-*ral*	hymn sung to a melody
coda	*koh*-duh	passage added to the final section of a musical piece
concerto	kun-*chayr*-toh	musical piece for a solo instrument and orchestra
librettist	lih-*bret*-ist	writer of song lyrics for a musical
libretto	lih-*breh*-toh	the words or text for an opera, oratorio, etc.
minstrel	*min*-strul	traveling entertainer of the medieval period
nocturne	*nahk*-tern	slow, quiet, lyrical piece
overture	*oh*-ver-chur	instrumental introduction to a musical play or opera
reprise	rih-*preez*	repetition of a musical phrase

Explore Ten More Musical Words

Everyone needs inspiration, especially musicians and other artists. When capitalized, the word *Muse* refers to a source of inspiration. The term comes from the mythological Greek Muses, the nine children of Zeus (king of the gods) and Mnemosyne (the goddess of memory). Each Muse was said to rule over a certain art or science. For instance, the Muse Terpischore inspired dancers, while the Muse Polymnia inspired sacred songs. When written in lowercase, the word *muse* means "to ponder, brood, or contemplate."

Here are ten more important test-worthy words that concern music:

1. **bravo** (*brah*-vo) well done, good

2. **cantata** (can-*tah*-tah) type of choral music

3. **duet** (*doo*-et) musical composition for two voices or instruments

4. **finale** (fih-*nal*-ee) the last piece, division, or movement in a musical work

5. **maestro** (*my*-stro) a famous conductor

6. **mandolin** (*man*-doh-lin) stringed instrument with a pear-shaped body

7. **quartet** (quar-*tet*) group of four musicians

8. **solo** (*so*-low) a song or other musical composition for one person

9. **soprano** (so-*prah*-no) the highest singing voice

10. **tarantella** (tar-en-*tell*-uh) a rapid, whirling Italian dance

Discover Five More Musical Terms

Everyone knows the word "fan," an enthusiastic supporter of a performance or person. It's a clipped word—a word formed by shortening another word. *Fan* comes from *fanatic,* which originally meant "a person inspired by a divinity." At first, the word meant "a man mad with wild notions of religion." Winston Churchill defined a *fan* as someone "who can't change his mind and won't change the subject." From Churchill's definition comes our present-day meaning: "an unreasonably zealous person."

Study the following five musical terms below. You'll likely see them on a standardized test.

Word	Pronunciation	Meaning
requiem	*rek*-wee-um	music for a funeral mass
sonata	suh-*nah*-tuh	musical piece composed for solo instrument
syncopation	sing-kuh-*pay*-shun	music with offbeats stressed
timbre	*tim*-ber	voice quality
troubadour	*troo*-buh-dor	musician of the medieval period; a wandering singer

Seventh-Inning Stretch: Multiple-Choice #1

Select the word that best completes each sentence. Then, write the letter of the word in the space. The answers appear on page 176.

1. The audience shouted _____ to show their appreciation of the soprano's magnificent performance.

    (A) "Bravo!"
    (B) "Anthem!"
    (C) "Chorale!"
    (D) "Coda!"
    (E) "Libretto!"

2. Harry Chapin's _____ "The Cat's in the Cradle" tells a sad story about a blighted father-son relationship.

    (A) chorale
    (B) coda
    (C) libretto
    (D) ballad
    (E) reprise

3. Latecomers were seated during the opera's _____, because the action had not yet begun.

(A) coda
(B) conclusion
(C) overture
(D) nocturne
(E) finale

4. During medieval days, the _____ was a traveling troubadour who made a living wandering from town to town, singing and playing musical selections.

(A) anthem
(B) minstrel
(C) chorale
(D) libretto
(E) coda

5. Frustrated at his lack of progress with the song, the _____ threw the paper across the room.

(A) coda
(B) librettist
(C) chorale
(D) libretto
(E) reprise

6. The two singers performed a lovely _____ together.

(A) solo
(B) trio
(C) mandolin
(D) quartet
(E) duet

7. Verdi wrote a famous _____, a somber funeral mass.

(A) anthem
(B) requiem
(C) chorale
(D) coda
(E) reprise

8. The _____ was so fast that the dancers were getting dizzy from all the twirling and whirling!

(A) chorale
(B) quartet
(C) coda
(D) reprise
(E) tarantella

9. The audience hoped the _____ would come soon because it was late and they wanted to get home.

(A) anthem
(B) finale
(C) chorale
(D) reprise
(E) mandolin

10. The concerto was too _____ and elaborate for the audience's taste, for they were expecting a much more simple piece.

(A) benevolent
(B) aria
(C) baroque
(D) anthem
(E) bipartisan

Give It a Try: Word Scramble

To complete the following acrostic, first unscramble each of the vocabulary words so that it matches its definition. Then, use the words to fill in the appropriate spaces on the corresponding lines. When you have completed the entire puzzle, another vocabulary word will read vertically in the circles. The answers appear on page 176.

Scramble	Definition
qabroue	ornate, elaborate
thenam	a short choral song of a serious nature
stiblretit	a writer of song lyrics for a musical
tibrleto	the words or text for an opera, oratorio, etc.
riaa	a song in an opera
udet	a musical composition for two performers

Enjoy Ten Words About the Theater

A performer's *repertory* (*reh*-per-tor-ee) is his or her collection of roles. It's also a theatrical company. The following ten words that entered English from French describe entertainment. As you read each word for the first time, cover the definition and try to guess the word's meaning.

1. **burlesque** (bur-*lesk*) a ludicrous parody

2. **cabaret** (ka-buh-*ray*) a dinner show

3. **debut** (day-*byoo*) an actor's first performance

4. **histrionics** (his-tree-*ah*-niks) overly dramatic acting

5. **impresario** (im-preh-*sahr*-ee-oh) a person who organizes or manages public entertainment

6. **marquee** (mar-*kee*) a sign on the front of a theater advertising a play

7. **pantomime** (*pan*-tuh-mym) acting without dialogue; often abbreviated "mime"

8. **pirouette** (peer-oo-*et*) to whirl on one foot

9. **proscenium** (pro-*see*-nee-um) the front part of a stage

10. **vaudeville** (*vawd*-vil) a variety show consisting of light, amusing acts

Time for Fun: Word-Find Puzzle

There are sixteen words hidden in this word-find puzzle. Many of the words have already been introduced in this chapter, but a few are new. To complete the puzzle, locate and circle all the words. (See the word list.) The words may be written forward, backward, or upside down. The answers appear on page 177. Good luck!

```
b  a  r  o  q  u  e  a  t  u  b  e  d  w  e  c
u  x  s  c  i  n  o  i  r  t  s  i  h  w  e  i
r  e  p  r  i  s  e  a  m  e  h  t  n  a  w  t
l  i  b  r  e  t  t  i  s  t  x  a  i  r  a  e
e  e  u  q  r  a  m  q  d  a  s  o  g  u  e  h
s  e  t  t  e  u  o  r  i  p  c  o  d  a  c  t
q  x  e  l  l  i  v  e  d  u  a  v  m  i  x  s
u  x  o  i  r  a  s  e  r  p  m  i  c  o  d  e
e  m  i  m  o  t  n  a  p  x  c  a  n  o  n  a
```

Word List

1. **burlesque:** a ludicrous parody
2. **reprise:** the repetition of a musical phrase
3. **librettist:** a writer of a song lyric for a musical
4. **marquee:** a theater sign
5. **pantomime:** acting with gestures rather than words
6. **pirouette:** whirling on one foot
7. **vaudeville:** a variety show consisting of light, amusing acts
8. **impresario:** a person who organizes or manages public entertainment
9. **histrionics:** overly dramatic acting
10. **debut:** an actor's first performance
11. **anthem:** a short, serious song
12. **aria:** a song in an opera
13. **coda:** a passage added to the final section of a musical piece
14. **baroque:** ornate, elaborate
15. **canon:** a musical round (repeated verse)
16. **aesthetic:** the appreciation of beauty

Paint Words About Art

By 1759, the Seven Years' War and Louis XV's costly mistress, Madame de Pompadour, had left France on the brink of bankruptcy. Hoping for a miracle, Madame de Pompadour convinced Louis XV to replace the finance minister with a friend of hers, Étienne de Silhouette. The new appointee immediately instituted a series of stringent reforms. The nobility poked fun at many of the petty regulations, especially the rules calling for coats without folds and snuffboxes made of wood (instead of ivory and gold). At the same time, there had also been a revival of the ancient art of tracing the outlines of shadows. Since these shadow profiles replaced many costly paintings, they sneeringly came to be called *à la Silhouette*. Étienne de Silhouette lost his job within the year, but his name has become permanently attached to this art form.

Below are additional test-worthy words about art. Study them by using the method or methods that best work for you.

Word	Pronunciation	Meaning
arabesque	ar-a-*besk*	fanciful interlaced patterns
armature	*ar*-muh-cher	a skeleton of a sculpture
bas-relief	*bah*-rih-leef	sculpture in which the figures project from the background
burnish	*ber*-nish	to rub or polish to a high gloss
caricature	*kayr*-ih-kuh-choor	cartoon in which the character is ridiculed or parodied through exaggeration
chiaroscuro	kee-ahr-uh-*skyoor*-oh	shading to give a three-dimensional appearance
curator	*kyur*-ay-ter	person in charge of the artwork in a museum
docent	*doh*-sint	tour guide at a museum
emboss	em-*baws*	to create raised figures or designs on a surface
etch	*ech*	to engrave a design with acid
festoon	fes-*toon*	a decorative design of looped, curved lines
fresco	*fres*-koh	mural painting on plaster
gilded	*gil*-did	covered with a gold finish
medium	*mee*-dee-um	material used to create a picture or sculpture
montage	mahn-*tahzh*	combination of several pictures
mosaic	moh-*zay*-ik	tiled art work
palette	*pal*-ut	artist's paints; a wooden board used by a painter to hold paint while painting
patina	puh-*tee*-nuh	green film on the surface of bronze
relief	rih-*leef*	raised; projecting from a background surface
varnish	*var*-nish	protective coating over paint

172

Seventh-Inning Stretch: Multiple-Choice #2

Select the correct meaning for each of the following boldfaced words. Circle your choice. The answers appear on page 177.

1. **gilded**

   (A) covered with money
   (B) covered with a green finish
   (C) worthless
   (D) covered with a gold finish
   (E) antique

2. **caricature**

   (A) protective coating over paint
   (B) a decorative design of looped, curved lines
   (C) cartoon in which the character is ridiculed or parodied through exaggeration
   (D) shading to give a three-dimensional appearance
   (E) a skeleton of a sculpture

3. **arabesque**

   (A) varnish
   (B) fresco
   (C) elaborate dance
   (D) protective coating over paint
   (E) fanciful interlaced patterns

4. **emboss**

   (A) to circumscribe
   (B) to shade to give a three-dimensional appearance
   (C) to etch
   (D) to engrave a design with acid
   (E) to create raised figures or designs on a surface

5. **chiaroscuro**

   (A) shading to give a three-dimensional appearance
   (B) damaged art work
   (C) a decorative design of looped, curved lines
   (D) fresco
   (E) Spanish folk dance

6. **curator**

   (A) person in charge of the artwork in a museum
   (B) docent
   (C) museum tour guide
   (D) artist's paints
   (E) protective coating over paint

7. **mosaic**

   (A) combination of several pictures
   (B) tiled art work
   (C) varnish
   (D) montage
   (E) artist's paints

8. **fresco**

   (A) miniature
   (B) mural painting on plaster
   (C) artist's paints
   (D) patina
   (E) relief

9. **medium**

   (A) bas-relief
   (B) not rare
   (C) material used to create a picture or sculpture
   (D) armature
   (E) patina

10. **burnish**

    (A) varnish
    (B) to discard through burning
    (C) to praise
    (D) to frame
    (E) to rub or polish to a high gloss

Build Up Words About Architecture

In the Middle Ages, the short upright columns that supported handrails were made in circles, swelling to a pear-shape on the bottom. The handrails looked like the flowers of the wild pomegranate, called *balaustra* in Italian. Because of the flower-like appearance of the handrails, they came to be called *balaustras*. The French took the name and spelled it *balustra*, which became *baluster* in English. Careless speech soon turned the word into the familiar term *banister*.

Below are some challenging words about architecture. They tend to appear on standardized tests. Use some of the mnemonic skills (memory tricks) that you learned on Day 3 to remember them. Write the words on word cards to study in your spare moments.

Word	Pronunciation	Meaning
arcade	ar-*kade*	arched passageway; shops
balcony	*bal*-co-nee	a gallery
catacomb	*kat*-uh-com	tomb
colonnade	*kol*-oh-nade	columns
corridor	*cor*-ih-door	hallway
frieze	*freeze*	decorative band
grotto	*grah*-toe	cave
loggia	*low*-gee-uh	gallery
mezzanine	meh-zuh-*neen*	lowest balcony
pedestal	*ped*-uh-stall	base or support
piazza	pee-*ah*-suh	plaza
portico	*pour*-tih-koe	porch
rotunda	roh-*tun*-duh	round building
stucco	*stuh*-koe	thick wall finish, like plaster
villa	*vil*-uh	country estate

Don't confuse *pizza* and *piazza*. To set the record straight, *pizza* is the delicious bread, sauce, and cheese pie; *piazza* is a plaza.

Seventh-Inning Stretch: Word-Definition Match

Match each word with its definition. Then, write the letter of your choice in the space provided. The answers appear on page 177.

_____	1. grotto	a.	gallery
_____	2. catacomb	b.	round building
_____	3. mezzanine	c.	cave
_____	4. portico	d.	thick wall finish, like plaster
_____	5. stucco	e.	columns
_____	6. rotunda	f.	plaza
_____	7. piazza	g.	lowest balcony
_____	8. frieze	h.	tomb
_____	9. loggia	i.	porch
_____	10. colonnade	j.	decorative band

Answers and Explanations

Find the Right Definition (page 166)

1. a category of artistic achievement
2. true-to-life artistic representation
3. a very skilled artist
4. an assortment
5. travesty; satire
6. made up of a variety of sources and styles
7. large painting applied directly to a wall
8. modern; current; up-to-date
9. selected portion of a passage
10. the appreciation of beauty

Synonyms and Antonyms (page 166)

(Possible answers)

Word	Synonym	Antonym
contemporary	modern	old-fashioned
excerpt	portion	whole
eclectic	variety	identical
parody	satire	drama
realism	true-to-life	unrealistic
virtuoso	skilled artist	amateur
mural	large painting	miniature

Multiple-Choice #1 (page 168)

1. A
2. D
3. C
4. B
5. B
6. E
7. B
8. E
9. B
10. C

Word Scramble (page 170)

baroque
anthem
librettist
libretto
aria
duet

Reading down: **ballad**

Word-Find Puzzle (page 171)

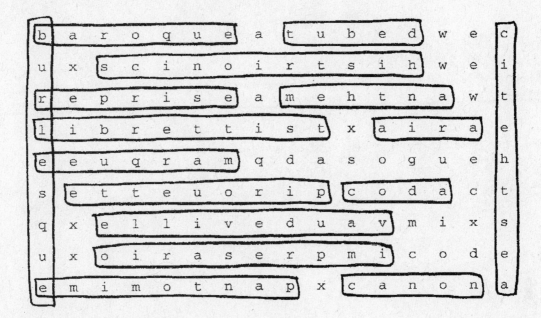

Multiple-Choice #2 (page 173)

1. D	6. A
2. C	7. B
3. E	8. B
4. E	9. C
5. A	10. E

Word-Definition Match (page 175)

1. c	6. b
2. h	7. f
3. g	8. j
4. i	9. a
5. d	10. e

Part V

Collect More Valuable Words

Day 13

Delve into Test-worthy Words About Hardships

The eighteenth-century French physician Joseph-Ignace Guillotin did not invent the guillotine, but, unfortunately, his name is forever connected to the beheading machine made famous during the French Revolution (1789–1799). The truth is that Dr. Guillotin was actually opposed to the death penalty, and in 1789 he petitioned the French National Assembly for a more humane and less painful method of execution than what existed at the time for everyone except the wealthy and nobility. Dr. Guillotin suggested the use of a mechanism that would behead painlessly. This decapitating device, originally called the Louisette or Louison after technical expert Dr. Antoine Louis, became known instead as the *guillotine,* and it became the most popular form of execution in France and many parts of Europe, especially during the French Revolution.

But don't worry . . . you won't lose your head over the words you'll learn today. Memorize them to help ensure that you have the words you need to get out of today's tight spots—standardized tests!

Learn Ten Words About Tough Times

The following ten words all describe difficult situations. As you have learned in earlier days, grouping words by a common theme makes them easier to learn. Read the words, parts of speech, pronunciations, and definitions through once. The second time, read the words, say them, and use them in a sentence. This will help fix them in your mind.

Word	Part of Speech	Pronunciation	Meaning
convoluted	adjective	kon-vuh-*loo*-tid	complex
cryptic	adjective	*krip*-tik	hard to understand
dilatory	adjective	*dil*-uh-tor-ee	always late
futile	adjective	*few*-tul	pointless
impede	verb	im-*peed*	block; thwart
listless	adjective	*list*-less	lethargic; sluggish
obscure	adjective	ub-*skur*	relatively unknown

Learn Ten Words About Tough Times—continued

Word	Part of Speech	Pronunciation	Meaning
obscure	verb	ub-*skur*	to hide
quandary	noun	*kwon*-dree	state of uncertainty
slander	noun	*slan*-der	false statements
spurious	adjective	*sper*-ee-us	fake

Seventh-Inning Stretch: Multiple-Choice #1

Select the correct meaning for each of the following boldfaced words. Circle your choice. The answers appear on page 192.

1. **spurious**

   (A) actual
   (B) reject
   (C) authentic
   (D) fake
   (E) obscure

2. **dilatory**

   (A) always early
   (B) inconsiderate
   (C) always late
   (D) dilated; enlarged
   (E) vicious

3. **quandary**

   (A) credence
   (B) belief
   (C) assurance
   (D) hostility
   (E) dilemma

4. **obscure**

   (A) crystal-clear
   (B) crystalline
   (C) fastidious
   (D) perverse
   (E) cryptic

5. **convoluted**

   (A) complex
   (B) futile
   (C) hostile
   (D) lethargic
   (E) fake

6. **listless**

   (A) lethargic
   (B) energetic
   (C) hostile
   (D) dilatory
   (E) convoluted

7. **slander**

   (A) support
   (B) defamation
   (C) suspicion
   (D) extol
   (E) ignore

8. **futile**

   (A) vicious
   (B) pointless
   (C) depraved
   (D) vile
   (E) immoral

9. **impede**

   (A) encode
   (B) encourage
   (C) thwart
   (D) facilitate
   (E) denounce

10. **cryptic**

   (A) cruel
   (B) grim
   (C) indecisive
   (D) easy to understand
   (E) hard to understand

Give It a Try: Synonyms and Antonyms

To play this game, find a *synonym* (word that means the same) and an *antonym* (word that means the opposite) for each of the following vocabulary words. If you want to boost your vocabulary even more, try to come up with more than one synonym and antonym for each word. The answers appear on page 192.

Word	Synonym	Antonym
convoluted	_____	_____
cryptic	_____	_____
dilatory	_____	_____
futile	_____	_____
impede	_____	_____
listless	_____	_____
obscure	_____	_____
quandry	_____	_____
slander	_____	_____
spurious	_____	_____

Master Ten More Words for Difficult Times

A *quisling* is a traitor, a person who betrays his or her country. It comes from the name of Vidkun Quisling (1887–1945), a Norwegian army officer turned fascist who collaborated with the Nazis during World War II.

The following ten words also describe troublesome situations. See how many of these words are familiar to you already. That will give you a leg up on your studying!

1. **condemn** (kun-*dem*) denounce; criticize
2. **discredit** (dis-*cred*-it) cause to be doubted
3. **disparage** (dis-*pair*-uj) to belittle
4. **impinge** (im-*pinj*) interfere with
5. **lament** (luh-*ment*) mourn
6. **melancholy** (*mel*-un-kaw-lee) depression; sadness
7. **pejorative** (puh-*jor*-uh-tiv) disparaging; rude
8. **plagiarism** (*play*-juh-riz-um) literary theft; the act of passing someone else's ideas or writing as your own
9. **truncated** (*trun*-kay-tid) shortened
10. **vilify** (*vil*-uh-fy) slander; defame

Time for Fun: Word-Find Puzzle

There are fifteen words hidden in this word-find puzzle. Many of the words have already been introduced in this chapter, but a few are new. To complete the puzzle, locate and circle all the words. (See the word list below.) The words may be written forward, backward, or upside down. The answers appear on page 193. Good luck!

```
d  i  s  p  a  r  a  g  e  d  l  t  q  u  s
i  m  p  e  d  e  c  a  r  s  s  r  u  y  p
s  e  v  i  t  a  r  o  j  e  p  u  a  r  u
c  o  n  d  e  m  n  n  e  w  o  n  n  o  r
r  e  d  n  a  l  s  h  a  r  d  c  d  t  i
e  y  l  o  h  c  n  a  l  e  m  a  a  a  o
d  i  v  i  l  i  f  y  g  h  i  t  r  l  u
i  m  p  i  n  g  e  t  i  m  e  e  y  i  s
t  n  e  m  a  l  l  i  n  g  s  d  e  d  z
c  o  n  v  o  l  u  t  e  d  t  r  o  u  b
```

Word List

1. **condemn:** denounce; criticize
2. **discredit:** cause to be doubted
3. **disparage:** to belittle
4. **impinge:** interfere with
5. **lament:** mourn
6. **melancholy:** depression; sadness
7. **pejorative:** disparaging; rude
8. **quandary:** state of uncertainty
9. **truncated:** shortened
10. **vilify:** slander; defame
11. **impede:** block; thwart
12. **slander:** false charges
13. **dilatory:** always late
14. **convoluted:** complex
15. **spurious:** fake

Seventh-Inning Stretch: Word-Definition Match

Match each vocabulary word to its definition. Write the letter of your response in the blank. The answers appear on page 193.

_____	1. brittle	a.	famous for bad deeds; infamous
_____	2. deleterious	b.	an ungrateful person
_____	3. enmity	c.	fragile
_____	4. notorious	d.	wild
_____	5. pugnacious	e.	deserving blame or censure
_____	6. reprehensible	f.	harmful
_____	7. ingrate	g.	belligerent; defiant
_____	8. incorrigible	h.	cannot be reformed
_____	9. fractious	i.	hatred
_____	10. feral	j.	rude

It's Your Turn: Rebel Razers and Rabble Rousers

The following vocabulary game contains words about destruction and rebellion. Decide which of the following three numbered words or phrases best describes each word in the list that follows. Write the number of your answer choice on the line to the left of each entry. The answers appear on page 193.

> 1. demolish
> 2. rebel
> 3. break or injure

_____ abrogate _____ lacerate

_____ annihilate _____ maim

_____ apostate _____ quisling

_____ expunge _____ rend

_____ incendiary _____ renegade

Give It a Try: It's All in the Altitude

All the words you'll learn today describe the dark side of the human condition. Let's relieve the gloom with some words that describe highs as well as lows! The following game concerns words that describe highs and lows.

For each word below, determine whether the word is closer in meaning to *high* or *low*. Indicate your choice by writing "H" for "high" or "L" for "low" on the line to the left of each word. The answers appear on page 194.

```
H — high
L — low
```

____ abyss	____ nadir
____ alluvial	____ pinnacle
____ apex	____ sublime
____ appraise	____ usury
____ excelsior	____ zenith
____ fathom	

Consider Ten More Words About Worries

A *scapegoat* is a person who is blamed for the mistakes of others. The word began as two words, *escape goat*. The Bible (Leviticus XVI, 10) describes the Hebrew ceremony of sacrificing a goat and then allowing a second one, bearing the sins of the people, to escape into the desert. The goat that "escaped" became the "escape goat." Today, the connotation is a bit different: a *scapegoat* is "a whipping boy, often a victim of hatred and prejudice."

Since you've been studying so hard, you won't need a scapegoat! Keep up the good work by learning the following ten words. They all have a negative connotation (emotional overtone).

1. **apprehension** (ap-ruh-*hen*-shun) anxiety; worry

2. **heinous** (*hay*-nus) atrocious; horrendous

3. **malfeasance** (mal-*feez*-uns) misconduct, especially by a public official

4. **malice** (*mal*-us) hostility; bitterness

5. **ominous** (*ah*-mih-nus) frightening; menacing

6. **putrid** (*pyoo*-trid) rotten

7. **rancorous** (*rank*-er-us) bitter; resentful

8. **timorous** (*tim*-uh-rus) timid

9. **toxic** (*tox*-sik) poisonous

10. **trepidation** (trep-uh-*day*-shun) agitation; consternation; fear

Give It a Try: Word Scramble

To complete the following acrostic, first unscramble each vocabulary word so that it matches its definition. Then, use the words to fill in the appropriate spaces on the corresponding lines. When you have completed the entire puzzle, another vocabulary word will read vertically in the circles. The answers appear on page 194.

oticx	poisonous
piemde	block; thwart
lcmaaeasfne	misconduct, especially by a public official
smioonu	frightening; menacing
angreede	traitor
bsrocue	relatively unknown
ysuur	illegal rate of interest
leansdr	false statements

Time for Fun: True or False

In the space provided, write **T** if the definition of each word is true and **F** if it is false. The answers appear on page 194.

_____ 1. apprehension   anxiety; worry

_____ 2. heinous   atrocious; horrendous

_____ 3. malfeasance   extreme anger

_____ 4. malice   philanthropy

_____ 5. ominous   misconduct, especially by a public official

_____ 6. putrid   rotten

_____ 7. rancorous   bitter; resentful

_____ 8. timorous   confident

_____ 9. toxic   poisonous

_____ 10. trepidation   agitation; consternation; fear

Moan Over More Terms for Woe

This time, there are sentences to help you see how the words are used in context. After you read these sentences, try to create some of your own. This will help you remember the words, especially those that are totally new to you.

1. **anathema** (uh-*na*-theh-muh) n. a person or thing condemned, accused, damned, cursed, or generally loathed. A similar word is *pariah*: an outcast.

    The adulteress Hester Prynne, the main character in *The Scarlet Letter,* is probably the best-known example of an anathema.

    Note: Do not confuse *anathema* with *anesthesia*: any drug that dulls the senses.

2. **bane** (bayn) n. any cause of ruin or destruction

    The woman grew to abhor her vituperative husband; among friends, she would refer to him hyperbolically as "the bane of my existence."

3. **beleaguer** (beh-*lee*-ger) v. to surround; besiege

    Beleaguered by enemy troops, the weary soldiers finally admitted defeat and surrendered their garrison.

4. **besmirch** (bih-*smerch*) v. to soil or tarnish, especially a person's honor or reputation; to defile. Similar words include *denigrate, deprecate,* and *calumniate.*

    One pejorative remark about the city councilman by the popular local newspaper columnist forever besmirched his reputation among the townspeople.

5. **censure** (*sen*-sher) n. strong expression of disapproval; an official reprimand. Similar words include *reproach, reproof, stricture,* and *condemnation.*

    The town's newspapers were unanimous in their censure of the proposed tax hikes.

    In 1834, the Senate censured President Andrew Jackson for withholding documents related to his actions in removing U.S. funds from the Bank of the United States.

6. **chagrin** (shuh-*grin*) n. irritation marked by disappointment or humiliation. A closely related word is *vexation* (irritation, annoyance, or provocation).

    His favorite team lost the big game, much to his chagrin since he had bet a large sum of money that his team would win.

7. **chicanery** (shih-*kay*-nuh-ree) n. trickery or deception, usually used to gain an advantage or to evade. Similar words include *guile, knavery, disingenuousness,* and *artifice.*

    Some unscrupulous knaves would resort to any sort of chicanery in order to fleece an unwitting dupe of his last dollar.

8. **choleric** (kuh-*layr*-ik) adj. tempermental; hotheaded. Similar words include *mercurial, peevish,* and *acrimonious.*

    Just beneath his affable and disarming veneer lay a choleric and dangerous psychopath.

    Although *choleric* is unrelated to *caloric,* both words involve the notion of heat (a calorie is a unit of measure for heat).

9. **churlish** (*cher*-lish) adj. crude; crass; vulgar. Similar words include *boorish, impudent,* and *insolent.*

    His churlish and uncivilized demeanor seems more befitting the Dark Ages than this age; I want nothing to do with the churl.

10. **deprecate** (*dep*-ruh-kayt) v. to express disapproval of. Similar words include *reprove, reprimand, rebuke*, and *reprobate*.

> "The friends of humanity will deprecate war, wheresoever it may appear."
> —George Washington

Deprecation does not necessarily involve blame, criticism, or punishment. Here are similar words that do carry one or more of these meanings:

> *castigate:* to punish in order to correct or reform
> *censure:* to strongly disapprove, criticize, or blame
> *reproach:* to find fault with; blame; criticize

11. **indigent** (*in*-dih-junt) adj. poor; destitute; impoverished. A synonym of indigent is *impecunious* (pecuniary: pertaining to money).

> An indigent person is sometimes referred to as a pauper.

Do not confuse indigent with the following:

> *indigenous:* native to or characterizing a particular region
> *indulgent:* permissive; tolerating

12. **inexorable** (in-*ek*-sor-uh-bul) adj. relentless; unyielding; merciless. A similar word is *implacable:* incapable of being pacified or appeased.

> No B-rated science fiction epic is complete without the inexorable attack of the grotesque monster, impervious to bullets and bombs but capitulating to the charms of a pretty girl.

> "What other dungeon is so dark as one's own heart! What jailer so inexorable as one's self!" —Nathaniel Hawthorne

13. **renege** (rih-*nig*) v. to go back on one's promise or word

> The world abounds with renegers: spouses reneging on their wedding vows, politicians reneging on their campaign promises, and dieters reneging on their pledge to cut calories.

> "Nations don't literally renege on their debts; they either postpone them indefinitely . . . or else pay them off in depreciated currency."
> —Roger Bridwell

> A renegade (traitor or deserter) is a person who reneges on his or her loyalty.

14. **salient** (*say*-lee-unt) adj. prominent or conspicuous

The word is usually used to describe features or characteristics. Note the two related but distinct meanings of the word, as underscored by these two sentences:

> The most salient feature of my house is its orange color.

> At the end of his sermon, the preacher reiterated what he considered to be the most salient points for the congregation to remember.

In this sentence, the word might carry either meaning:

> The personal ads were resplendent with such salient words as adventurous, petite, spiritual, and, perhaps most salient of all, single.

15. **supercilious** (soo-per-*sil*-ee-us) adj. disdainful in a haughty and arrogant way. Similar words include *haughty, consequential*, and *patronizing*.

> While stopped at the traffic light, the supercilious socialite in her brand-new luxury car glanced disdainfully to her left at the beat-up old sedan and at the car's driver.

> Imagining a supercilious person raising his or her eyebrows is helpful in understanding the definitions of this word.

16. **umbrage** (*um*-brij) n. anger; resentment; sense of having been maligned or insulted

> Similar words include *vexation, animosity*, and *spite*. The word is derived from the astronomical term *umbra,* which refers to the darkest shadow formed by an eclipse. Accordingly, a person with umbrage is ensconced in a dark shadow of anger and resentment.

> "The patient who sees SOB on his chart should not take umbrage, as it is usually intended to mean 'short of breath.'" —William Safire

17. **wanton** (*wahn*-tun) adj. without regard for what is morally right; reckless; unjustifiable. A closely related word is *want*: lack or scarcity. A wanton person demonstrates a want of scruples.

> In criminal law, the prosecution must prove that a defendant accused of first-degree murder acted with wanton disregard for human life.

> "If you suppress the exorbitant love of pleasure and money, idle curiosity, iniquitous purpose, and wanton mirth, what a stillness there would be in the greatest cities."—Jean de La Bruyere

Seventh-Inning Stretch: Multiple-Choice #2

Select the word that best completes each sentence. Write the letter of the word in the space. The answers appear on page 194.

1. The teenager thought that her life would be perfect were it not for acne, which was the _____ of her existence.

   (A) besmirch
   (B) wanton
   (C) compensation
   (D) merit
   (E) bane

2. Despite the use of exercise, diet, Botox, and plastic surgery, the passage of time is _____ and we all look old eventually.

   (A) supercilious
   (B) churlish
   (C) inexorable
   (D) wanton
   (E) salient

3. The CEO's reputation was _____ when it was discovered that he had his hand in the till—to the tune of $30 million.

    (A) encroached
    (B) beleaguered
    (C) besmirched
    (D) lamented
    (E) ameliorated

4. If you can't keep a promise, don't make it, but never _____ on your word.

    (A) lament
    (B) deprecate
    (C) beleaguer
    (D) wanton
    (E) renege

5. My boyfriend is _____ by nature: even the smallest slights make him very angry.

    (A) choleric
    (B) serene
    (C) melancholy
    (D) supercilious
    (E) salient

6. We knew the carnival tricks were the most blatant _____, but we didn't mind getting fooled as long as we were entertained as well.

    (A) anathema
    (B) chicanery
    (C) plagiarism
    (D) ingrate
    (E) mishap

7. I thought I had lost my keys, but to my _____, they were in my pocket the whole time!

    (A) plagiarism
    (B) anathema
    (C) wanton
    (D) chagrin
    (E) chaos

8. Since we knew the hobo was _____, we dropped a $10 bill into his outstretched palm.

    (A) indigent
    (B) wanton
    (C) churlish
    (D) supercilious
    (E) salient

9. President Clinton was _____ by the Senate for his contemptible behavior with a certain intern.

    (A) churlished
    (B) beleaguered
    (C) censured
    (D) lamented
    (E) lauded

10. No insult was intended, but the child was so sensitive that she took great _____ anyway and refused to speak to anyone for a week.

    (A) plagiarism
    (B) rapture
    (C) umbrage
    (D) quandary
    (E) slander

Answers and Explanations

Multiple-Choice #1 (page 182)

1. D	6. A
2. C	7. B
3. E	8. B
4. E	9. C
5. A	10. E

Synonyms and Antonyms (page 183)

(Possible answers)

Word	Synonym	Antonym
convoluted	complex	simple; plain; easy; clear
cryptic	hard to understand	easy to understand; simple
dilatory	always late	prompt
futile	pointless	effectual; productive
impede	block; thwart	assist
listless	lethargic; sluggish	energetic
obscure	relatively unknown	famous
quandry	state of uncertainty	certainty
slander	defamation	truth
spurious	fake	authentic; real; actual

Word-Find Puzzle (page 184)

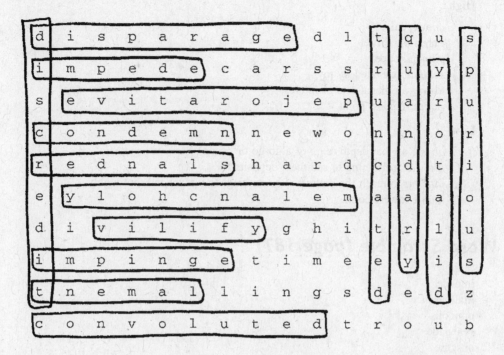

Word-Definition Match (page 185)

1. c	6. e
2. f	7. b
3. i	8. h
4. a	9. j
5. g	10. d

Rebel Razers and Rabble Rousers (page 185)

1. **demolish**

   abrogate: to set aside
   annihilate: to demolish
   expunge: to obliterate

2. **rebel**

   apostate: a person who abandons a faith or cause
   incendiary: a person who willfully stirs up strife
   quisling: a traitor
   renegade: a traitor

3. **break or injure**

   lacerate: to wound
   maim: to mutilate
   rend: to tear violently

It's All in the Altitude (page 186)

High

> *apex:* peak
> *excelsior:* loftier
> *pinnacle:* apex
> *sublime:* elevated by joy
> *usury:* an illegal rate of interest
> *zenith:* highest point

Low

> *abyss:* a great depth (e.g., of a gorge or ocean)
> *alluvial:* pertaining to sediment deposits
> *fathom:* to reach the bottom of something; to understand thoroughly
> *nadir:* lowest point

Word Scramble (page 187)

toxic
impede
malfeasance
ominous
renegade
obscure
usury
slander

Reading down: **timorous**

True or False (page 187)

1. T   6. T
2. T   7. T
3. F   8. F
4. F   9. T
5. F   10. T

Multiple-Choice #2 (page 190)

1. E   6. B
2. C   7. D
3. C   8. A
4. E   9. C
5. A   10. C

Day 14

Explore Test-worthy Words About Behavior

In 1740, Admiral Vernon of the British fleet decided to water down the navy's rum. Needless to say, the sailors weren't pleased. To get some small measure of revenge, they nicknamed the Admiral "Old Grog" after the stiff wool grogram coats he wore. The term "grog" soon began to mean the watered-down drink itself. When you were drunk on this grog, you were "groggy," a word still in use today.

Today you'll learn test-worthy words that have to do with the way we act. As always, try to use the techniques you learned on Day 3 to help you remember these words.

Learn Words About Conduct

Today, the word *etiquette* refers to the conventional requirements of social behavior. Commonly, the word is used to refer to manners. Originally, an *etiquette* was a target attached to a post. Children used it in games. Later, it was a military order prescribing the duties of the day. Then the paper card itself became the etiquette, the equivalent of a "ticket." (This is what the word means in French today.) Still later the word came to mean a card that set out the procedures to be observed at the royal court. With the passage of time, it came to be linked to the manners themselves.

The following ten words refer to behavior. Try to use each word in a sentence to fix it in your memory.

Word	Pronunciation	Definition
assimilate	uh-*sim*-il-ate	fit in
dubious	*doo*-bee-us	doubtful
egregious	uh-*gree*-jus	offensive
elusive	ee-*loo*-sive	evasive; intangible
gratuitous	grah-*too*-ih-tus	unwarranted
inherent	in-*her*-ent	inborn
innate	in-*ayt*	inborn
inveterate	in-*vet*-uh-rit	deep-rooted; done by habit
proximity	prahk-*sim*-ih-tee	closeness
transient	*trans*-zee-ent	passing away with time

Discover Ten Words About Comportment

Comportment is a fancy word for "behavior." See? You learned a new word just like that! Below are ten more test-worthy words about human actions and behavior. As you study, pronounce each word and link it to a synonym. This will make it more likely that you'll remember the words, come test time.

1. **affable** (*af*-uh-bul) adjective, easy-going; good-natured

2. **amenable** (uh-*meen*-uh-bul) adjective, agreeable; docile

3. **chastise** (*chas*-tyz) verb, to discipline; to rebuke

4. **clandestine** (klan-*des*-tin) adjective, secretive; hidden

5. **decorous** (*dek*-er-us) adjective, proper; well-mannered

6. **disdain** (dis-*dayn*) verb, to scorn; to treat with contempt

7. **disingenuous** (dis-in-*jen*-yoo-us) adjective, crafty; Machiavellian

8. **disport** (dis-*port*) verb, to carry away, comfort, entertain; to divert or amuse

9. **fabricated** (*fab*-ruh-kay-tid) verb, made; created

10. **hypocrisy** (hih-*pok*-ruh-see) noun, insincerity; pretense of virtue

Seventh-Inning Stretch: Word-Definition Match

Match the word to its definition. You may wish to say the word aloud as you look for the match. Remember: saying the words will help you remember them! Then, write the letter of your answer in the space provided. The answers appear on page 209.

_____ 1. gratuitous	a. insincerity; pretense of virtue
_____ 2. affable	b. passing away with time
_____ 3. proximity	c. unwarranted
_____ 4. innate	d. offensive
_____ 5. transient	e. crafty; Machiavellian
_____ 6. disingenuous	f. closeness
_____ 7. hypocrisy	g. deep-rooted; done by habit
_____ 8. disport	h. easy-going; good-natured
_____ 9. egregious	i. inborn
_____ 10. inveterate	j. to comfort or entertain; to amuse

Time for Fun: Word-Find Puzzle

There are fourteen words hidden in this word-find puzzle. Many of the words have already been introduced in this chapter, but a few are new. To complete the puzzle, locate and circle all the words. (See the word list below.) The words may be written forward, backward, or upside down. The answers appear on page 209. Good luck!

```
i  n  h  e  r  e  n  t  a  j  e  a  s  e  s
n  e  g  r  e  g  i  o  u  s  i  m  u  l  u
b  e  t  a  l  i  m  i  s  s  a  e  o  u  o
e  t  a  r  e  t  e  v  n  i  p  n  r  s  i
f  g  r  a  t  u  i  t  o  u  s  a  o  i  b
e  n  i  t  s  e  d  n  a  l  c  b  c  v  u
n  i  a  d  s  i  d  w  a  r  y  l  e  e  d
t  r  a  n  s  i  e  n  t  o  s  e  d  u  s
d  i  s  i  n  g  e  n  u  o  u  s  e  e  e
```

Word List

1. **clandestine:** secretive; hidden
2. **inherent:** inborn
3. **transient:** passing away with time
4. **inveterate:** deep-rooted; done by habit
5. **disdain:** contempt; scorn
6. **gratuitous:** unwarranted
7. **assimilate:** fit in
8. **egregious:** offensive
9. **wary:** watchful
10. **amenable:** agreeable; docile
11. **decorous:** proper; well-mannered
12. **elusive:** evasive; intangible
13. **dubious:** doubtful
14. **disingenuous:** crafty; Machiavellian

Study the Way We Are

The following ten test-worthy words are popular with test makers because they're also useful in life. As you read this chart, see how many of these terms you would use in your everyday life . . . after tests!

Word	Pronunciation	Meaning
dogged	*dog*-id	stubbornly determined
enthrall	en-*thrawl*	to fascinate
exemplary	eg-*zemp*-luh-ree	outstanding
laudatory	*law*-duh-tor-ee	giving praise
staid	*stayd*	serious
stoic	*stow*-ik	impassive; self-possessed
surreptitious	ser-ep-*tish*-us	sneaky
tenacity	ten-*ass*-uh-tee	persistence
vitality	vy-*tah*-lih-tee	energetic
wary	*wair*-ee	watchful

Seventh-Inning Stretch: Multiple-Choice #1

Select the correct meaning for each of the following boldfaced words. Circle your choice. The answers appear on page 209.

1. **stoic**

   (A) decorous
   (B) egregious
   (C) disingenuous
   (D) impassive; self-possessed
   (E) sensitive

2. **surreptitious**

   (A) susceptible
   (B) decorous
   (C) sneaky
   (D) disingenuous
   (E) egregious

3. **vitality**

   (A) sluggishness
   (B) inactivity
   (C) viciousness
   (D) irony
   (E) spunk

4. **dogged**

   (A) dog-like
   (B) egregious
   (C) disingenuous
   (D) decorous
   (E) stubbornly determined

5. **staid**

   (A) serious
   (B) stiff
   (C) disingenuous
   (D) egregious
   (E) decorous

6. **wary**

   (A) watchful
   (B) disingenuous
   (C) decorous
   (D) egregious
   (E) negligent

7. **enthrall**

   (A) imprison
   (B) fascinate
   (C) repel
   (D) disgust
   (E) interest mildly

8. **exemplary**

   (A) inconspicuous
   (B) outstanding
   (C) hypocrisy
   (D) commonplace
   (E) ordinary

9. **laudatory**

   (A) hypocrisy
   (B) egregious
   (C) giving praise
   (D) potent
   (E) brutal

10. **tenacity**

   (A) city-like
   (B) rural area
   (C) tough
   (D) hypocrisy
   (E) persistence

See How Words of a Feather Flock Together

Animals have contributed their share of words and expressions, too. Here are some examples: *beetle-browed* (an angry, gloomy person), *behemoth* (someone of enormous size), *caterpillar* (an amusement park ride), and *chameleon* (a person who changes opinion).

Study the following terms for animal groups. They will help you correctly identify masses of animals.

Word	Animal Group
brood	group of chickens
covey	family of game birds
drove	group of sheep or oxen
flock	group of birds
gaggle	flock of geese
gam	group of whales
herd	group of animals
pride	group of lions
school	group of fish
shoal	group of fish
stable	group of horses
swarm	body of bees

It's Your Turn: Fill-in-the-Blank

Play this game by writing in the term for the group in which each animal travels. The answers appear on page 210.

A _____ of chickens

A _____ of birds

A _____ of geese

A _____ of lions

A _____ of whales

A _____ or a _____ of fish

A _____ of horses

A _____ of bees

Give It a Try: Rock and Roll

The following words all concern motion. To play this game, determine which of the following three phrases best describes each of the words in the list that follows. Write the number of your answer choice on the line to the left of each entry. The answers appear on page 210.

> 1. to swing or rock
> 2. to spin or rotate
> 3. to twitch or vibrate

___ bandy   ___ quake

___ gyrate   ___ undulate

___ oscillate   ___ vacillate

___ pirouette   ___ whirl

More Words About Human Nature

Since human nature is endlessly varied, it's no wonder that we have so many words to describe it! The following list also includes synonyms and antonyms for each vocabulary word.

adept (uh-*dept*) adjective, skillful; competent

    Synonyms: proficient; able; adroit; deft

    Antonyms: incompetent; loutish; inept

aplomb (uh-*plahm*) noun, poise; composure

    Synonyms: assurance; intrepidity; impassivity; unflappability; imperturbability

    Antonyms: intemperance; irascibility; petulance

balk (*bawk*) verb, to stop; to refuse to continue

Synonyms: demur; spurn; shun; desist; halt; falter; stammer; suspend

Antonyms: advance; proceed; persevere; persist; endure; dogged; indefatigable

boisterous (*boy*-ster-us) adjective, loud, rough, or violent

Synonyms: clamorous; tumultuous; obstreperous; rambunctious; riotous; turbulent

Antonyms: sedate; staid; reconciled; subdued; placid; tranquil

bovine (*boh*-vyn) adjective, cowlike; dull or inactive

Synonyms: inert; loutish; slothful; torpid; indolent; languid; phlegmatic; listless

Antonyms: astir; exuberant; animated; vivacious; effervescent; ebullient

brusque (*brusk*) adjective, abrupt or blunt in speech

Synonyms: curt; bluff; crude; frank; boorish; sententious; terse

Antonyms: tactful; suave; glib

candid (*can*-did) adjective, sincere and forthright

Synonyms: frank; ingenuous; guileless; earnest; fervent

Antonyms: hypocritical; sanctimonious; ingenuous; equivocal; mendacious; devious

dapper (*dap*-er) adjective, neat; trim

Synonyms: fashionable; smart; natty; fastidious

Antonyms: disheveled; unkempt; tousled; slovenly; rumpled; disarrayed

debonair (deh-boh-*nayr*) adjective, courteous; charming

Synonyms: dashing; ambrosial; rakish; genteel; gallant; urbane; amiable; complaisant

Antonyms: impudent; impertinent; insolent; flippant; churlish; boorish; unceremonious

deft (*deft*) adjective, proficient; skilled

Synonyms: adroit; adept; dexterous

Antonyms: maladroit; inept; gauche

Time for Fun: Synonyms and Antonyms

This time, complete the chart by writing a *synonym* and an *antonym* for each word. Remember: a *synonym* means the same; an *antonym* has the opposite meaning. Try to list at least two synonyms and two antonyms for each vocabulary word. The answers appear on page 210.

Word	Synonym	Antonym
dapper	_____	_____
deft	_____	_____
aplomb	_____	_____
debonair	_____	_____
candid	_____	_____
balk	_____	_____
adept	_____	_____
bovine	_____	_____
brusque	_____	_____
boisterous	_____	_____

Enjoy Words About Behavior with a French Flair

How many English words with French origins do you see on standardized tests? Here are ten words that entered English from French. They not only appear on standardized tests but are especially handy in social situations, too!

Word	Pronunciation	Meaning
bon mot	bon-*mo*	clever saying
bourgeois	bush-*wah*	middle class
charlatan	*shar*-lah-ten	faker, quack
faux pas	foh-*pah*	social blunder
gauche	*gohsh*	socially inept
genteel	jen-*teel*	elegant, refined
nonchalance	non-shah-*lans*	indifference
raconteur	rah-con-*tour*	expert storyteller
rapport	rah-*por*	harmony, accord
repartee	rey-par-*tay*	witty talk

Rehearse Words About the Act and the Actor

In medieval days, a *cavalier* was a gallant on horseback. The word came to refer to a man courting members of the opposite sex. However, men on horseback look down on those who do not ride. Their attitude is haughty, and so *cavalier* came to mean "disdainful, arrogant."

As the example of *cavalier* shows, language is a living thing. Therefore, words often change meaning. Catch the following words before they change their meaning!

1. **exhort** (eg-*zort*) verb, to urge by words; to caution or advise strongly

2. **dissemble** (dih-*sem*-bul) verb, to hide, conceal, or disguise

3. **gambol** (*gam*-bul) verb, to skip or leap playfully

4. **impassive** (im-*pas*-iv) adjective, composed; without emotion; reserved

5. **ingratiate** (in-*gray*-shee-ayt) verb, to gain favor with another; to become popular with

6. **insouciant** (in-*soo*-see-int) adjective, unconcerned; without a care; carefree; jaunty

7. **predilection** (preh-duh-*lik*-shun) noun, partiality; preference

8. **rakish** (*ray*-kish) adjective, stylish; chic

9. **redress** (ree-*dres*) verb, setting right that which is wrong; compensation or remedy for a wrong

10. **reproach** (ree-*prohch*) verb, to find fault with; blame; scold

Give It a Try: Word Scramble

Game time! First unscramble each of the words so that it matches its definition. Then, use the words to fill the appropriate spaces on the corresponding line. When you have completed the entire puzzle, another test-worthy word will read vertically in the circles. This puzzle uses words from the entire chapter. The answers appear on page 211.

Scramble	Definition
aikrsh	stylish; chic
rxheot	to caution
cpoedriletin	partiality; preference
erssdre	setting right that which is wrong
aocilslte	swing
pmloab	assurance; intrepidity
acnddi	sincere and forthright
yprshociy	insincerity; pretense of virtue

Get in Your Last Licks

Here are six more words to help you hit the top of the charts on all your vocabulary tests.

jaded (*jay*-did) adjective, weary

    Synonyms: enervated; spent; cloyed; depleted

    Antonyms: invigorated; revitalized; enlivened

jaunty (*jawn*-tee) adjective, carefree; lighthearted

    Synonyms: insouciant; jocund; jocose; jovial; blithe

    Antonyms: dour; sullen; morose; somber; doleful; melancholy; lugubrious; saturnine

jocose (joh-*kohs*) adjective, playful; lighthearted

    Synonyms: jocular; jocund; waggish; jovial; facetious; blithe; trifling; buoyant; halcyon

    Antonyms: somber; demure; staid; sedate; stern; grim; lugubrious; pensive; saturnine

jubilant (*joo*-buh-lunt) adjective, rejoicing; joyful

    Synonyms: elated; exuberant; exultant; reveling; frolicsome

    Antonyms: depressed; sad

inscrutable (in-*skroo*-tuh-bul) adjective, mysterious

    Synonyms: impervious; impermeable; hermetic; enigmatic; cryptic; abstruse; recondite

    Antonyms: pervious; permeable; porous; pregnable; fathomable; ascertainable

misconstrue (mis-kun-*stroo*) verb, to misunderstand or misinterpret

    Synonyms: distort; pervert; err

    Antonyms: discern; fathom; conceive; assimilate

Seventh-Inning Stretch: Multiple-Choice #2

Complete each sentence with the word that fits best. Write the letter of the word in the blank. The answers appear on page 211.

1. Despite the extreme pain, the child remained _____ and didn't even shed a tear.

   (A) bovine
   (B) candid
   (C) insouciant
   (D) impassive
   (E) clandestine

2. With a dashing, _____ grin, the old-time movie actor prepared to pick up the star-struck ingenue.

   (A) brusque
   (B) clandestine
   (C) jaunty
   (D) erudite
   (E) biennial

3. We all knew the rumors of her misdeeds, but we could find no proof because her behavior was beyond _____.

   (A) jocose
   (B) bovine
   (C) clandestine
   (D) brusque
   (E) reproach

4. The liar could _____ so well that no one knew when—or even if—he was ever telling the truth.

   (A) expunge
   (B) embalm
   (C) embark
   (D) chastise
   (E) dissemble

5. The children liked to skip, leap, and _____ around the playground.

   (A) gambol
   (B) fabricate
   (C) chastise
   (D) envenom
   (E) reimburse

6. With a weary sigh, the world traveler realized that he was _____ by too many wondrous sights, sounds, and experiences.

   (A) jaded
   (B) insouciant
   (C) jocose
   (D) fabricated
   (E) chastised

7. The soccer fans were _____ when their team won the World Cup. In their joy, they rushed from the stands onto the field.

   (A) clandestine
   (B) jubilant
   (C) insouciant
   (D) fabricated
   (E) chastised

8. According to the cartoon, bears have a _____ for picnic baskets filled with goodies.

   (A) clandestine
   (B) predilection
   (C) syllogism
   (D) syndicate
   (E) philanthropy

9. After all the Botox injections, her face was an _____ mask, devoid of all emotion.

   (A) alias
   (B) audible
   (C) inscrutable
   (D) insouciant
   (E) antebellum

10. The model wore the outlandish hat with just the right _____ tilt and so it looked quite dashing and glamorous.

   (A) carnivorous
   (B) antebellum
   (C) audible
   (D) brusque
   (E) rakish

Rush Once More into the Breach!

Let's finish up with ten more terms for unwanted behaviors. Study the synonyms and antonyms as well as the boldface vocabulary words.

obtuse (ahb-*toos*) adjective, slow to understand

Synonyms: undiscerning; doltish; dull; dimwitted; moronic

Antonyms: perspicacious; keen; astute; discerning

pallid (*pal*-id) noun, pale

Synonyms: sallow; wan; ashen; anemic; waxen; blanched

Antonyms: flushed; ruddy; rosy; cerise; rubicund; sanguine

pan (*pan*) verb, to criticize harshly

Synonyms: censure; reprove; chastise; reprimand; reproach; remonstrate; inveigh

Antonyms: acclaim; extol; plaudit; laud; hail; adulate; commend; eulogize

puerile (*pyoor*-yl) adjective, childish

Synonyms: callow; nubile; fledgling; pubescent; juvenile; green

Antonyms: hoary; grizzled; ancient; antique; decrepit; doddering

scurrilous (*sker*-uh-lis) adjective, obscene; indecent

Synonyms: lewd; vulgar; uncouth; indecorous; lascivious; licentious; unsavory; libertine; bawdy; ribald

Antonyms: seemly; decorous; befitting; scrupulous; genteel; courtly

vainglorious (vayn-*glor*-ee-us) adjective, boastful

Synonyms: vain; boastful; conceited; egotistical; haughty; pompous; arrogant

Antonyms: retiring; unpretentious; unobtrusive; decorous

vapid (*vap*-id) adjective, boring

Synonyms: insipid; stale; banal; mundane; prosaic; phlegmatic; insouciant

Antonyms: effervescent; ebullient; vivacious; savory

vaunt (*vawnt*) verb, to boast

Synonyms: brag; flaunt; gloat; tout; brandish; publicize

Antonyms: lament; mourn; grieve

vitriolic (vit-ree-*ah*-lik) adjective, sarcastic; caustic

Synonyms: scathing; sardonic; acerbic; mordant; trenchant; acrimonious; pungent

Antonyms: soothing; tropical; temperate

wastrel (*way*-strul) adjective, extremely or lavishly wasteful, especially with money

Synonyms: prodigal; spendthrift; squanderer; profligate

Antonyms: frugal; penurious; sparing; provident; thrifty; parsimonious; miserly

Seventh-Inning Stretch: Multiple-Choice #3

Choose the correct word to complete each sentence. Write the letter of the word in the space provided. The answers appear on page 211.

1. The boss's sardonic and _____ words lingered in the air long after the actual quarrel had ended.

   (A) insouciant
   (B) vitriolic
   (C) laudatory
   (D) mundane
   (E) boring

2. The starlet was so banal and _____ that even the talk show host showed signs of falling asleep during their interview.

   (A) vapid
   (B) effervescent
   (C) vivacious
   (D) ebullient
   (E) profligate

3. My girlfriend is such a _____ with money that she's sure to be broke before she's thirty years old!

   (A) thrifty
   (B) parsimonious
   (C) miserly
   (D) penurious
   (E) wastrel

4. The slander was so _____ that there was no question the victim would litigate and surely emerge victorious.

   (A) decorous
   (B) genteel
   (C) courtly
   (D) scurrilous
   (E) scrupulous

5. The _____ prank was certainly not what we expected from a sophisticated professional like him!

   (A) puerile
   (B) sophisticated
   (C) urbane
   (D) mature
   (E) clever

6. After a bad case of the flu, my friend was _____ and ashen, so pale that she looked like she had seen a ghost.

   (A) pallid
   (B) ruddy
   (C) rubicund
   (D) sanguine
   (E) obtuse

7. The critic _____ the movie but fans didn't think it was bad at all and eagerly lined up to see it over and over.

   (A) acclaimed
   (B) lauded
   (C) hailed
   (D) commended
   (E) panned

8. Richie was very _____ when it came to subtle jokes so we knew that he'd be slow to understand the joke that Heather told.

   (A) perspicacious
   (B) obtuse
   (C) discerning
   (D) astute
   (E) keen

9. Resting should make people more energetic, but it often has the opposite effect, leaving them _____ and sluggish.

   (A) lethargic
   (B) vivacious
   (C) ebullient
   (D) effervescent
   (E) zealous

10. The _____ general rarely stopped boasting about his success on the battlefield—and off.

    (A) modest
    (B) unobtrusive
    (C) decorous
    (D) unpretentious
    (E) vainglorious

Answers and Explanations

Word-Definition Match (page 196)

1. c	6. e
2. h	7. a
3. f	8. j
4. i	9. d
5. b	10. g

Word-Find Puzzle (page 197)

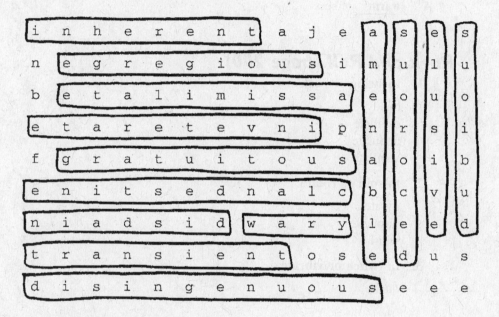

Multiple-Choice #1 (page 198)

1. D	6. A
2. C	7. B
3. E	8. B
4. E	9. C
5. A	10. E

Fill-in-the-Blank (page 200)

A **brood** of chickens

A **flock** of birds

A **gaggle** of geese

A **pride** of lions

A **gam** of whales

A **school** or a **shoal** of fish

A **stable** of horses

A **swarm** of bees

Rock and Roll (page 200)

1. **to swing or rock**

   bandy
   oscillate
   undulate
   vacillate

2. **to spin or rotate**

   gyrate
   pirouette
   whirl

3. **to twitch or vibrate**

   quake

Synonyms and Antonyms (page 202)

(Possible answers)

Word	Synonym	Antonym
dapper	spruce; smart	disheveled; unkempt
deft	adroit; adept	maladroit; inept
aplomb	assurance; intrepidity	irascibility; petulance
debonair	dashing; rakish	impudent; impertinent
candid	frank; ingenuous	hypocritical; sanctimonious
balk	demur; spurn	advance; proceed
adept	proficient; able	incompetent; inept
bovine	loutish; slothful	astir; exuberant
brusque	bluff; crude	tactful; suave
boisterous	riotous; turbulent	sedate; staid

Word Scramble (page 203)

rakish
exhort
predilection
redress
oscillate
aplomb
candid
hypocrisy

Reading down: **reproach**

Multiple-Choice #2 (pages 205–206)

1. D	6. A
2. C	7. B
3. E	8. B
4. E	9. C
5. A	10. E

Multiple-Choice #3 (pages 207–208)

1. B	6. A
2. A	7. E
3. E	8. B
4. D	9. A
5. A	10. E

Day 15

Unmask the Great Pretenders: Test-worthy Words That Can Fool You

Today, we'll talk about test-worthy words that can fool you. Some of these words are tricky because they look like words with different meanings. Other words can be deceptive because they don't seem to mean what they say. However, all the words are alike because they are likely to appear on standardized vocabulary tests!

Learn Fifteen Words That Look Deceptively Familiar

There's an interesting dish called *Welsh Rabbit* or *Welsh Rarebit*. Looking at the words, you would assume the dish contains rabbit. Actually, Welsh Rabbit is a bread-and-cheese dish, like a cheesy French toast. Not a bit of rabbit in it!

The following words can be equally tricky because they all look like other words. For example, the word *whet* from the following list looks (and sounds) like *wet*. However, the words have absolutely nothing in common at all, as you'll soon find out. As you've learned already, try making some word cards or using the words in a sentence. These techniques will help you learn the words more easily and remember them longer.

Word	Pronunciation	Meaning	Often Confused With . . .
abject	*ab*-jekt	utterly hopeless	object
motif	moh-*teef*	repeated element	motive
beatific	bee-uh-*tif*-ik	blissful	beautiful, beat
concomitant	kahn-*kam*-ih-tunt	accompanying; connected	commitment
dissemble	dis-*sem*-bul	disguise; lie	disassemble
enervate	*en*-er-vayt	weaken; debilitate	interview
feint	*faynt*	deceptive movement	faint

Learn Fifteen Words That Look Deceptively Familiar—*continued*

Word	Pronunciation	Meaning	Often Confused With . . .
fraught	*frawt*	filled with	fought
friable	*fry*-uh-bul	easily crumbled	fry
querulous	*kwer*-oh-lus	petulant	queer
reproach	re-*proach*	to scold or blame	reapproach
reprobate	*re*-pro-bayt	unscrupulous person	reappropriate
protean	*proh*-tee-un	changeable	protein
whet	*weht*	to sharpen	wet
unwonted	un-*wohn*-tid	unusual or rare	unwanted

Time for Fun: Unmask the Tricksters!

Each of the fifteen words in this list look a bit like a more common word with which you are probably familiar. However, the two words are unrelated in meaning. To play this game, choose the word that is nearest in meaning to the word in boldface. The answers appear on page 221.

1. **abject**
   - (a) hopeless
   - (b) argue
   - (c) goal
2. **motif**
   - (a) repeated element
   - (b) massive
   - (c) morose
3. **beatific**
   - (a) bold
   - (b) attractive
   - (c) blissful
4. **concomitant**
   - (a) anxious
   - b) accompanying
   - (c) strong
5. **dissemble**
   - (a) destroy
   - (b) disguise
   - (c) compare
6. **enervate**
   - (a) interfere
   - (b) weaken
   - (c) invigorate
7. **feint**
   - (a) modesty
   - (b) dizziness
   - (c) sham
8. **fraught**
   - (a) fearful
   - (b) full
   - (c) imagined
9. **friable**
   - (a) sturdy
   - (b) fragile
   - (c) flexible
10. **querulous**
    - (a) whining
    - (b) meddling
    - (c) eccentric
11. **reproach**
    - (a) retreat
    - (b) scold
    - (c) return
12. **reprobate**
    - (a) ashamed
    - (b) unscrupulous
    - (c) likely
13. **protean**
    - (a) sturdy
    - (b) fragile
    - (c) changeable

14. **whet**
    (a) to sharpen   (b) to moisten   (c) to consume
15. **unwonted**
    (a) commonplace   (b) rare   (c) not welcome

Decode the Top Twelve Teasers

Here are twelve more teasers. Meet them now and get to know them well. Then you can be sure that they won't fake you out on a standardized vocabulary test!

Word	Part of Speech	Pronunciation	Definition
accost	uh-*kawst*	verb	approach boldly
consequential	kahn-sih-*kwen*-chul	adjective	self-important; pompous
copious	*koh*-pee-us	adjective	abundant; plentiful
factotum	fak-*toh*-tum	noun	a handyman
leaven	*leh*-vun	verb	to rise
potable	*poh*-tuh-bul	adjective	drinkable
privation	prih-*vay*-shun	noun	hardship; destitution
refractory	rih-*frak*-tuh-ree	adjective	unmanageable; unruly
restive	*res*-tiv	adjective	restless; impatient
touchstone	*tuch*-stohn	noun	measure
untoward	un-*tord*	adjective	unfavorable or unfortunate
wizened	*wih*-zind	adjective	shriveled; withered

Give It a Try: Synonyms and Antonyms

Complete the following chart by writing a synonym and an antonym for each word. S-t-r-e-t-c-h your brain by writing as many synonyms and antonyms as you can. The answers appear on page 221.

Word	Synonyms	Antonyms
restive	_____	_____
accost	_____	_____
consequential	_____	_____
copious	_____	_____
wizened	_____	_____
potable	_____	_____
privation	_____	_____
refractory	_____	_____
untoward	_____	_____
leaven	_____	_____

Seventh-Inning Stretch: Multiple Choice

For each word in bold letters, select the word among the choices that is nearest in meaning. Some of the words have been covered in this lesson, while others may be new to you. The answers appear on page 222.

1. **accost**

    (A) evaluate
    (B) accumulate
    (C) confront
    (D) ignore

2. **factotum**

    (A) veracity
    (B) handyman
    (C) directory
    (D) factory

3. **leaven**

    (A) joking
    (B) fighting
    (C) healing
    (D) cause to rise

4. **consequential**

    (A) arrogant
    (B) satisfying
    (C) shocking
    (D) useless

5. **officious**

    (A) savage
    (B) angry
    (C) pleasant
    (D) authoritative

6. **copious**

    (A) tearful
    (B) imitated
    (C) endured
    (D) abundant

7. **potable**

    (A) drinkable
    (B) movable
    (C) credible
    (D) drunken

8. **decorous**

    (A) layered
    (B) demonic
    (C) gaudy
    (D) respectful

9. **privation**

    (A) solitude
    (B) hardship
    (C) panic
    (D) rank in the military

10. **noisome**

    (A) odorous
    (B) loud
    (C) friendly
    (D) hostile

11. **factitious**

    (A) bothersome
    (B) manufactured
    (C) detailed
    (D) foreign

12. **redress**

    (A) repair
    (B) conceal
    (C) confront
    (D) ignore

Tame the Top Ten Test-worthy Taunters

These bad boys can trip up unwary test takers. Study these words carefully so you know them when you take the GED, PSAT/NMSQT, SAT, ACT, or TOEFL.

1. **aggrandize** (uh-*gran*-dyz) verb, to make larger, more powerful or important, or wealthier

2. **amass** (uh-*mas*) verb, to collect or accumulate

3. **belated** (buh-*lay*-tid) adjective, late

4. **coalesce** (koh-uh-*les*) verb, unite; come together to form a whole

5. **contagion** (kun-*tay*-jun) noun, communicable disease

6. **efficacy** (*ef*-ih-kih-see) adjective, capability; efficiency

7. **evince** (ee-*vins*) verb, to demonstrate clearly or convincingly

8. **exigency** (*ek*-zih-jin-see) noun, urgency

9. **forestall** (for-*stahl*) verb, to prevent in advance

10. **frenetic** (fruh-*neh*-tik) adjective, agitated; frantic

Give It a Try: Word Scramble

To complete the following acrostic, first unscramble each of the vocabulary words so that it matches its definition. Then, use the words to fill in the appropriate spaces on the corresponding lines. When you have completed the entire puzzle, another vocabulary word will read vertically in the circles. The answers appear on page 222.

ncgotaion	communicable disease
qosebuious	overly servile or obedient
gzadgranie	to make larger, more powerful or important, or wealthier
enavle	to rise
yeficfac	capability; efficiency
isnale	pertaining to salt
cnslteqouenia	self-important; pompous
inceev	to demonstrate clearly or convincingly

Domesticate a Dozen Dirties

The following twelve words have misled many an unwary test taker. Learn these words so you can distinguish between them when it counts—on a standardized test!

Word	Pronunciation	Part of Speech	Definition
funereal	fyoo-*neer*-ee-ul	adjective	sorrowful; solemn; sad
guile	*gyl*	noun	deceit; fraud
insular	*in*-suh-ler	adjective	narrow-minded
largess	lahr-*jes*	noun	generosity
maculated	*mak*-yoo-lay-tid	adjective	spotted; stained
militate	*mil*-uh-tayt	verb	contemplate
nexus	*nek*-sus	noun	connection
polemic	puh-*lem*-ik	noun	controversy
politic	*pahl*-uh-tik	adjective	shrewd; expedient; judicious
quiescent	kwy-*es*-unt	adjective	quiet; inactive
remnant	*rem*-nunt	noun	left-over
requisite	*reh*-kwih-zit	adjective	necessary

Time for Fun: Word-Find Puzzle

There are fifteen words hidden in this puzzle. Many have already been introduced in this chapter, but a few are new. To complete the puzzle, locate and circle all the words. (See the word list on the next page.) They may be written forward, backward, or upside down. The answers appear on page 222. Good luck!

```
c o n t a g i o n h a p p y
f o r e q u i s i t e c y f
u n q u i e s c e n t o c r
n t s u x e n w h e t a a e
e t a t i l i m g i o l c n
r e m n a n t n c a l e i e
e l i u g a m a s s u s f t
a m p o l e m i c n y c f i
l g o p o l i t i c a e e c
```

Word List

1. **guile:** deceit; fraud
2. **militate:** contemplate
3. **requisite:** necessary
4. **funereal:** sorrowful; solemn; sad
5. **quiescent:** quiet; inactive
6. **nexus:** connection
7. **politic:** shrewd; expedient; judicious
8. **remnant:** left-over
9. **polemic:** controversy
10. **amass:** to collect or accumulate
11. **whet:** to sharpen
12. **coalesce:** unite; come together to form a whole
13. **efficacy:** capability; efficiency
14. **frenetic:** agitated; frantic
15. **contagion:** communicable disease

Seventh-Inning Stretch: Game Time #1

Let's finish today's work with some fun. To play the following two games, match each numbered word in the left column with its lettered definition in the right column. Some of the words will be familiar, while others may be new to you. The answers appear on page 223.

_____ 1. calumny	a. command or order
_____ 2. conundrum	b. dabbler in the arts
_____ 3. debauch	c. excessive pride
_____ 4. dilettante	d. group with a common purpose
_____ 5. fiat	e. commonplace or everyday
_____ 6. gossamer	f. line up sequentially
_____ 7. queue	g. puzzle or mystery
_____ 8. hubris	h. malicious statement
_____ 9. insouciant	i. corrupt by sensuality
_____ 10. apparition	j. having a foul odor
_____ 11. milieu	k. sheer and light
_____ 12. peccadillo	l. slight offense
_____ 13. phalanx	m. a ghost
_____ 14. quotidian	n. surroundings or environment
_____ 15. noisome	o. unconcerned or carefree

Seventh-Inning Stretch: Game Time #2

The answers appear on page 223.

_____	1. abject	a.	surpass
_____	2. adventitious	b.	abolish
_____	3. exceed	c.	prevent
_____	4. turgid	d.	admiration
_____	5. enervate	e.	by chance
_____	6. obeisance	f.	complaining or whining
_____	7. undulate	g.	relief or assistance
_____	8. obviate	h.	deadly
_____	9. protean	i.	to move in a wavelike motion
_____	10. virulent	j.	swollen
_____	11. predilection	k.	demonstration of respect
_____	12. querulous	l.	deprive of vitality
_____	13. succor	m.	preference
_____	14. adulation	n.	utterly hopeless
_____	15. abrogate	o.	versatile

Answers and Explanations

Unmask the Tricksters! (pages 214–215)

1. **The correct answer is (a). Abject** means utterly hopeless (as in abject poverty).

2. **The correct answer is (a). Motif** means a basic element repeated throughout the work.

3. **The correct answer is (c). Beatific** means blissful.

4. **The correct answer is (b). Concomitant** means accompanying; connected.

5. **The correct answer is (b). Dissemble** means disguise; lie.

6. **The correct answer is (b). Enervate** means weaken; debilitate.

7. **The correct answer is (c). Feint** means a deceptive movement; sham.

8. **The correct answer is (b). Fraught** means filled with.

9. **The correct answer is (b). Friable** means easily crumbled.

10. **The correct answer is (a). Querulous** means petulant.

11. **The correct answer is (b). Reproach** means to scold or blame.

12. **The correct answer is (b). Reprobate** means an unscrupulous person.

13. **The correct answer is (c). Protean** means the ability to take many forms or perform many functions; versatile; variable; changeable; mutable.

14. **The correct answer is (a). Whet** means to sharpen; make keen; intensify.

15. **The correct answer is (b). Unwonted** means not customary; not habitual; unusual or rare.

Synonyms and Antonyms (page 215)

(Possible answers)

Word	Synonyms	Antonyms
restive	restless; impatient	patient
accost	approach boldly	avoid
consequential	self-important; pompous	modest; meek
copious	abundant; plentiful	scarce
wizened	shriveled; withered	lush
potable	drinkable	poisoned
privation	hardship; destitution	affluence
refractory	unmanageable; unruly	docile; submissive
untoward	unfavorable or unfortunate	favorable
leaven	to rise	to fall

Multiple Choice (page 216)

1. C	5. D	9. B
2. B	6. D	10. A
3. D	7. A	11. B
4. A	8. D	12. A

Word Scramble (page 217)

contagion
obsequious
aggrandize
leaven
efficacy
saline
consequential
evince

Reading down: **coalesce**

Word-Find Puzzle (page 218)

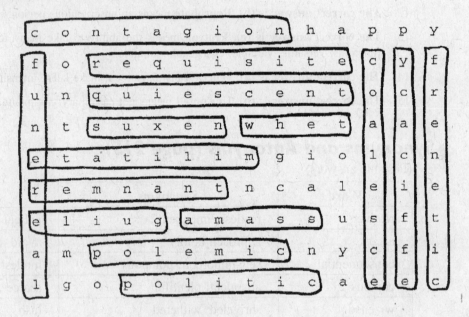

Game Time #1 (page 219)

1. h	6. k	11. n
2. g	7. f	12. l
3. i	8. c	13. d
4. b	9. o	14. e
5. a	10. m	15. j

Game Time #2 (page 220)

1. n	6. k	11. m
2. e	7. i	12. f
3. a	8. c	13. g
4. j	9. o	14. d
5. l	10. h	15. b

Day 16

Study 100 Key SAT or ACT Words

Some words keep showing up on standardized tests such as the SAT or ACT because they are especially useful in college speech and writing. As a result, test makers love them—and by the time you finish this chapter, you will, too. So let's talk about words that you are highly likely to encounter on the SAT or ACT. To help you learn these words more easily, they are grouped according to their part of speech.

Learn Twenty Vital Test-worthy Nouns

When asked why he robbed banks, famous thief Willie Sutton is said to have replied: "Because that's where the money is." When asked why you take standardized tests, the answer is: "Because standardized tests are generally required for college and grad school admission, as well as for certain careers." Learning these twenty test-worthy nouns can help you do your best on test day.

Word	Pronunciation	Meaning
cacophony	kuh-*kahf*-uh-nee	tremendous noise, disharmonious sound
kinetic	kih-*neh*-tik	motion
rancor	*rang*-ker	deep, bitter resentment
caliper	*kal*-uh-per	instrument used to measure the thickness of an object
parsimony	*pahr*-sih-moh-nee	frugality, stinginess
aberration	ab-uh-*rey*-shuhn	something that differs from the norm
rectitude	*rek*-tih-tood, -tyood	uprightness, extreme morality
duress	dyoo-*res*	force
serendipity	ser-uhn-*dip*-ih-tee	luck, finding good things without looking for them
temerity	tuh-*mer*-ih-tee	audacity, recklessness

Learn Twenty Vital Test-worthy Nouns—*continued*

Word	Pronunciation	Meaning
grandiloquence	gran-*dil*-uh-kwehns	lofty, pompous language
dearth	durth	lack, scarcity
surfeit	*sur*-fit	overabundant supply or indulgence
umbrage	*uhm*-brij	resentment, offense
collusion	kuh-*loo*-zhun	conspiracy
utopia	yoo-*toh*-pee-uh	imaginary and remote place of perfection
behemoth	bih-*hee*-muhth	something of tremendous power or size
travesty	*trav*-uh-stee	grossly inferior imitation
complicity	kum-*plih*-sih-tee	participation in a crime
debacle	dey-*bah*-kuhl, duh-*bak*-uhl	disastrous failure, disruption

Administered by the College Board, the SAT is a 4-hour standardized test divided into three sections: math, critical reading, and writing. The SAT is used chiefly as a factor in college admissions, and, to a much lesser extent, as a factor in admissions to elite academic summer programs and private high schools.

Give It a Try: Puzzle Me This!

Complete the following crossword puzzle with the twenty test-worthy words that you just learned. If you're feeling smug, do the puzzle in ink rather than pencil. The answers appear on page 238.

ACROSS
1. Pompous language
3. Recklessness
5. Bitter resentment
10. Scarcity
11. Participation in a crime
13. Resentment
14. A conspiracy
16. Force
18. A grossly inferior imitation
19. Luck

DOWN
2. Something that differs from the norm
4. Motion
6. Disharmonious sound
7. Stinginess
8. Uprightness, extreme morality
9. Something of tremendous power or size
10. A disastrous failure
12. Instrument used to measure the thickness of an object
15. An overabundance
17. An imaginary and remote place of perfection

Time for Fun: Word-Find Puzzle #1

To really own a word, you have to practice using it. That's what these games, puzzles, and activities help you do. For example, there are twenty words hidden in this word-find puzzle. All twenty words were defined in "Learn Twenty Vital Test-worthy Nouns," but you'll find the definitions here, too. To complete the puzzle, locate and circle all the words. (See the word list on the next page.) The words may be written forward, backward, diagonally, or upside down. The answers appear on page 239. Good luck!

```
d  s  z  b  e  h  e  m  o  t  h  u  c  o  g  w  s  f
w  y  l  x  n  k  i  s  s  n  q  t  g  y  i  g  t  v
g  t  c  n  b  o  m  g  p  f  l  o  c  s  t  r  d  w
b  s  i  d  k  h  i  p  q  f  u  p  v  q  e  a  i  b
s  e  t  f  m  n  n  t  g  u  d  i  a  a  m  n  s  v
u  v  e  t  v  w  e  f  a  u  s  a  p  w  e  d  v  d
r  a  n  n  q  j  y  l  m  r  k  e  c  d  r  i  y  a
f  r  i  o  r  w  t  x  j  y  r  l  f  y  i  l  s  r
e  t  k  i  a  y  i  y  x  n  d  e  l  b  t  o  u  e
i  s  a  s  n  t  p  u  e  o  e  w  b  e  y  q  b  c
t  g  i  u  c  i  i  m  l  h  a  c  w  a  t  u  q  t
g  c  k  l  o  c  d  b  c  p  r  z  i  d  g  e  x  i
g  g  b  l  r  i  n  r  a  o  t  e  s  z  z  n  s  t
w  t  p  o  q  l  e  a  b  c  h  w  p  u  v  c  s  u
b  x  w  c  e  p  r  g  e  a  x  q  w  a  o  e  e  d
z  i  b  b  j  m  e  e  d  c  a  l  i  p  e  r  r  e
a  z  f  j  o  o  s  m  q  d  a  x  m  e  m  f  u  d
z  t  b  s  o  c  p  a  r  s  i  m  o  n  y  j  d  l
```

Word List

1. **aberration:** something that differs from the norm
2. **behemoth:** something of tremendous power or size
3. **cacophony:** tremendous noise, disharmonious sound
4. **caliper:** instrument used to measure the thickness of an object
5. **collusion:** conspiracy
6. **complicity:** participation in a crime
7. **dearth:** lack, scarcity
8. **debacle:** disastrous failure, disruption
9. **duress:** force
10. **grandiloquence:** lofty, pompous language
11. **kinetic:** motion
12. **parsimony:** frugality, stinginess
13. **rancor:** deep, bitter resentment
14. **rectitude:** uprightness, extreme morality
15. **serendipity:** luck, finding good things without looking for them
16. **surfeit:** overabundant supply or indulgence
17. **temerity:** audacity, recklessness
18. **travesty:** grossly inferior imitation
19. **umbrage:** resentment, offense
20. **utopia:** imaginary and remote place of perfection

Make Ten More Nouns Your Own

In 1823, Scottish chemist Charles Macintosh discovered that the newfangled substance called "rubber" could be dissolved with the chemical naphtha and painted on cloth to create a waterproof covering. Clothing made with this fabric came to be called *mackintoshes* (raincoats).

Here are ten more test-worthy nouns. They're not waterproof, but they *are* useful on tests and in daily conversation. Use the memory tricks you learned earlier to make it easier to remember these words.

1. **abstinence** (*ab*-stih-nehns) self denial
2. **bourgeois** (bore-*zhwah*) a middle-class person, capitalist
3. **dissonance** (*dis*-oh-nans) discord
4. **edict** (*ee*-dihkt) an order, decree
5. **guile** (*gy*-uhl) deceitful behavior

6. **hegemony** (*heh*-jih-moh-nee) domination over others

7. **hiatus** (hy-*ay*-tuhs) a break or gap in duration or continuity

8. **iniquity** (ih-*nih*-kwih-tee) evil, wickedness

9. **medley** (*mehd*-lee) a mixture of differing things

10. **translucent** (trans-*loo*-sehnt) the property or state of allowing the passage of light

Give It a Try: Synonyms and Antonyms

Complete this puzzle by writing a synonym (word that means the same) and an antonym (word that means the opposite) for each of these ten words. See if you can come up with more than one synonym and antonym for each word. The answers appear on page 240.

Word	Synonym	Antonym
1. abstinence		
2. bourgeois		
3. dissonance		
4. edict		
5. guile		
6. hegemony		
7. hiatus		
8. iniquity		
9. medley		
10. translucent		

Visualize Twenty Vital Verbs

We don't want to slight words that show action or state of being, so here are twenty important verbs.

1. **abase** (uh-*beys*) to humiliate, to degrade

2. **abdicate** (*ab*-di-kayt) to give up a position, usually one of leadership

3. **balk** (bawk) to stop

4. **carouse** (kuh-*rouz*) to party, to celebrate

5. **extort** (eks-*tort*) to demand payment based on threats

6. **extradite** (*eks*-truh-dyt) to give up a fugitive from one state or country to another

7. **forge** (forj) to counterfeit

8. **goad** (gohd) to urge on

9. **immerse** (ih-*murs*) to absorb, to deeply involve, to engross

10. **mitigate** (*mit*-ih-gayt) to alleviate

11. **modulate** (*moj*-uh-layt) to change, to transform

12. **mollify** (*mol*-uh-fy) to appease

13. **procure** (pro-*kyoor*) to purchase

14. **sanction** (*sank*-shun) to give approval

15. **solder** (*sah*-der) to join metal with melted metal

16. **transgress** (tranz-*gress*) to violate

17. **transmute** (tranz-*myoot*) to change or alter in form

18. **underwrite** (*un*-der-ryt) to offer insurance

19. **venerate** (*ven*-uh-rayt) to regard with respect or to honor

20. **vituperate** (vy-*too*-puh-rayt) to berate

Seventh-Inning Stretch: Make a Match

Below are ten verbs from the list that you just studied. To complete this game, match each word to its definition. Consider pronouncing the word aloud as you write it, because this will help you fix it more firmly in your mind. Then write the letter of your answer in the space provided. The answers appear on page 240.

_____ 1. extradite

_____ 2. sanction

_____ 3. vituperate

_____ 4. transgress

_____ 5. underwrite

_____ 6. mitigate

_____ 7. balk

_____ 8. abdicate

_____ 9. goad

_____ 10. modulate

a. to stop

b. to change

c. to alleviate

d. to give up a fugitive from one state or country to another

e. to urge on

f. to violate

g. to give approval

h. to give up a position, usually one of leadership

i. to berate

j. to offer insurance

Give It a Try: Puzzle Me This—Take 2!

Complete the following crossword puzzle with ten of the test-worthy verbs that you just learned. The answers appear on page 241.

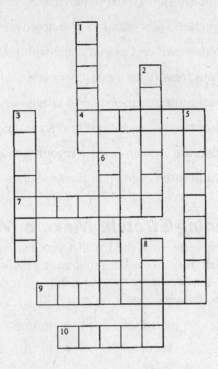

ACROSS

4. To demand payment based on threats
7. To absorb
9. To regard with respect or to honor
10. To counterfeit

DOWN

1. To join metal with melted metal
2. To purchase
3. To appease
5. To change or alter in form
6. To celebrate
8. To humiliate

Crack Fifteen Virtuous Verbs

Verbs are useful in life as well as on tests, so here are fifteen more to help you get ahead. Use the techniques that you learned earlier to help you memorize these words and their meanings.

Word	Pronunciation	Definition
emulate	*em*-yoo-layt	to imitate
expurgate	*ek*-sper-gayt	to remove offensive or incorrect parts, usually of a book
immerse	ih-*murs*	to absorb, deeply involve
mitigate	*mit*-ih-gayt	to alleviate
mollify	*mol*-uh-fy	to soften in temper
nurture	*nur*-cher	to assist the development of
obfuscate	*ob*-fuh-skayt, ob-*fuhs*-kayt	to render incomprehensible
oscillate	*os*-uh-layt	to sway
palliate	*pal*-ee-ayt	to relieve
permeate	*pur*-mee-ayt	to saturate
perplex	per-*pleks*	to confuse
quell	kwel	to control
rail	reyl	to scold
satiate	*say*-shee-ayt	to satisfy (as a need or desire) fully
transgress	trans-*gres*	to violate

Seventh-Inning Stretch: Multiple Choice

Select the correct meaning for each of the following boldfaced verbs. Circle your choice. The answers appear on page 242.

1. **oscillate**

   (A) satisfy
   (B) annoy
   (C) to soften in temper
   (D) swing back and forth
   (E) to render incomprehensible

2. **satiate**

   (A) relieve
   (B) compensate
   (C) qualify
   (D) clinch
   (E) quench

3. **rail**

   (A) reprimand
   (B) relieve
   (C) review
   (D) renew
   (E) rewrite

4. **obfuscate**

   (A) confuse
   (B) refine
   (C) clarify
   (D) explain
   (E) simplify

5. **expurgate**

(A) assist
(B) saturate
(C) abridge
(D) berate
(E) pardon

When applied to a business setting, a *dingbat* (*ding*-bat) is used to refer to a small symbol such as an arrow, pointing finger, and so forth, which is part of a typeface. For example: ☞. In general speech, the word *dingbat* refers to a crackpot or a weirdo.

Discover Ten Test-worthy Adjectives

Remember that an *adjective* is a word that modifies (describes) a noun or a pronoun. Adjectives are arranged in specific order before a noun, as follows: opinion, dimension, age, shape, color, origin, and material. Thus, we say *delicious hot vegetable* soup, not *hot delicious vegetable* soup or *vegetable delicious hot* soup.

Here are ten test-worthy adjectives arranged on a chart. As you read them, mentally arrange them in order in a sentence.

Word	Pronunciation	Meaning
fiscal	*fis*-kul	the finances of a government or business
ribald	*ry*-buld	obscene; indecent; mocking
prudent	*proo*-dent	having common sense
serene	suh-*reen*	calm
whimsical	*wihm*-zuh-kul	unpredictable
tenuous	*ten*-yoo-us	weak
trivial	*trih*-vee-ul	insignificant
prurient	*proor*-ee-uhnt	eliciting or possessing an extraordinary interest in sex
obstreperous	uhb-*strep*-er-uhs	noisy, unruly
deferential	def-uh-*ren*-shuhl	showing respect for another's authority

Master Fifteen More Adjectives You'll Likely Encounter on the SAT or ACT

One of the great strengths of English is its welcoming attitude toward new words. People coin new English words daily, and some of them even become a permanent part of our language. For example, *fantabulous* is a new adjective that means "beyond fabulous." Can you guess which two words were combined to form this new word? (They're *fantastic* and *fabulous*.) Perhaps this clever word will endure; perhaps not.

Below are fifteen test-worthy adjectives that have withstood the test of time. As a result, it is virtually guaranteed that you will see some of these words on the standardized tests that you take.

1. **desiccated** (*deh*-sih-kayt-id) dried up, dehydrated

2. **capacious** (kuh-*pay*-shus) very spacious

3. **puerile** (*pure*-ill) juvenile, immature

4. **banal** (buh-*nal*) commonplace

5. **rancid** (*rant*-sid) spoiled

6. **sacrosanct** (*sa*-croh-sankt) holy

7. **pugnacious** (pug-*nay*-shus) quarrelsome, combative

8. **taciturn** (*ta*-suh-tern) not inclined to talk

9. **torpid** (*tor*-pid) lethargic

10. **benign** (be-*nyn*) mild

11. **prosaic** (pro-*zay*-ik) plain

12. **sanctimonious** (sank-te-*moh*-nee-us) hypocritical

13. **benevolent** (be-*ne*-ve-lent) compassionate

14. **bashful** (*bash*-fil) shy

15. **vicarious** (vy-*ker*-ee-us) experiencing something through someone else

---

Ginormous is a newly coined adjective that means "extremely large." It's a blend of *gigantic* and *enormous.*

Give It a Try: Chart It!

Complete this puzzle by writing a synonym (word that means the same) and an antonym (word that means the opposite) for each of these ten adjectives. See if you can come up with more than one synonym and antonym for each adjective. The answers appear on page 242.

Word	Synonym	Antonym
1. serene		
2. prosaic		
3. prudent		
4. bashful		
5. deferential		
6. ribald		
7. torpid		
8. benign		
9. capacious		
10. trivial		

Study Ten More Critical SAT or ACT Words

Economics has been called "the dismal science." Learning the following ten test-worthy words from the financial field can keep you cheerful—especially when you see your high score on standardized vocabulary tests!

1. **accrue** (uh-*kroo*) verb, to accumulate interest over time

2. **actuary** (*ak*-choo-ayr-ee) noun, an expert on statistics

3. **amortize** (*am*-or-tyz) verb, to gradually reduce or write off the cost or value of (as an asset)

4. **appraise** (uh-*prayz*) verb, to assess the market value of an asset

5. **arbitrage** (*ar*-bih-trahzh) verb, to take advantage of differing prices for a commodity

6. **arrears** (uh-*reers*) noun, an unpaid and overdue debt

7. **contraband** (*kahn*-truh-band) noun, goods illegally transported across a border

8. **embargo** (em-*bar*-goh) noun, an official prohibition or restriction of foreign trade by one nation against another

9. **entrepreneur** (*ahn*-truh-pruh-ner) noun, someone who takes a risk in a business venture

10. **escrow** (*es*-kroh) noun, a temporary account established to hold funds pending the completion of an investment

Time for Fun: Word-Find Puzzle #2

This word-find puzzle has all ten words you just learned. As with the other word-find puzzles that you have enjoyed in this book, to complete the puzzle, locate and circle all the words. (See the word list below.) The words may be written forward, backward, diagonally, or upside down. The answers appear on page 243. Good luck!

```
o  y  t  a  c  c  r  u  e  a  z  a  t
l  r  g  r  x  u  w  x  b  f  a  r  e
h  a  h  u  a  z  x  v  q  b  r  b  m
h  u  d  e  o  r  d  l  l  w  x  i  b
h  t  n  n  j  j  r  v  g  d  v  t  a
a  c  a  e  t  e  r  e  m  a  e  r  r
m  a  b  r  k  y  l  j  a  a  u  a  g
o  v  a  p  c  j  j  w  m  r  g  g  o
r  o  r  e  a  p  p  r  a  i  s  e  g
t  g  t  r  j  o  c  q  p  x  a  b  a
i  j  n  t  v  o  m  v  r  m  m  n  k
z  b  o  n  k  w  o  r  c  s  e  u  x
e  s  c  e  e  w  d  z  m  l  b  m  n
```

Word List

1. **accrue:** to accumulate or be added periodically
2. **actuary:** person who calculates insurance and annuity premiums, reserves, and dividends
3. **amortize:** to gradually reduce or write off the cost or value of (as an asset)
4. **appraise:** to evaluate the worth, significance, or status of
5. **arbitrage:** the purchase of a stock or takeover target especially with a view to selling it profitably to the raider
6. **arrears:** an unpaid or overdue debt
7. **contraband:** illegal or prohibited traffic in goods
8. **embargo:** a legal prohibition on commerce
9. **entrepreneur:** one who organizes, manages, and assumes the risks of a business or enterprise
10. **escrow:** a deed, bond, money, or piece of property held in trust by a third party to be turned over to the grantee upon fulfillment of a condition

Answers and Explanations

Puzzle Me This! (page 227)

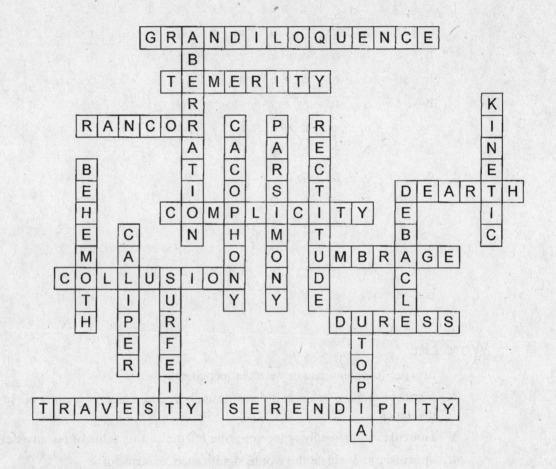

Word-Find Puzzle #1 (page 228)

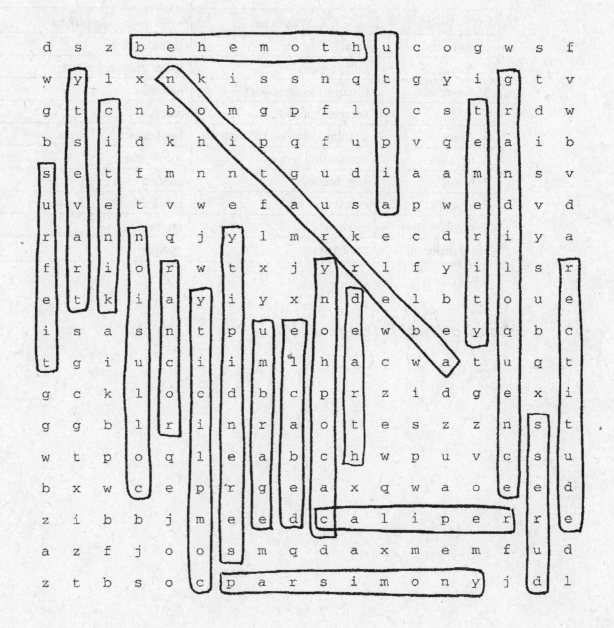

Synonyms and Antonyms (page 230)

(Possible answers)

Word	Synonym	Antonym
1. abstinence	denial	indulgence
2. bourgeois	middle class	lower class/upper class
3. dissonance	discord, disagreement	harmony
4. edict	decree, demand	edict
5. guile	cunning, slyness, cleverness	frankness
6. hegemony	domination, control	subjugation
7. hiatus	gap, break	continuation
8. iniquity	evilness	goodness
9. medley	mixture	mixture
10. translucent	transparent	opaque

Make a Match (page 231)

1. d   6. c
2. g   7. a
3. i   8. h
4. f   9. e
5. j   10. b

Seventh-Inning Stretch: Puzzle Me This—Take 2!
(page 232)

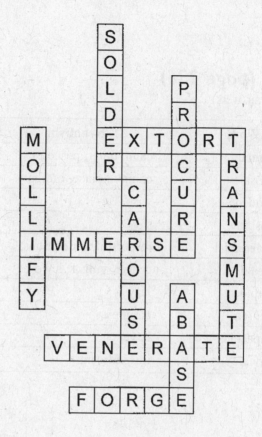

Multiple Choice (page 233–234)

1. D
2. E
3. A
4. A
5. C

Chart It! (page 236)

(Possible answers)

Word	Synonym	Antonym
1. serene	calm, quiet, peaceful	bustling
2. prosaic	commonplace, ordinary	extraordinary
3. prudent	wise	foolhardy
4. bashful	shy	outgoing
5. deferential	respectful, obsequious	disrespectful
6. ribald	coarse, vulgar, lewd	refined
7. torpid	lazy	energetic
8. benign	harmless	harmful
9. capacious	large	small
10. trivial	insignificant	important

Word-Find Puzzle #2 (page 237)

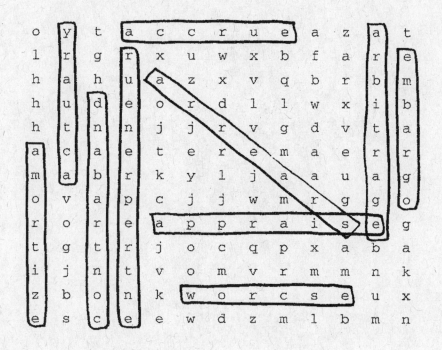

Part VI

Go for the Gold! Puzzles and Games to Win with Words

Day 17:
Practice Makes Perfect

Day 18:
Have Some Fun While You Boost Your Vocabulary

Day 17

Practice Makes Perfect

It's obvious that you can't use a new word in your speech and writing until you learn it. Learning new words doesn't have to be *arduous*. (Notice the test-worthy synonym for *difficult*!) In fact, learning new words can be a lot of fun. Have some fun now with these vocabulary puzzles. Most of the words in these puzzles have already been introduced in this book, but some are new, so you can learn even more words.

In 1812, the governor of Massachusetts, Elbridge Gerry, conspired with his political party to change the boundaries of the voting districts to enhance his own political power. When a newspaper editor noticed that one such rigged district looked like a salamander, he coined the term *gerrymander* to describe the practice of dividing a state, or any other geographic district, into election districts to give one political party a majority.

Puzzle #1

Complete the following crossword puzzle with twenty test-worthy words you have already learned. The clues are on the next page. If you're feeling smug, do the puzzle in ink rather than pencil. The answers appear on page 259.

ACROSS

3. A word or phrase describing a person; a derogatory word or phrase used to show contempt
6. Inclination
7. Noisy fight
9. Fiery, passionate
12. Following or occurring after death
16. Made worse
17. Businessperson
18. Corner
19. Large, roomy
20. Light brown

DOWN

1. Profusion of words
2. Hairpiece
4. Voice box
5. Tomb
8. Carefree
10. Soiled; made filthy
11. A waterfall
13. Swamp
14. Payment
15. Leadership

Puzzle #2

In the space provided, write **T** if the definition is true and **F** if it is false. The answers appear on page 260.

_____	1. debacle	a disastrous failure, disruption
_____	2. conciliatory	friendly, agreeable
_____	3. denude	to strip bare
_____	4. solvent	able to pay one's debts
_____	5. misnomer	a wrong name or designation
_____	6. fastidious	exact; meticulous
_____	7. zenith	the highest point, culminating point
_____	8. bountiful	plentiful
_____	9. vocation	occupation or profession
_____	10. pragmatic	practical
_____	11. promulgated	publish or disseminate widely
_____	12. abstemious	moderate, sober
_____	13. hierarchy	a group organized by rank
_____	14. embellish	to decorate or make beautiful
_____	15. allegation	assertion, claim

Puzzle #3

There are twenty words hidden in this word-find puzzle. Every word begins with "S." To complete the puzzle, locate and circle all the words. (See the word list on the next page.) The words may be written forward, backward, diagonally, or upside down. The answers appear on page 260. Good luck!

```
s  o  l  i  l  o  q  u  y  k  q  j  k  m  t  v  m  h
o  e  h  p  d  o  n  a  r  p  o  s  a  e  b  l  n  d
l  d  c  w  u  w  i  t  s  o  m  n  o  l  e  n  t  e
o  u  s  e  v  b  d  z  c  t  u  j  x  n  a  p  j  d
l  c  p  p  d  x  l  f  x  g  e  v  c  v  e  u  b  e
r  a  z  k  u  e  l  a  n  i  m  i  l  b  u  s  g  s
p  s  c  c  i  r  o  m  o  h  p  o  s  v  w  o  e  r
e  s  y  i  z  e  i  l  n  g  i  e  r  e  v  o  s  e
b  s  o  n  r  s  n  o  c  q  s  u  r  p  l  u  s  p
i  e  s  l  o  t  i  y  u  l  z  m  s  e  o  d  c  u
d  u  o  e  u  p  e  i  g  s  d  m  i  y  r  b  j  s
y  h  e  v  c  b  s  m  o  f  i  z  s  s  n  b  j  x
f  t  j  x  e  t  l  i  m  l  h  j  o  z  w  t  b  y
e  n  l  s  o  y  g  e  s  y  w  o  i  f  a  y  a  a
p  w  n  y  e  l  d  n  i  w  s  g  b  v  h  w  x  x
u  g  d  a  y  d  i  s  b  u  s  z  m  j  e  h  a  k
t  m  d  a  o  s  e  c  q  j  j  h  y  m  z  s  x  n
s  x  t  p  a  w  g  d  j  p  n  r  s  r  o  y  x  u
```

The Twenty Hidden Words for Puzzle #3

1. secede
2. sect
3. soliloquy
4. solo
5. soluble
6. somnolent
7. sophomoric
8. soprano
9. sovereign
10. spurious
11. stupefy
12. subliminal
13. subsidy
14. supersede
15. surplus
16. swindle
17. symbiosis
18. symmetrical
19. synopsis
20. syntax

Puzzle #4

Complete this chart by finding the prefix in each word, defining the prefix, and then using that clue to define each word. The answers appear on page 261.

Word	Prefix	Prefix Meaning	Word Meaning
amoral			
catalyst			
circumference			
cohabit			
discredit			
disinter			
extraterrestrial			
intractable			
malcontent			
misnomer			
multifaceted			
multiform			
philharmonic			
polyglot			
reacquaint			

Puzzle #5

To complete this puzzle, match each word to its definition. Then, write your answers in the space provided. The answers appear on page 261.

_____	1. nomenclature	a.	to talk together; prattle
_____	2. font	b.	bubbling; lively
_____	3. meticulous	c.	statement
_____	4. ignominious	d.	system of naming
_____	5. prolix	e.	a long, usually abusive, argument
_____	6. extradited	f.	precise
_____	7. vacillation	g.	to give up a fugitive from one state or nation to another
_____	8. diatribe		
_____	9. herbivore	h.	needlessly prolonged or drawn out
_____	10. assertion	i.	clever, pithy saying; aphorism
_____	11. effervescent	j.	indecision
_____	12. cogent	k.	typeface
_____	13. epithet	l.	disgracing one's name
_____	14. confabulate	m.	convincing; compelling
_____	15. epigram	n.	plant eater
		o.	nasty word or phrase used to show contempt

Puzzle #6

To complete the following acrostic, first unscramble each of the vocabulary words so that it matches its definition. Then, use the words to fill in the appropriate spaces on the corresponding lines. When you have completed the entire puzzle, another test-worthy word will read vertically in the circles. The answers appear on page 261.

lmbativaen	uncertain
treplee	filled to capacity
vbneneolet	generous
annei	silly or nonsensical; vacuous
enstuou	weak
tnaaleocmri	to make new again
mplea	a large amount
ibarld	obscene; indecent; mocking
eny	desire; urge

Puzzle #7

Match each occupation in the left column with the definition in the right column. Write the matching letter on the line next to each entry in the left column. The answers appear on page 262.

_____ 1. actuary		a. missionary
_____ 2. apostle		b. teller, cashier
_____ 3. bard		c. storyteller
_____ 4. barrister		d. clerk
_____ 5. concierge		e. troubadour
_____ 6. conservator		f. handyman
_____ 7. courtesan		g. statistician
_____ 8. curator		h. hotel employee
_____ 9. despot		i. wine dealer
_____ 10. factotum		j. farmer
_____ 11. impresario		k. mistress
_____ 12. incumbent		l. sponsor
_____ 13. osteopath		m. lawyer
_____ 14. purser		n. chiropractor
_____ 15. raconteur		o. fiduciary
_____ 16. scrivener		p. candidate
_____ 17. vintner		q. docent
_____ 18. yeoman		r. potentate

Puzzle #8

Complete the following crossword puzzle with ten test-worthy words that begin with "B." Every one of these words has appeared in the book, so you're getting a great review! The answers appear on page 262.

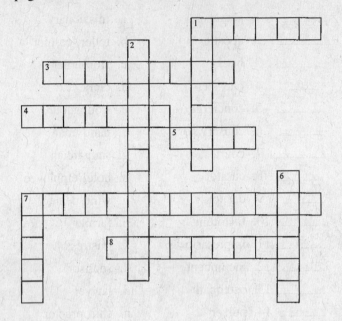

ACROSS

1. Self-service meal
3. A ludicrous parody
4. Feast
5. Floating marker
7. Cooperation between political parties
8. Infinite

DOWN

1. Abrupt, impatient
2. Blessing
6. Prejudiced
7. Well done

Puzzle #9

Match each word with its definition. Write the letter of your choice in the space provided. The answers appear on page 262.

_____	1. permeated	a. silly or nonsensical
_____	2. omnipotent	b. humble
_____	3. novice	c. absorbed
_____	4. naïve	d. to soothe
_____	5. mollify	e. wildly excited
_____	6. modest	f. average
_____	7. mediocrity	g. beginner
_____	8. maverick	h. all powerful
_____	9. inane	i. lacking sophistication
_____	10. frenetic	j. nonconformist

Puzzle #10

Select the correct meaning for each of the following boldfaced words. Circle your choice. The answers appear on page 262.

1. **delude**

   (A) deceive
   (B) exhort
   (C) ingratiate
   (D) gambol
   (E) reproach

2. **colloquial**

   (A) bourgeois
   (B) cryptic
   (C) gauche
   (D) informal
   (E) genteel

3. **malign**

   (A) to speak badly of another with the intent to harm
   (B) to redress
   (C) to soothe
   (D) to talk together
   (E) to strip bare

4. **dementia**

   (A) a faux pas
   (B) a predilection
   (C) a loss of mental abilities or powers
   (D) a raconteur
   (E) a bon mot

5. **denouement**

   (A) factotum
   (B) privation
   (C) conclusion
   (D) touchstone
   (E) contagion

6. **malcontent**

   (A) a consequential event
   (B) a potable drink
   (C) a refractory individual
   (D) an untoward event
   (E) a dissatisfied person

7. **amoral**

   (A) copious
   (B) unscrupulous
   (C) restive
   (D) wizened
   (E) impassive

8. **perdition**

   (A) largess
   (B) guile
   (C) nexus
   (D) polemic
   (E) ruin

9. **premonition**

   (A) a forewarning
   (B) a remnant
   (C) an actuary
   (D) an entrepreneur
   (E) a pundit

10. **dialectic**

    (A) compendium
    (B) insectivore
    (C) argument through critical discussion
    (D) fraud
    (E) jurisprudence

Answers and Explanations

Puzzle #1 (page 248)

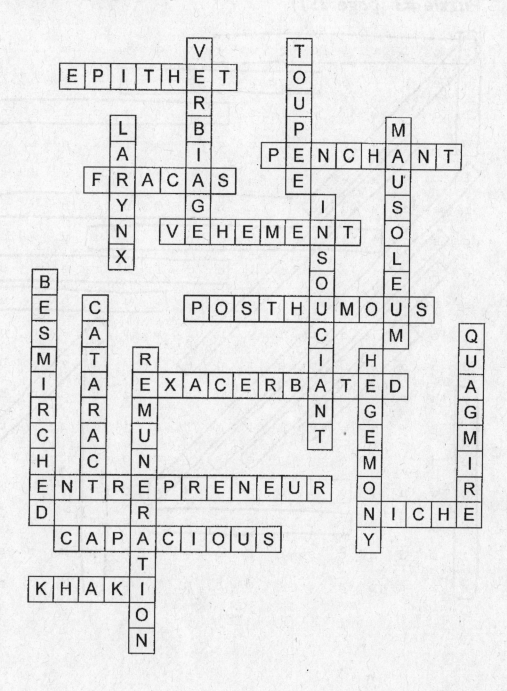

Puzzle #2 (page 250)

Every answer is true.

Puzzle #3 (page 251)

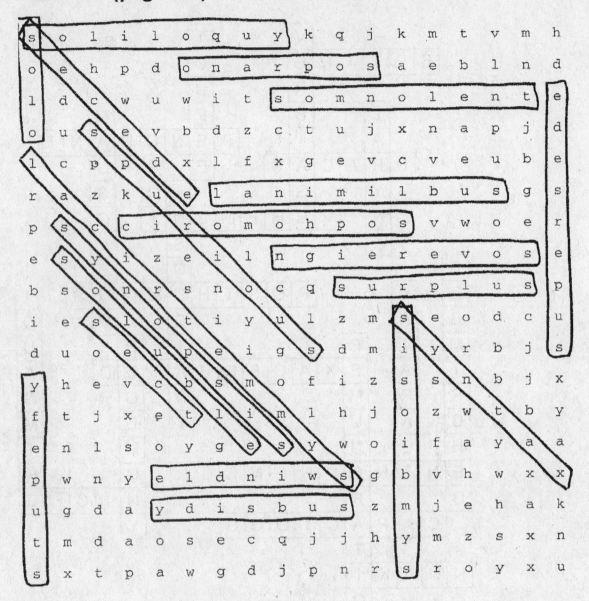

Puzzle #4 (page 253)

Word	Prefix	Prefix Meaning	Word Meaning
amoral	a	not	not moral
catalyst	cata	down, against, or wholly	reactant
circumference	circa	around	the outer boundary of something
cohabit	co	with	live together
discredit	dis	not	to cause to be doubted
disinter	dis	not	to unearth
extraterrestrial	extra	more than	alien (not of this place)
intractable	in	not	hard to handle; unmanageable
malcontent	mal	evil	a dissatisfied person
misnomer	mis	not	wrong name
multifaceted	multi	many	having many sides or aspects
multiform	multi	many	having many different forms
philharmonic	phil	love of	fond of music
polyglot	poly	many	speaking many languages
reacquaint	re	again	meet again

Puzzle #5 (page 254)

1. d	6. g	11. b
2. k	7. j	12. m
3. f	8. e	13. o
4. l	9. n	14. a
5. h	10. c	15. i

Puzzle #6 (page 254)

ambivalent
replete
benevolent
inane
tenuous
reclamation
ample
ribald
yen

Reading down: **arbitrary**

Puzzle #7 (page 255)

1. g	7. k	13. n
2. a	8. q	14. b
3. e	9. r	15. c
4. m	10. f	16. d
5. h	11. l	17. i
6. o	12. p	18. j

Puzzle #8 (page 256)

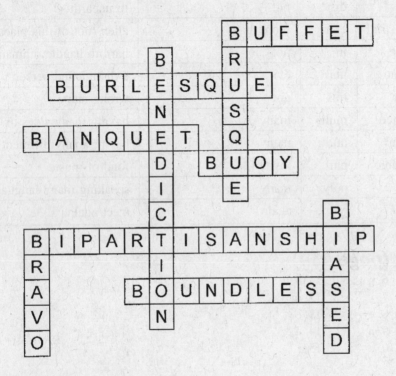

Puzzle #9 (page 257)

1. c	6. b
2. h	7. f
3. g	8. j
4. i	9. a
5. d	10. e

Puzzle #10 (pages 257–258)

1. A	6. E
2. D	7. B
3. A	8. E
4. C	9. A
5. C	10. C

Day 18

Have Some Fun While You Boost Your Vocabulary

Earlier in this book you learned that you can figure out many unfamiliar words by taking them apart. Sometimes, you can use your knowledge of prefixes, roots, and suffixes to decode new words. For example, the word "malaria" contains the prefix *mal* (bad) and the root *aria* (air). Thus, *malaria* literally means "bad air." The ancient Romans believed that the "bad air" around swamps caused people to become very ill with fevers and chills. We now know that the Romans were close but not exactly right: it is not the air around swamps that makes people ill; rather, it is the mosquitoes that breed in the stagnant water and then infect people with the disease.

You have learned many ways to define new words. Use these methods now as you enjoy the vocabulary games in this chapter. You have already encountered many of the words in these games earlier in this book, but you'll find some new ones as well so you can expand your vocabulary even more.

Game #1

Complete this chart by finding the root in each word, defining the root, and then using that clue to define each word. Then see how many other words you can list that have the same root. The answers appear on page 275.

Word	Root	Root Meaning	Word Meaning	Words with the Same Root
nominal				
omnivore				
pendulous				
eloquent				
discredit				
dehydrate				
nominate				
cogitate				
repulsion				
abducted				
decapitate				
genocide				
loquacious				
calligraphy				
chronicle				
panacea				
pedometer				
insecticide				
cosmopolitan				
theology				

Game #2

Select the correct meaning for each of the following boldfaced words. Circle your choice. The answers appear on page 275.

1. **abstemious**

   (A) absent
   (B) implacable
   (C) polygamous
   (D) temperate
   (E) polychromatic

2. **poignant**

   (A) polychromatic
   (B) passionate
   (C) emotional
   (D) implacable
   (E) miserable

3. **alleviate**

   (A) to augment
   (B) to pervade
   (C) to ignore
   (D) to eschew
   (E) to ease pain or a burden

4. **alienated**

   (A) jovial
   (B) polite
   (C) convivial
   (D) hostile
   (E) asocial

5. **opulent**

   (A) rich
   (B) insolvent
   (C) indigent
   (D) precocious
   (E) implacable

6. **ambiguous**

   (A) open to more than one interpretation
   (B) precocious
   (C) clear-cut
   (D) lucid
   (E) rancorous

7. **ornate**

   (A) implacable
   (B) very fancy
   (C) plain
   (D) drab
   (E) misanthropic

8. **ostentatious**

   (A) cynical
   (B) pretentious; showy
   (C) implacable
   (D) antagonistic
   (E) embittered

9. **florid**

   (A) hideous
   (B) supercilious
   (C) excessively ornate
   (D) dismal
   (E) acrimonious

10. **embellish**

    (A) to leave
    (B) to pervade
    (C) to transcend
    (D) to neglect
    (E) to decorate

Game #3

Complete the following chart by writing a synonym and an antonym for each test-worthy word. Try to write as many synonyms and antonyms for each word as you can. The answers appear on page 276.

Word	Synonyms	Antonyms
alleviate		
poignant		
embellish		
florid		
ambiguous		
opulent		
alienated		
ornate		
ostentatious		
abstemious		
boisterous		
enigmatic		
imperious		
indigent		
vivacious		

Game #4

To play this vocabulary game, write the synonym and antonym for each word. (Remember that a *synonym* means the same; an *antonym* means the opposite.) Try to think of more than one word for each category. You may wish to say the word aloud as you look for the match. Remember: saying the words will help you remember them. Then write your answers in the spaces provided. The answers appear on pages 276–277.

Word	Synonym	Antonym
ominous		
condemn		
melancholy		
adept		
aplomb		
balk		
boisterous		
truncated		
vilify		
wanton		
enthrall		
putrid		
choleric		
exemplary		
candid		
dapper		
debonair		
deft		
jaded		
misconstrue		

Game #5

Complete the following crossword puzzle with fifteen test-worthy words that you have already learned. Good luck! The answers appear on page 277.

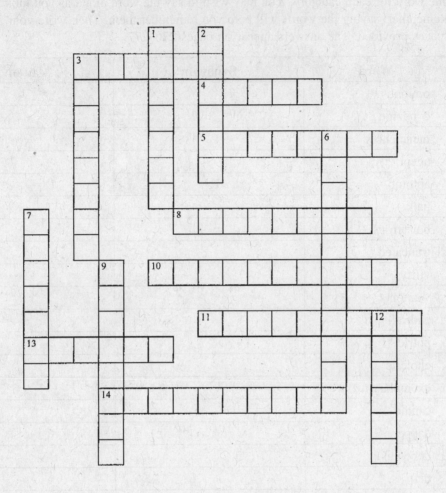

ACROSS

   3. To go back on one's promise or word

   4. To collect or accumulate

   5. Urgency

   8. Unite

  10. Unconcerned; carefree; jaunty

  11. Faker, quack

  13. Stylish; chic

  14. To make larger

DOWN

   1. Late

   2. To rise

   3. Witty talk

   6. Indifference

   7. Harmony, accord

   9. Capability

  12. Approach boldly

Game #6

To play this game, match each test-worthy word to its definition. Then, write your answers in the space provided. The answers appear on page 278.

_____	1. ambivalent	a.	a large amount
_____	2. auspicious	b.	a place of retreat
_____	3. austere	c.	unsure
_____	4. benign	d.	generous
_____	5. benevolent	e.	strict
_____	6. asylum	f.	shrewd
_____	7. astute	g.	promising
_____	8. ape	h.	subject to judgment
_____	9. ample	i.	mimic
_____	10. arbitrary	j.	harmless

According to legend, the wealthy and debonair Griswold Lorillard was at a party in the then-luxurious community of Tuxedo, New York, when he decided to have the tails removed from his formal coat. Voila! A new fashion was born. Can you guess what this evening suit is called?

Game #7

Complete each sentence with the word that fits best. Write the letter of the word in the blank. The answers appear on page 278.

1. The technician used a _____ to measure the thickness of the metal plate.

   (A) transistor
   (B) transformer
   (C) masonry
   (D) notary
   (E) caliper

2. When the _____ on the utility blew during the storm, the neighborhood was plunged into darkness.

   (A) transformer
   (B) masonry
   (C) notary
   (D) proxy
   (E) solvent

3. The _____ kitchen counter looked like thick, expensive marble, not a thin plastic veneer.

   (A) solvent
   (B) vocation
   (C) laminate
   (D) embalmed
   (E) extradited

4. The _____ at the new home was a combination of brick, interlocking pavers, and macadam.

   (A) notary
   (B) proxy
   (C) solvent
   (D) misanthrope
   (E) masonry

5. The jogger used a _____ to measure the number of steps he took on his morning jog.

   (A) pedometer
   (B) barometer
   (C) hydrometer
   (D) thermometer
   (E) altimeter

6. It is hard to keep your _____ on an ocean liner during a hurricane.

   (A) equilibrium
   (B) notary
   (C) solvent
   (D) vocation
   (E) proxy

7. According to the _____ , we were in for a strong storm that evening.

   (A) barometer
   (B) hydrometer
   (C) pedometer
   (D) thermometer
   (E) altimeter

8. After years of testing, the prototype aircraft was finally _____ and ready for its maiden voyage.

   (A) vocational
   (B) operational
   (C) intermittent
   (D) incoherent
   (E) unintelligible

9. The jeweler applied a dab of hot _____ to repair the broken ring.

   (A) vocation
   (B) arrears
   (C) contraband
   (D) solder
   (E) pedagogy

10. The doctor used a _____ to determine if the child had a fever.

    (A) pedometer
    (B) barometer
    (C) hydrometer
    (D) altimeter
    (E) thermometer

11. The child's interest _____ because she is fickle and not used to concentrating on one task at a time.

    (A) wallows
    (B) vindicates
    (C) wanes
    (D) validates
    (E) promulgates

12. Chris is a daredevil and has a _____ for high-risk sports such as sky-diving.

    (A) portent
    (B) polemic
    (C) propensity
    (D) munificence
    (E) nadir

13. His _____ personality made him difficult to get along with and resulted in a great many misunderstandings and quarrels.

    (A) contentious
    (B) compliant
    (C) contemporaneous
    (D) innocuous
    (E) reputable

14. When she realized that the insurgents would succeed in their plan to overthrow her government, the queen decided to _____ her throne.

    (A) abhor
    (B) disport
    (C) disinter
    (D) refurbish
    (E) abdicate

15. With a(n) _____ look in her eye, the child announced that she was going to cross the street all by herself.

    (A) ribald
    (B) resolute
    (C) sedentary
    (D) antiseptic
    (E) circuitous

Game #8

To complete the following acrostic, first unscramble each of the vocabulary words so that it matches its definition. Then, use the words to fill in the appropriate spaces on the corresponding lines. When you have completed the entire puzzle, another vocabulary word will read vertically in the circles. The answers appear on page 278.

oacurtr	organizes museum exhibits	⬡⬜⬜⬜⬜⬜
mmbuodsan	go-between in conflicts between governments and citizens	⬡⬜⬜⬜⬜⬜⬜⬜
benotgiale	transferable	⬡⬜⬜⬜⬜⬜⬜⬜⬜
smaxtiderit	person who prepares, stuffs, and displays animal skins	⬡⬜⬜⬜⬜⬜⬜⬜⬜⬜
uoreacntr	story teller	⬡⬜⬜⬜⬜⬜⬜⬜
cuacre	to accumulate interest over time	⬡⬜⬜⬜⬜
artbrrise	lawyer	⬡⬜⬜⬜⬜⬜⬜⬜
zmaortie	reduction in value of an asset over time	⬡⬜⬜⬜⬜⬜⬜
enmcryoanc	the field of magic and sorcery	⬡⬜⬜⬜⬜⬜⬜⬜⬜⬜
eodspt	tyrant	⬡⬜⬜⬜⬜

Game #9

The following words concern strength and weakness. For each word below, determine whether the word suggests strength or weakness. Indicate your choice by sorting the following words into two columns. The answers appear on page 278.

Word Box			
debility	efficacy	flaccid	impregnable
decrepit	sinewy	lassitude	emasculate
stalwart	enervation	dominion	languor
potency	intensity		

Strength	Weakness
_____	_____
_____	_____
_____	_____
_____	_____
_____	_____
_____	_____

Game #10

Select the correct meaning for each of the following boldfaced words. Circle your choice. The answers appear on page 278.

1. **dilatory**

   (A) listless
   (B) futile
   (C) remiss
   (D) arid
   (E) commensurate

2. **congenial**

   (A) genetic
   (B) garish
   (C) spurious
   (D) obscure
   (E) pleasantly agreeable

3. **garrulous**

   (A) supercilious
   (B) loquacious
   (C) salient
   (D) magnanimous
   (E) lurid

4. **disingenuous**

   (A) multifarious
   (B) Machiavellian
   (C) morose
   (D) nebulous
   (E) nascent

5. jaunty

   (A) blithe
   (B) nocturnal
   (C) noisome
   (D) nefarious
   (E) brazen

6. inscrutable

   (A) vainglorious
   (B) vitriolic
   (C) enigmatic
   (D) pallid
   (E) hapless

7. vituperate

   (A) berate
   (B) inundate
   (C) pillage
   (D) ameliorate
   (E) amalgamate

8. heinous

   (A) atrocious
   (B) ambiguous
   (C) amicable
   (D) anachronistic
   (E) amorous

9. anathema

   (A) restitution
   (B) gourmand
   (C) bard
   (D) analgesic
   (E) pariah

10. besmirch

   (A) surmise
   (B) truncate
   (C) undulate
   (D) defile
   (E) upbraid

Answers and Explanations

Game #1 (page 264)
(Possible answers)

Word	Root	Root Meaning	Word Meaning	Words with the Same Root
nominal	nomen	name	so-called	nominee
omnivore	vor	eat	eats everything	carnivore, herbivore
pendulous	pend	hanging	hanging loosely, swinging	pendant
eloquent	loqu	speech	expressive, fluent speech	circumlocution
discredit	cred	believe	cause to be doubted	credit, credible
dehydrate	hydro	water	lose water	hydration
nominate	nomen	name	name someone for an office	nomenclature
cogitate	cog	think	to think or meditate	cognition
repulsion	puls	send	send back	propulsion
abducted	duct	send	kidnap	deduct
decapitate	capit	head	cut off someone's head	capital
genocide	cide	killing	killing a race of people	matricide, patricide
loquacious	loqu	speech	talkative	obloquy, locution
calligraphy	graphy	writing	beautiful writing	graphology
chronicle	chron	time	historical record	chronological
panacea	pan	all	a cure-all	pandemic
pedometer	ped	foot	device for measuring steps	pedestrian
insecticide	cide	killing	killing insects	homicide, fratricide, infanticide
cosmopolitan	polit	citizen	citizen of the world	politics
theology	theo	god	study of god	theocracy

Game #2 (page 265)

1. D	6. A
2. C	7. B
3. E	8. B
4. E	9. C
5. A	10. E

Game #3 (page 266)
(Suggested answers)

Word	Synonyms	Antonyms
alleviate	relieve	aggravate
poignant	emotional	insipid
embellish	to decorate	mar; spoil; disfigure
florid	showy, gaudy	plain
ambiguous	unclear	clear; lucid
opulent	rich	indigent
alienated	hostile, asocial	gregarious; social
ornate	very fancy	very plain
ostentatious	pretentious	unadorned
abstemious	temperate	intemperate; greedy
boisterous	loud and full of energy	quiet, withdrawn
enigmatic	mystifying, cryptic	open, clear
imperious	commanding, domineering	shy, withdrawn
indigent	poor; destitute; impoverished	rich, wealthy
vivacious	lively, sprightly	languid

Game #4 (page 267)
(Suggested answers)

Word	Synonyms	Antonyms
ominous	frightening; menacing	promising, hopeful
condemn	denounce; criticize	praise
melancholy	depression; sadness	happiness
adept	skillful; competent, proficient; able; adroit; deft	incompetent; loutish; inept
aplomb	poise; composure	intemperance; irascibility; petulance
balk	demur; spurn; shun; desist; halt; falter; stammer; suspend	advance; proceed; persevere; persist; endure; dogged; indefatigable
boisterous	clamorous; tumultuous; obstreperous; rambunctious; riotous; turbulent	sedate; staid; reconciled; subdued; placid; tranquil
truncated	shortened	lengthened, increased
vilify	slander; defame	compliment, praise
wanton	reckless; unjustifiable	careful, cautious
enthrall	fascinate	bore

Game #4—continued

Word	Synonyms	Antonyms
putrid	rotten	fresh
choleric	temperamental; hotheaded	calm, prudent
exemplary	outstanding	mediocre, substandard
candid	sincere, forthright, frank; ingenuous; guileless; earnest; fervent	hypocritical; sanctimonious; ingenuous; equivocal; mendacious; devious
dapper	spruce; smart; natty; fastidious	disheveled; unkempt; tousled; slovenly; rumpled; disarrayed
debonair	courteous; charming, dashing; ambrosial; rakish; genteel; gallant; urbane; amiable; complaisant	impudent; impertinent; insolent; flippant; churlish; boorish; unceremonious
deft	proficient; skilled, adroit; adept; dexterous	maladroit; inept; gauche
jaded	weary, enervated; spent; cloyed; depleted	invigorated; revitalized; enlivened
misconstrue	distort; pervert; err, misunderstand, misinterpret	discern; fathom; conceive; assimilate

Game #5 (page 268)

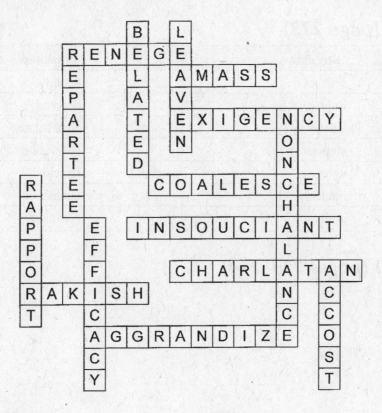

Game #6 (page 269)

1. c	6. b
2. g	7. f
3. e	8. i
4. j	9. a
5. d	10. h

Game #7 (pages 270–271)

1. E	6. A	11. C
2. A	7. A	12. C
3. C	8. B	13. A
4. E	9. D	14. E
5. A	10. E	15. B

Game #8 (page 272)

curator
ombudsman
negotiable
taxidermist
raconteur
accrue
barrister
amortize
necromancy
despot
Reading down: **contraband**

Game #9 (page 273)

Strength	Weakness
efficacy	debility
impregnable	decrepit
sinewy	emasculate
stalwart	enervation
potency	flaccid
intensity	languor
dominion	lassitude

Game #10 (pages 273–274)

1. C	6. C
2. E	7. A
3. B	8. A
4. B	9. E
5. A	10. D

Ultimate Success Word List

Use the Words You Learn

Vocabulary *as such* is not tested on exams like the PSAT/NMSQT, GED, SAT, TOEFL, or ACT. But as you learned earlier, there are plenty of *indirect* and *hidden* vocabulary questions on the exams:

1. **Reading comprehension passages** include vocabulary-in-context questions. These focus on particular words in the passage and ask you to determine their meaning in the passage. Sometimes the words chosen are obviously hard words (*latent, replete,* and *eminent,* to name three real examples). More often they are seemingly easy words that are tricky because they have many possible meanings (*camp, idea,* and *hard,* for example). In both cases, the broader, more varied, and more accurate your vocabulary knowledge, the better your chances of answering these questions quickly and correctly.

2. The better your vocabulary knowledge, the easier you'll find it to understand both **critical reading passages** and **sentence completion items** (which are, in effect, mini-reading passages, each one sentence long). Even an occasional math item is made a little more complicated by the use of a challenging vocabulary word.

So vocabulary knowledge makes a clear and significant difference in your performance on standardized tests. Fortunately, the kinds of words that regularly appear on exams like the SAT, GED, ACT, TOEFL, and PSAT/NMSQT fall into definite patterns.

These exams are basically tests of "book learning." They are written and edited by bookish people for the benefit of the other bookish people who run colleges and universities. They're designed to test your ability to handle the kinds of bookish tasks college students usually have to master: reading textbooks, finding information in reference books, deciphering scholarly journals, studying research abstracts, and writing impressive-sounding term papers.

So the hard words on the tests are hard words of a particular sort: bookish hard words that deal, broadly speaking, with the manipulation and communication of *ideas*—words like *ambiguous, amplify, arbitrary,* and *arcane.* The better you master this sort of vocabulary, the better you'll do on your exam.

Happily, you don't need to find these words on your own. We've done the hard work for you. By examining actual exams from the last several years, we've been able to come up with a list of the words most commonly used in reading passages and sentence completions, including both the question stems and the answer choices. This list has become the *Ultimate Success Word List*. It includes about 500 primary words that are most likely to appear in one form or another on the SAT, GED, ACT, TOEFL, and PSAT/NMSQT. It also includes hundreds of related words—words that are either variants of the primary words (*ambiguity* as a variant of *ambiguous*, for example) or that share a common word root (like *ample*, *amplify*, and *amplitude*). Many of these words have already been covered in this book; some even appear in the flashcards at the back. By placing them all in a single location, however, we hope to give you one more tool to enhance your vocabulary study.

A

abbreviate (verb) to make briefer, to shorten. *Because time was running out, the speaker had to abbreviate his remarks.* **abbreviation** (noun).

abrasive (adjective) irritating, grinding, rough. *The manager's rude, abrasive way of criticizing the workers was bad for morale.* **abrasion** (noun).

abridge (verb) to shorten, to reduce. *The Bill of Rights is designed to prevent Congress from abridging the rights of Americans.* **abridgment** (noun).

absolve (verb) to free from guilt, to exonerate. *The criminal jury absolved Mr. Callahan of the murder of his neighbor.* **absolution** (noun).

abstain (verb) to refrain, to hold back. *After his heart attack, he was warned by the doctor to abstain from smoking, drinking, and overeating.* **abstinence** (noun), **abstemious** (adjective).

accentuate (verb) to emphasize, to stress. *The overcast skies and chill winds accentuated our gloomy mood.* **accentuation** (noun).

acrimonious (adjective) biting, harsh, caustic. *The election campaign became acrimonious, as the candidates traded insults and accusations.* **acrimony** (noun).

adaptable (adjective) able to be changed to be suitable for a new purpose. *Some scientists say that the mammals outlived the dinosaurs because they were more adaptable to a changing climate.* **adapt** (verb), **adaptation** (noun).

adulation (noun) extreme admiration. *Few young actors have received greater adulation than did Marlon Brando after his performance in* A Streetcar Named Desire. **adulate** (verb), **adulatory** (adjective).

adversary (noun) an enemy or opponent. *When the former Soviet Union became an American ally, the United States lost a major adversary.* **adversarial** (adjective).

adversity (noun) misfortune. *It's easy to be patient and generous when things are going well; a person's true character is revealed under adversity.* **adverse** (adjective).

aesthetic (adjective) relating to art or beauty. *Mapplethorpe's photos may be attacked on moral grounds, but no one questions their aesthetic value—they are beautiful.* **aestheticism** (noun).

affected (adjective) false, artificial. *At one time, Japanese women were taught to speak in an affected high-pitched voice, which was thought girlishly attractive.* **affect** (verb), **affectation** (noun).

aggressive (adjective)   forceful, energetic, and attacking. *A football player needs a more aggressive style of play than a soccer player.* **aggression** (noun).

alacrity (noun)   promptness, speed. *Thrilled with the job offer, he accepted with alacrity—"Before they can change their minds!" he thought.* **alacritous** (adjective).

allege (verb)   to state without proof. *Some have alleged that Foster was murdered, but all the evidence points to suicide.* **allegation** (noun).

alleviate (verb)   to make lighter or more bearable. *Although no cure for AIDS has been found, doctors are able to alleviate the suffering of those with the disease.* **alleviation** (noun).

ambiguous (adjective)   having two or more possible meanings. *The phrase, "Let's table that discussion" is ambiguous; some think it means, "Let's discuss it now," while others think it means, "Let's save it for later."* **ambiguity** (noun).

ambivalent (adjective)   having two or more contradictory feelings or attitudes; uncertain. *She was ambivalent toward her impending marriage; at times she was eager to go ahead, while at other times she wanted to call it off.* **ambivalence** (noun).

amiable (adjective)   likable, agreeable, friendly. *He was an amiable lab partner, always smiling, on time, and ready to work.* **amiability** (noun).

amicable (adjective)   friendly, peaceable. *Although they agreed to divorce, their settlement was amicable and they remained friends afterward.*

amplify (verb)   to enlarge, expand, or increase. *Uncertain as to whether they understood, the students asked the teacher to amplify his explanation.* **amplification** (noun).

anachronistic (adjective)   out of the proper time. *The reference, in Shakespeare's* Julius Caesar *to "the clock striking twelve" is anachronistic, since there were no striking timepieces in ancient Rome.* **anachronism** (noun).

anarchy (noun)   absence of law or order. *For several months after the Nazi government was destroyed, there was no effective government in parts of Germany, and anarchy ruled.* **anarchic** (adjective).

anomaly (noun)   something different or irregular. *The tiny planet Pluto, orbiting next to the giants Jupiter, Saturn, and Neptune, has long appeared to be an anomaly.* **anomalous** (adjective).

antagonism (noun)   hostility, conflict, opposition. *As more and more reporters investigated the Watergate scandal, antagonism between Nixon and the press increased.* **antagonistic** (adjective), **antagonize** (verb).

antiseptic (adjective)   fighting infection; extremely clean. *A wound should be washed with an antiseptic solution. The all-white offices were bare and almost antiseptic in their starkness.*

apathy (noun)   lack of interest, concern, or emotion. *Tom's apathy toward his job could be seen in his lateness, his sloppy work, and his overall poor attitude.* **apathetic** (adjective).

arable (adjective)   able to be cultivated for growing crops. *Rocky New England has relatively little arable farmland.*

arbiter (noun)   someone able to settle disputes; a judge or referee. *The public is the ultimate arbiter of commercial value; it decides what sells and what doesn't.*

arbitrary (adjective)   based on random or merely personal preference. *Both computers cost the same and had the same features, so in the end I made an arbitrary decision about which one to buy.*

arcane (adjective)   little-known, mysterious, obscure. *Eliot's* Waste Land *is filled with arcane lore, including quotations in Latin, Greek, French, German, and Sanskrit.* **arcana** (noun, plural).

ardor (noun)   a strong feeling of passion, energy, or zeal. *The young revolutionary proclaimed his convictions with an ardor that excited the crowd.* **ardent** (adjective).

arid (adjective)   very dry; boring and meaningless. *The arid climate of Arizona makes farming difficult. Some find the law a fascinating topic, but for me it is an arid discipline.* **aridity** (noun).

ascetic (adjective)   practicing strict self-discipline for moral or spiritual reasons. *The so-called Desert Fathers were hermits who lived an ascetic life of fasting, study, and prayer.* **asceticism** (verb).

assiduous (adjective)   working with care, attention, and diligence. *Although Karen is not a naturally gifted math student, by assiduous study she managed to earn an A in trigonometry.* **assiduity** (noun).

astute (adjective)   observant, intelligent, and shrewd. *Safire's years of experience in Washington and his personal acquaintance with many political insiders made him an astute commentator on politics.*

atypical (adjective)   not typical; unusual. *In* The Razor's Edge, *Bill Murray, best known as a comic actor, gave an atypical dramatic performance.*

audacious (adjective)   bold, daring, adventurous. *Her plan to cross the Atlantic single-handed in a 12-foot sailboat was audacious, if not reckless.* **audacity** (noun).

audible (adjective)   able to be heard. *Although she whispered, her voice was picked up by the microphone, and her words were audible throughout the theater.* **audibility** (noun).

auspicious (adjective)   promising good fortune; propitious. *The news that a team of British climbers had reached the summit of Everest seemed an auspicious sign for the reign of newly crowned Queen Elizabeth II.*

authoritarian (adjective)   favoring or demanding blind obedience to leaders. *Despite Americans' belief in democracy, the American government has supported authoritarian regimes in other countries.* **authoritarianism** (noun)

B

belated (adjective)   delayed past the proper time. *She called her mother on January 5th to offer her a belated "Happy New Year."*

belie (verb)   to present a false or contradictory appearance. *Lena Horne's youthful appearance belies her long, distinguished career in show business.*

benevolent (adjective)   wishing or doing good. *In old age, Carnegie used his wealth for benevolent purposes, donating large sums to found libraries and schools.* **benevolence** (noun).

berate (verb)   to scold or criticize harshly. *The judge angrily berated the two lawyers for their unprofessional behavior.*

bereft (adjective)   lacking or deprived of something. *Bereft of parental love, orphans sometimes grow up to be insecure.*

bombastic (adjective)   inflated or pompous in style. *Old-fashioned bombastic political speeches don't work on television, which demands a more intimate style of communication.* **bombast** (noun).

bourgeois (adjective)   middle class or reflecting middle-class values. *The Dadaists of the 1920s produced art deliberately designed to offend bourgeois art collectors, with their taste for respectable, refined, uncontroversial pictures.* **bourgeois** (noun).

buttress (noun)   something that supports or strengthens; a projecting structure of masrony or wood. *The endorsement of the American Medical Association is a powerful buttress for the claims made about this new medicine. The buttress on the south wall of the Medieval castle was beginning to crumble.* **buttress** (verb).

C

camaraderie (noun)   a spirit of friendship. *Spending long days and nights together on the road, the members of a traveling theater group develop a strong sense of camaraderie.*

candor (noun)   openness, honesty, frankness. *In his memoir about the Vietnam War, former defense secretary McNamara described his mistakes with remarkable candor.* **candid** (adjective).

capricious (adjective)   unpredictable, whimsical. *The pop star Madonna has changed her image so many times that each new transformation now appears capricious rather than purposeful.* **caprice** (noun).

carnivorous (adjective)   meat-eating. *The long, dagger-like teeth of the Tyrannosaurus make it obvious that this was a carnivorous dinosaur.* **carnivore** (noun).

carping (adjective)   unfairly or excessively critical; querulous. *New York is famous for its demanding critics, but none is harder to please than the carping John Simon, said to have single-handedly destroyed many acting careers.* **carp** (verb).

catalytic (adjective)   bringing about, causing, or producing some result. *The conditions for revolution existed in America by 1765; the disputes about taxation that arose later were the catalytic events that sparked the rebellion.* **catalyze** (verb).

caustic (adjective)   burning, corrosive. *No one was safe when the satirist H. L. Mencken unleashed his caustic wit.*

censure (noun)   blame, condemnation. *The news that the senator had harassed several women brought censure from many feminists.* **censure** (verb).

chaos (noun)   disorder, confusion, chance. *The first few moments after the explosion were pure chaos: no one was sure what had happened, and the area was filled with people running and yelling.* **chaotic** (adjective).

circuitous (adjective)   winding or indirect. *We drove to the cottage by a circuitous route so we could see as much of the surrounding countryside as possible.*

circumlocution (noun)   speaking in a roundabout way; wordiness. *Legal documents often contain circumlocutions that make them difficult to understand.*

circumscribe (verb)   to define by a limit or boundary. *Originally, the role of the executive branch of government was clearly circumscribed, but that role has greatly expanded over time.* **circumscription** (noun).

circumvent (verb) to get around. *When Jerry was caught speeding, he tried to circumvent the law by offering the police officer a bribe.*

clandestine (adjective) secret, surreptitious. *As a member of the underground, Balas took part in clandestine meetings to discuss ways of sabotaging the Nazi forces.*

cloying (adjective) overly sweet or sentimental. *The deathbed scenes in the novels of Dickens are famously cloying: as Oscar Wilde said, "One would need a heart of stone to read the death of Little Nell without laughing."*

cogent (adjective) forceful and convincing. *The committee members were won over to the project by the cogent arguments of the chairman.* **cogency** (noun).

cognizant (adjective) aware, mindful. *Cognizant of the fact that it was getting late, the master of ceremonies cut short the last speech.* **cognizance** (noun).

cohesive (adjective) sticking together, unified. *An effective military unit must be a cohesive team, all its members working together for a common goal.* **cohere** (verb), **cohesion** (noun).

collaborate (verb) to work together. *To create a truly successful movie, the director, writers, actors, and many others must collaborate closely.* **collaboration** (noun), **collaborative** (adjective).

colloquial (adjective) informal in language; conversational. *Some expressions from Shakespeare, such as the use of thou and thee, sound formal today but were colloquial English in Shakespeare's time.*

competent (adjective) having the skill and knowledge needed for a particular task; capable. *Any competent lawyer can draw up a will.* **competence** (noun).

complacent (adjective) smug, self-satisfied. *Until recently, American auto makers were complacent, believing that they would continue to be successful with little effort.* **complacency** (noun).

composure (noun) calm, self-assurance. *The president managed to keep his composure during his speech even when the teleprompter broke down, leaving him without a script.* **composed** (adjective).

conciliatory (adjective) seeking agreement, compromise, or reconciliation. *As a conciliatory gesture, the union leaders agreed to postpone a strike and to continue negotiations with management.* **conciliate** (verb), **conciliation** (noun).

concise (adjective) expressed briefly and simply; succinct. *Less than a page long, the Bill of Rights is a concise statement of the freedoms enjoyed by all Americans.* **concision** (noun).

condescending (adjective)   having an attitude of superiority toward another; patronizing. *"What a cute little car!" she remarked in a condescending style. "I suppose it's the nicest one someone like you could afford!"* **condescension** (noun).

condolence (noun)   pity for someone else's sorrow or loss; sympathy. *After the sudden death of Princess Diana, thousands of messages of condolence were sent to her family.* **condole** (verb).

confidant (noun)   someone entrusted with another's secrets. *No one knew about Janee's engagement except Sarah, her confidant.* **confide** (verb), **confidential** (adjective).

conformity (noun)   agreement with or adherence to custom or rule. *In my high school, conformity was the rule: everyone dressed the same, talked the same, and listened to the same music.* **conform** (verb), **conformist** (noun, adjective).

consensus (noun)   general agreement among a group. *Among Quakers, voting traditionally is not used; instead, discussion continues until the entire group forms a consensus.*

consolation (noun)   relief or comfort in sorrow or suffering. *Although we miss our dog very much, it is a consolation to know that she died quickly, without suffering.* **console** (verb).

consternation (noun)   shock, amazement, dismay. *When a voice in the back of the church shouted out, "I know why they should not be married!" the entire gathering was thrown into consternation.*

consummate (verb)   to complete, finish, or perfect. *The deal was consummated with a handshake and the payment of the agreed-upon fee.* **consummate** (adjective), **consummation** (noun).

contaminate (verb)   to make impure. *Chemicals dumped in a nearby forest had seeped into the soil and contaminated the local water supply.* **contamination** (noun).

contemporary (adjective)   modern, current; from the same time. *I prefer old-fashioned furniture rather than contemporary styles. The composer Vivaldi was roughly contemporary with Bach.* **contemporary** (noun).

contrite (adjective)   sorry for past misdeeds. *The public is often willing to forgive celebrities who are involved in some scandal, as long as they appear contrite.* **contrition** (noun).

conundrum (noun)   a riddle, puzzle, or problem. *The question of why an all-powerful, all-loving God allows evil to exist is a conundrum many philosophers have pondered.*

convergence (noun)   the act of coming together in unity or similarity. *A remarkable example of evolutionary convergence can be seen in the shark and the dolphin, two sea creatures that developed from different origins to become very similar in form.* **converge** (verb).

convoluted (adjective)   twisting, complicated, intricate. *Tax law has become so convoluted that it's easy for people to accidentally violate it.* **convolute** (verb), **convolution** (noun).

corroborating (adjective)   supporting with evidence; confirming. *A passerby who had witnessed the crime gave corroborating testimony about the presence of the accused person.* **corroborate** (verb), **corroboration** (noun).

corrosive (adjective)   eating away, gnawing, or destroying. *Years of poverty and hard work had a corrosive effect on her beauty.* **corrode** (verb), **corrosion** (noun).

credulity (noun)   willingness to believe, even with little evidence. *Con artists fool people by taking advantage of their credulity.* **credulous** (adjective).

criterion (noun)   a standard of measurement or judgment. *In choosing a design for the new taxicabs, reliability will be our main criterion.* **criteria** (plural).

critique (noun)   a critical evaluation. *The editor gave a detailed critique of the manuscript, explaining its strengths and its weaknesses.* **critique** (verb).

culpable (adjective)   deserving blame, guilty. *Although he committed the crime, because he was mentally ill he should not be considered culpable for his actions.* **culpability** (noun).

cumulative (adjective)   made up of successive additions. *Smallpox was eliminated only through the cumulative efforts of several generations of doctors and scientists.* **accumulation** (noun), **accumulate** (verb).

curtail (verb)   to shorten. *The opening round of the golf tournament was curtailed by the thunderstorm.*

D

debased (adjective)   lowered in quality, character, or esteem. *The quality of TV journalism has been debased by the many new tabloid-style talk shows.* **debase** (verb).

debunk (verb)   to expose as false or worthless. *Magician James Randi loves to debunk psychics, mediums, clairvoyants, and others who claim supernatural powers.*

decorous (adjective)   having good taste; proper, appropriate. *Prior to her visit to Buckingham Palace, the young woman was instructed to demonstrate the most decorous behavior.* **decorum** (noun).

decry (verb)   to criticize or condemn. *The workers continued to decry the lack of safety in their factory.*

deduction (noun)   a logical conclusion, especially a specific conclusion based on general principles. *Based on what is known about the effects of greenhouse gases on atmospheric temperature, scientists have made several deductions about the likelihood of global warming.* **deduce** (verb).

delegate (verb)   to give authority or responsibility. *The president delegated the vice president to represent the administration at the peace talks.* **delegate** (noun).

deleterious (adjective)   harmful. *About thirty years ago, scientists proved that working with asbestos could be deleterious to one's health, producing cancer and other diseases.*

delineate (verb)   to outline or describe. *Naturalists had long suspected the fact of evolution, but Darwin was the first to delineate a process—natural selection—through which evolution could occur.*

demagogue (noun)   a leader who plays dishonestly on the prejudices and emotions of his followers. *Senator Joseph McCarthy was a demagogue who used the paranoia of the anti-Communist 1950s as a way of seizing fame and power in Washington.* **demagoguery** (noun).

demure (adjective)   modest or shy. *The demure heroines of Victorian fiction have given way to today's stronger, more opinionated, and more independent female characters.*

denigrate (verb)   to criticize or belittle. *The firm's new president tried to explain his plans for improving the company without seeming to denigrate the work of his predecessor.* **denigration** (noun).

depose (verb)   to remove from office, especially from a throne. *Iran was once ruled by a monarch called the Shah, who was deposed in 1979.*

derelict (adjective)   neglecting one's duty. *The train crash was blamed on a switchman who was derelict, having fallen asleep while on duty.* **dereliction** (noun).

derivative (adjective)   taken from a particular source. *When a person first writes poetry, her poems are apt to be derivative of whatever poetry she most enjoys reading.* **derivation** (noun), **derive** (verb).

desolate (adjective)   empty, lifeless, and deserted; hopeless, gloomy. *Robinson Crusoe was shipwrecked and had to learn to survive alone on a desolate island. The murder of her husband left Mary Lincoln desolate.* **desolation** (noun).

destitute (adjective)   very poor. *Years of rule by a dictator who stole the wealth of the country had left the people of the Philippines destitute.* **destitution** (noun).

deter (verb)   to discourage from acting. *The best way to deter crime is to ensure that criminals will receive swift and certain punishment.* **deterrence** (noun), **deterrent** (adjective).

detractor (noun) someone who belittles or disparages. *Neil Diamond has many detractors who consider his music boring, inane, and sentimental.* **detract** (verb).

deviate (verb)   to depart from a standard or norm. *Having agreed upon a spending budget for the company, we mustn't deviate from it; if we do, we may run out of money soon.* **deviation** (noun).

devious (adjective)   tricky, deceptive. *The CEO's devious financial tactics were designed to enrich his firm while confusing or misleading government regulators.*

didactic (adjective)   intended to teach, instructive. *The children's TV show* Sesame Street *is designed to be both entertaining and didactic.*

diffident (adjective)   hesitant, reserved, shy. *Someone with a diffident personality should pursue a career that involves little public contact.* **diffidence** (noun).

diffuse (verb)   to spread out, to scatter. *The red dye quickly became diffused through the water, turning it a very pale pink.* **diffusion** (noun).

digress (verb)   to wander from the main path or the main topic. *My high school biology teacher loved to digress from science into personal anecdotes about his college adventures.* **digression** (noun), **digressive** (adjective).

dilatory (adjective)   delaying, procrastinating. *The lawyer used various dilatory tactics, hoping that his opponent would get tired of waiting for a trial and drop the case.*

diligent (adjective)   working hard and steadily. *Through diligent efforts, the townspeople were able to clear away the debris from the flood in a matter of days.* **diligence** (noun).

diminutive (adjective)   unusually small, tiny. *Children are fond of Shetland ponies because their diminutive size makes them easy to ride.* **diminution** (noun).

discern (verb)   to detect, notice, or observe. *I could discern the shape of a whale off the starboard bow, but it was too far away to determine its size or species.* **discernment** (noun).

disclose (verb)   to make known; to reveal. *Election laws require candidates to disclose the names of those who contribute large sums of money to their campaigns.* **disclosure** (noun).

discomfit (verb)   to frustrate, thwart, or embarrass. *Discomfited by the interviewer's unexpected question, Peter could only stammer in reply.* **discomfiture** (noun).

disconcert (verb)   to confuse or embarrass. *When the hallway bells began to ring halfway through her lecture, the speaker was disconcerted and didn't know what to do.*

discredit (verb)   to cause disbelief in the accuracy of some statement or the reliability of a person. *Although many people still believe in UFOs, among scientists the reports of "alien encounters" have been thoroughly discredited.*

discreet (adjective)   showing good judgment in speech and behavior. *Be discreet when discussing confidential business matters— don't talk among strangers on the elevator, for example.* **discretion** (noun).

discrepancy (noun)   a difference or variance between two or more things. *The discrepancies between the two witnesses' stories show that one of them must be lying.* **discrepant** (adjective).

disdain (noun)   contempt, scorn. *The professor could not hide his disdain for those students who were perpetually late to his class.* **disdain** (verb), **disdainful** (adjective).

disingenuous (adjective)   pretending to be candid, simple, and frank. *When Texas billionaire H. Ross Perot ran for president, many considered his "jest plain folks" style disingenuous.*

disparage (verb)   to speak disrespectfully about, to belittle. *Many political ads today both praise their own candidate and disparage his or her opponent.* **disparagement** (noun), **disparaging** (adjective).

disparity (noun)   difference in quality or kind. *There is often a disparity between the kind of high-quality television people say they want and the low-brow programs they actually watch.* **disparate** (adjective).

disregard (verb)   to ignore, to neglect. *If you don't write a will, when you die, your survivors may disregard your wishes about how your property should be handled.* **disregard** (noun).

disruptive (adjective)   causing disorder, interrupting. *When the senator spoke at our college, angry demonstrators picketed, heckled, and engaged in other disruptive activities.* **disrupt** (verb), **disruption** (noun).

dissemble (verb)   to pretend, to simulate. *When the police questioned her about the crime, she dissembled innocence.*

dissipate (verb)   to spread out or scatter. *The windows and doors were opened, allowing the smoke that had filled the room to dissipate.* **dissipation** (noun).

dissonance (noun) lack of music harmony; lack of agreement between ideas. *Most modern music is characterized by dissonance, which many listeners find hard to enjoy. There is a noticeable dissonance between two common beliefs of most conservatives: their faith in unfettered free markets and their preference for traditional social values.* **dissonant** (adjective).

diverge (verb) to move in different directions. *Frost's poem* The Road Less Traveled *tells of the choice he made when "Two roads diverged in a yellow wood."* **divergence** (noun), **divergent** (adjective).

diversion (noun) a distraction or pastime. *During the two hours he spent in the doctor's waiting room, his hand-held computer game was a welcome diversion.* **divert** (verb).

divination (noun) the art of predicting the future. *In ancient Greece, people wanting to know their fate would visit the priests at Delphi, supposedly skilled at divination.* **divine** (verb).

divisive (adjective) causing disagreement or disunity. *Throughout history, race has been the most divisive issue in American society.*

divulge (verb) to reveal. *The people who count the votes for the Oscar awards are under strict orders not to divulge the names of the winners.*

dogmatic (adjective) holding firmly to a particular set of beliefs with little or no basis. *Believers in Marxist doctrine tend to be dogmatic, ignoring evidence that contradicts their beliefs.* **dogmatism** (noun).

dominant (adjective) greatest in importance or power. *Turner's* Frontier Thesis *suggests that the existence of the frontier had a dominant influence on American culture.* **dominate** (verb), **domination** (noun).

dubious (adjective) doubtful, uncertain. *Despite the chairman's attempts to convince the committee members that his plan would succeed, most of them remained dubious.* **dubiety** (noun).

durable (adjective) long lasting. *Denim is a popular material for work clothes because it is strong and durable.*

duress (noun) compulsion or restraint. *Fearing that the police might beat him, he confessed to the crime, not willingly but under duress.*

E

eclectic (adjective) drawn from many sources; varied, heterogeneous. *The Mellon family art collection is an eclectic one, including works ranging from ancient Greek sculptures to modern paintings.* **eclecticism** (noun).

efficacious (adjective) able to produce a desired effect. *Though thousands of people today are taking herbal supplements to treat depression, researchers have not yet proved them efficacious.* **efficacy** (noun).

effrontery (noun) shameless boldness. *The sports world was shocked when a professional basketball player had the effrontery to choke his head coach during a practice session.*

effusive (adjective) pouring forth one's emotions very freely. *Having won the Oscar for Best Actress, Sally Field gave an effusive acceptance speech in which she marveled, "You like me! You really like me!"* **effusion** (noun).

egotism (noun) excessive concern with oneself; conceit. *Robert's egotism was so great that all he could talk about was the importance—and the brilliance—of his own opinions.* **egotistic** (adjective).

egregious (adjective) obvious, conspicuous, flagrant. *It's hard to imagine how the editor could allow such an egregious error to appear.*

elated (adjective) excited and happy; exultant. *When the Arizona Cardinals' last, desperate pass was dropped, the elated fans of the Pittsburgh Steelers began to celebrate.* **elate** (verb), **elation** (noun).

elliptical (adjective) very terse or concise in writing or speech; difficult to understand. *Rather than speak plainly, she hinted at her meaning through a series of nods, gestures, and elliptical half sentences.*

elusive (adjective) hard to capture, grasp, or understand. *Though everyone thinks they know what "justice" is, when you try to define the concept precisely, it proves to be quite elusive.*

embezzle (verb) to steal money or property that has been entrusted to your care. *The church treasurer was found to have embezzled thousands of dollars by writing phony checks on the church bank account.* **embezzlement** (noun).

emend (verb) to correct. *Before the letter is mailed, please emend the two spelling errors.* **emendation** (noun).

emigrate (verb) to leave one place or country to settle elsewhere. *Millions of Irish emigrated to the New World in the wake of the great Irish famines of the 1840s.* **emigrant** (noun), **emigration** (noun).

eminent (adjective) noteworthy, famous. *Vaclav Havel was an eminent author before being elected president of the Czech Republic.* **eminence** (noun).

emissary (noun)   someone who represents another. *In an effort to avoid a military showdown, Carter was sent as an emissary to Korea to negotiate a settlement.*

emollient (noun)   something that softens or soothes. *She used a hand cream as an emollient on her dry, work-roughened hands.* **emollient** (adjective).

empathy (noun)   imaginative sharing of the feelings, thoughts, or experiences of another. *It's easy for a parent to have empathy for the sorrow of another parent whose child has died.* **empathetic** (adjective).

empirical (adjective)   based on experience or personal observation. *Although many people believe in ESP, scientists have found no empirical evidence of its existence.* **empiricism** (noun).

emulate (verb)   to imitate or copy. *The British band Oasis admitted their desire to emulate their idols, the Beatles.* **emulation** (noun).

encroach (verb)   to go beyond acceptable limits; to trespass. *By quietly seizing more and more authority, Robert Moses continually encroached on the powers of other government leaders.* **encroachment** (noun).

enervate (verb)   to reduce the energy or strength of someone or something. *The extended exposure to the sun along with dehydration enervated the shipwrecked crew, leaving them almost too weak to spot the passing vessel.*

engender (verb)   to produce, to cause. *Countless disagreements over the proper use of national forests have engendered feelings of hostility between ranchers and environmentalists.*

enhance (verb)   to improve in value or quality. *New kitchen appliances will enhance your house and increase the amount of money you'll make when you sell it.* **enhancement** (noun).

enmity (noun)   hatred, hostility, ill will. *Long-standing enmity, like that between the Protestants and Catholics in Northern Ireland, is difficult to overcome.*

enthrall (verb)   to enchant or charm. *The Swedish singer Jenny Lind enthralled American audiences in the nineteenth century with her beauty and talent.*

ephemeral (adjective)   quickly disappearing; transient. *Stardom in pop music is ephemeral; many of the top acts of ten years ago are forgotten today.*

equanimity (noun)   calmness of mind, especially under stress. *FDR had the gift of facing the great crises of his presidency—the Depression and the Second World War—with equanimity and even humor.*

eradicate (verb) to destroy completely. *American society has failed to eradicate racism, although some of its worst effects have been reduced.*

espouse (verb) to take up as a cause; to adopt. *No politician in America today will openly espouse racism, although some behave and speak in racially prejudiced ways.*

euphoric (adjective) a feeling of extreme happiness and well-being; elation. *One often feels euphoric during the earliest days of a new love affair.* **euphoria** (noun).

evanescent (adjective) vanishing like a vapor; fragile and transient. *As she walked by, the evanescent fragrance of her perfume reached me for just an instant.*

exacerbate (verb) to make worse or more severe. *The roads in our town already have too much traffic; building a new shopping mall will exacerbate the problem.*

exasperate (verb) to irritate or annoy. *Because she was trying to study, Sharon was exasperated by the yelling of her neighbors' children.*

exculpate (verb) to free from blame or guilt. *When someone else confessed to the crime, the previous suspect was exculpated.* **exculpation** (noun), **exculpatory** (adjective).

exemplary (adjective) worthy to serve as a model. *The Baldrige Award is given to a company with exemplary standards of excellence in products and service.* **exemplar** (noun), **exemplify** (verb).

exonerate (verb) to free from blame. *Although the truck driver was suspected at first of being involved in the bombing, later evidence exonerated him.* **exoneration** (noun), **exonerative** (adjective).

expansive (adjective) broad and large; speaking openly and freely. *The LBJ Ranch is located on an expansive tract of land in Texas. Over dinner, she became expansive in describing her dreams for the future.*

expedite (verb) to carry out promptly. *As the flood waters rose, the governor ordered state agencies to expedite their rescue efforts.*

expertise (noun) skill, mastery. *The software company was eager to hire new graduates with programming expertise.*

expiate (verb) to atone for. *The president's apology to the survivors of the notorious Tuskegee experiments was his attempt to expiate the nation's guilt over their mistreatment.* **expiation** (noun).

expropriate (verb) to seize ownership of. *When the Communists came to power in China, they expropriated most businesses and turned them over to government-appointed managers.* **expropriation** (noun).

extant (adjective) currently in existence. *Of the seven ancient Wonders of the World, only the pyramids of Egypt are still extant.*

extenuate (verb) to make less serious. *Karen's guilt is extenuated by the fact that she was only twelve when she committed the theft.* **extenuating** (adjective), **extenuation** (noun).

extol (verb) to greatly praise. *At the party convention, speaker after speaker rose to extol their candidate for the presidency.*

extricate (verb) to free from a difficult or complicated situation. *Much of the humor in the TV show* I Love Lucy *comes in watching Lucy try to extricate herself from the problems she creates by fibbing or trickery.* **extricable** (adjective).

extrinsic (adjective) not an innate part or aspect of something; external. *The high price of old baseball cards is due to extrinsic factors, such as the nostalgia felt by baseball fans for the stars of their youth, rather than the inherent beauty or value of the cards themselves.*

exuberant (adjective) wildly joyous and enthusiastic. *As the final seconds of the game ticked away, the fans of the winning team began an exuberant celebration.* **exuberance** (noun).

F

facile (adjective) easy; shallow or superficial. *The one-minute political commercial favors a candidate with facile opinions rather than serious, thoughtful solutions.* **facilitate** (verb), **facility** (noun).

fallacy (noun) an error in fact or logic. *It's a fallacy to think that "natural" means "healthful"; after all, the deadly poison arsenic is completely natural.* **fallacious** (adjective).

felicitous (adjective) pleasing, fortunate, apt. *The sudden blossoming of the dogwood trees on the morning of Matt's wedding seemed a felicitous sign of good luck.* **felicity** (noun).

feral (adjective) wild. *The garbage dump was inhabited by a pack of feral dogs that had escaped from their owners and become completely wild.*

fervent (adjective) full of intense feeling; ardent, zealous. *In the days just after his religious conversion, his piety was at its most fervent.* **fervid** (adjective), **fervor** (noun).

flagrant (adjective)   obviously wrong; offensive. *Nixon was forced to resign the presidency after a series of flagrant crimes against the U.S. Constitution.* **flagrancy** (noun).

flamboyant (adjective)   very colorful, showy, or elaborate. *At Mardi Gras, partygoers compete to show off the most wild and flamboyant outfits.*

florid (adjective)   flowery, fancy; reddish. *The grand ballroom was decorated in a florid style. Years of heavy drinking had given him a florid complexion.*

foppish (adjective)   describing a man who is foolishly vain about his dress or appearance. *The foppish character of the 1890s wore bright-colored spats and a top hat; in the 1980s, he wore fancy suspenders and a shirt with a contrasting collar.* **fop** (noun).

formidable (adjective)   awesome, impressive, or frightening. *According to his plaque in the Baseball Hall of Fame, pitcher Tom Seaver turned the New York Mets "from lovable losers into formidable foes."*

fortuitous (adjective)   lucky, fortunate. *Although the mayor claimed credit for the falling crime rate, it was really caused by several fortuitous trends.*

fractious (adjective)   troublesome, unruly. *Members of the British Parliament are often fractious, shouting insults and sarcastic questions during debates.*

fragility (noun)   the quality of being easy to break; delicacy, weakness. *Because of their fragility, few stained-glass windows from the early Middle Ages have survived.* **fragile** (adjective).

fraternize (verb)   to associate with on friendly terms. *Although baseball players aren't supposed to fraternize with their opponents, players from opposing teams often chat before games.* **fraternization** (noun).

frenetic (adjective)   chaotic, frantic. *The floor of the stock exchange, filled with traders shouting and gesturing, is a scene of frenetic activity.*

frivolity (noun)   lack of seriousness; levity. *The frivolity of the Mardi Gras carnival is in contrast to the seriousness of the religious season of Lent that follows.* **frivolous** (adjective).

frugal (adjective)   spending little. *With our last few dollars, we bought a frugal dinner: a loaf of bread and a piece of cheese.* **frugality** (noun).

fugitive (noun)   someone trying to escape. *When two prisoners broke out of the local jail, police were warned to keep an eye out for the fugitives.* **fugitive** (adjective).

G

gargantuan (adjective) huge, colossal. *The building of the Great Wall of China was one of the most gargantuan projects ever undertaken.*

genial (adjective) friendly, gracious. *A good host welcomes all visitors in a warm and genial fashion.*

grandiose (adjective) overly large, pretentious, or showy. *Among Hitler's grandiose plans for Berlin was a gigantic building with a dome several times larger than any ever built.* **grandiosity** (noun).

gratuitous (adjective) given freely or without cause. *Since her opinion was not requested, her harsh criticism of his singing seemed a gratuitous insult.*

gregarious (adjective) enjoying the company of others; sociable. *Naturally gregarious, Emily is a popular member of several clubs and a sought-after lunch companion.*

guileless (adjective) without cunning; innocent. *Deborah's guileless personality and complete honesty make it hard for her to survive in the harsh world of politics.*

gullible (adjective) easily fooled. *When the sweepstakes entry form arrived bearing the message, "You may be a winner!" my gullible neighbor tried to claim a prize.* **gullibility** (noun).

H

hackneyed (adjective) without originality, trite. *When someone invented the phrase, "No pain, no gain," it was clever, but now it is so commonly heard that it seems hackneyed.*

haughty (adjective) overly proud. *The fashion model strode down the runway, her hips thrust forward and a haughty expression, like a sneer, on her face.* **haughtiness** (noun).

hedonist (noun) someone who lives mainly to pursue pleasure. *Having inherited great wealth, he chose to live the life of a hedonist, traveling the world in luxury.* **hedonism** (noun), **hedonistic** (adjective).

heinous (adjective) very evil, hateful. *The massacre by Pol Pot of more than a million Cambodians is one of the twentieth century's most heinous crimes.*

hierarchy (noun) a ranking of people, things, or ideas from highest to lowest. *A cabinet secretary ranks just below the president and vice president in the hierarchy of the executive branch.* **hierarchical** (adjective).

hypocrisy (noun) a false pretense of virtue. *When the sexual misconduct of the television preacher was exposed, his followers were shocked at his hypocrisy.* **hypocritical** (adjective).

I

iconoclast (noun) someone who attacks traditional beliefs or institutions. *Comedian Stephen Colbert enjoys his reputation as an iconoclast, though people in power often resent his satirical jabs.* **iconoclasm** (noun), **iconoclastic** (adjective).

idiosyncratic (adjective) peculiar to an individual; eccentric. *Cyndi Lauper sings pop music in an idiosyncratic style, mingling high-pitched whoops and squeals with throaty gurgles.* **idiosyncrasy** (noun).

idolatry (noun) the worship of a person, thing, or institution as a god. *In Communist China, Chairman Mao was the subject of idolatry; his picture was displayed everywhere, and millions of Chinese memorized his sayings.* **idolatrous** (adjective).

impartial (adjective) fair, equal, unbiased. *If a judge is not impartial, then all of her rulings are questionable.* **impartiality** (noun).

impeccable (adjective) flawless. *The crooks printed impeccable copies of the Super Bowl tickets, making it impossible to distinguish them from the real ones.*

impetuous (adjective) acting hastily or impulsively. *Ben's resignation was an impetuous act; he did it without thinking, and he soon regretted it.* **impetuosity** (noun).

impinge (verb) to encroach upon, touch, or affect. *You have a right to do whatever you want, so long as your actions don't impinge on the rights of others.*

implicit (adjective) understood without being openly expressed; implied. *Although most clubs had no rules excluding minorities, many had an implicit understanding that no member of a minority group would be allowed to join.*

impute (verb) to credit or give responsibility to; to attribute. *Although Sarah's comments embarrassed me, I don't impute any ill will to her; I think she didn't realize what she was saying.* **imputation** (noun).

inarticulate (adjective) unable to speak or express oneself clearly and understandably. *A skilled athlete may be an inarticulate public speaker, as demonstrated by many post-game interviews.*

incisive (adjective) clear and direct expression. *Franklin settled the debate with a few incisive remarks that summed up the issue perfectly.*

incompatible (adjective)   unable to exist together; conflicting. *Many people hold seemingly incompatible beliefs: for example, supporting the death penalty while believing in the sacredness of human life.* **incompatibility** (noun).

inconsequential (adjective)   of little importance. *When the flat screen TV was delivered, it was a different shade of gray than I expected, but the difference was inconsequential.*

incontrovertible (adjective) impossible to question. *The fact that Sheila's fingerprints were the only ones on the murder weapon made her guilt seem incontrovertible.*

incorrigible (adjective)   impossible to manage or reform. *Lou is an incorrigible trickster, constantly playing practical jokes no matter how much his friends complain.*

incremental (adjective) increasing gradually by small amounts. *Although the initial cost of the Medicare program was small, the incremental expenses have grown to be very large.* **increment** (noun).

incriminate (verb)   to give evidence of guilt. *The fifth amendment to the Constitution says that no one is required to reveal information that would incriminate him in a crime.* **incriminating** (adjective).

incumbent (noun)   someone who occupies an office or position. *It is often difficult for a challenger to win a seat in Congress from the incumbent.* **incumbency** (noun), **incumbent** (adjective).

indeterminate (adjective)   not definitely known. *The college plans to enroll an indeterminate number of students; the size of the class will depend on the number of applicants and how many accept offers of admission.* **determine** (verb).

indifferent (adjective)   unconcerned, apathetic. *The mayor's small proposed budget for education suggests that he is indifferent to the needs of our schools.* **indifference** (noun).

indistinct (adjective) unclear, uncertain. *We could see boats on the water, but in the thick morning fog their shapes were indistinct.*

indomitable (adjective)   unable to be conquered or controlled. *The world admired the indomitable spirit of Nelson Mandela; he remained courageous despite years of imprisonment.*

induce (verb)   to cause. *The doctor prescribed a medicine that was supposed to induce a lowering of the blood pressure.* **induction** (noun).

ineffable (adjective)   difficult to describe or express. *He gazed in silence at the sunrise over the Taj Mahal, his eyes reflecting an ineffable sense of wonder.*

inevitable (adjective) unable to be avoided. *Once the Japanese attacked Pearl Harbor, American involvement in World War II was inevitable.* **inevitability** (noun).

inexorable (adjective) unable to be deterred; relentless. *It's difficult to imagine how the mythic character of Oedipus could have avoided his evil destiny; his fate appears inexorable.*

ingenious (adjective) showing cleverness and originality. *The Post-it® note is an ingenious solution to a common problem—how to mark papers without spoiling them.* **ingenuity** (noun).

inherent (adjective) naturally part of something. *Compromise is inherent in democracy, since everyone cannot get his way.* **inhere** (verb), **inherence** (noun).

innate (adjective) inborn, native. *Not everyone who takes piano lessons becomes a fine musician, which shows that music requires innate talent as well as training.*

innocuous (adjective) harmless, inoffensive. *I was surprised that Andrea took offense at such an innocuous joke.*

inoculate (verb) to prevent a disease by infusing with a disease-causing organism. *Pasteur found he could prevent rabies by inoculating patients with the virus that causes the disease.* **inoculation** (noun).

insipid (adjective) flavorless, uninteresting. *Some TV shows are so insipid that you can watch them while reading without missing a thing.* **insipidity** (noun).

insolence (noun) an attitude or behavior that is bold and disrespectful. *Some feel that news reporters who shout questions at the president are behaving with insolence.* **insolent** (adjective).

insular (adjective) narrow or isolated in attitude or viewpoint. *Americans are famous for their insular attitudes; they seem to think that nothing important has ever happened outside of their country.* **insularity** (noun).

insurgency (noun) uprising, rebellion. *The angry townspeople had begun an insurgency bordering on downright revolution; they were collecting arms, holding secret meetings, and refusing to pay certain taxes.* **insurgent** (adjective).

integrity (noun) honesty, uprightness; soundness, completeness. *"Honest Abe" Lincoln is considered a model of political integrity. Inspectors examined the building's support beams and foundation and found no reason to doubt its structural integrity.*

interlocutor (noun) someone taking part in a dialogue or conversation. *Annoyed by the constant questions from someone in the crowd, the speaker challenged his interlocutor to offer a better plan.* **interlocutory** (adjective).

interlude (noun)   an interrupting period or performance. *The two most dramatic scenes in* King Lear *are separated, strangely, by a comic interlude starring the king's jester.*

interminable (adjective)   endless or seemingly endless. *Addressing the United Nations, Castro announced, "We will be brief"—then delivered an interminable 4-hour speech.*

intransigent (adjective)   unwilling to compromise. *Despite the mediator's attempts to suggest a fair solution, the two parties were intransigent, forcing a showdown.* **intransigence** (noun).

intrepid (adjective)   fearless and resolute. *Only an intrepid adventurer is willing to undertake the long and dangerous trip by sled to the South Pole.* **intrepidity** (noun).

intrusive (adjective)   forcing a way in without being welcome. *The legal requirement of a search warrant is supposed to protect Americans from intrusive searches by the police.* **intrude** (verb), **intrusion** (noun).

intuitive (adjective)   known directly, without apparent thought or effort. *An experienced chess player sometimes has an intuitive sense of the best move to make, even if she can't explain it.* **intuit** (verb), **intuition** (noun).

inundate (verb)   to flood; to overwhelm. *As soon as playoff tickets went on sale, eager fans inundated the box office with orders.*

invariable (adjective)   unchanging, constant. *When writing a book, it was her invariable habit to rise at 6 and work at her desk from 7 to 12.* **invariability** (noun).

inversion (noun)   a turning backwards, inside-out, or upside-down; a reversal. *Latin poetry often features inversion of word order; for example, the first line of Virgil's* Aeneid: *"Arms and the man I sing."* **invert** (verb), **inverted** (adjective).

inveterate (adjective)   persistent, habitual. *It's very difficult for an inveterate gambler to give up the pastime.* **inveteracy** (noun).

invigorate (verb)   to give energy to, to stimulate. *As her car climbed the mountain road, Lucinda felt invigorated by the clear air and the cool breezes.*

invincible (adjective)   impossible to conquer or overcome. *For three years at the height of his career, boxer Mike Tyson seemed invincible.*

inviolable (adjective)   impossible to attack or trespass upon. *In the president's remote hideaway at Camp David, guarded by the Secret Service, his privacy is, for once, inviolable.*

irrational (adjective)   unreasonable. *Charles knew that his fear of insects was irrational, but he was unable to overcome it.* **irrationality** (noun).

irresolute (adjective)   uncertain how to act, indecisive. *The line in the ice cream shop grew as the irresolute child wavered between her two favorite ice cream flavors before finally choosing one.* **irresolution** (noun).

J

jeopardize (verb)   to put in danger. *Terrorist attacks jeopardize the fragile peace in the Middle East.* **jeopardy** (noun).

juxtapose (verb)   to put side by side. *Juxtaposing the two editorials revealed the enormous differences in the writers' opinions.* **juxtaposition** (noun).

L

languid (adjective)   without energy; slow, sluggish, listless. *The hot, humid weather of late August can make anyone feel languid.* **languish** (verb), **languor** (noun).

latent (adjective)   not currently obvious or active; hidden. *Although he had committed only a single act of violence, the psychiatrist who examined him said he had probably always had a latent tendency toward violence.* **latency** (noun).

laudatory (adjective)   giving praise. *The ads for the movie are filled with laudatory comments from critics.*

lenient (adjective)   mild, soothing, or forgiving. *The judge was known for his lenient disposition; he rarely imposed long jail sentences on criminals.* **leniency** (noun).

lethargic (adjective)   lacking energy; sluggish. *Visitors to the zoo are surprised that the lions appear so lethargic, but, in the wild, lions sleep up to 18 hours a day.* **lethargy** (noun).

liability (noun)   an obligation or debt; a weakness or drawback. *The insurance company had a liability of millions of dollars after the town was destroyed by a tornado. Slowness afoot is a serious liability in an aspiring basketball player.* **liable** (adjective).

lithe (adjective)   flexible and graceful. *The ballet dancer was almost as lithe as a cat.*

longevity (noun)   length of life; durability. *The reduction in early deaths from infectious diseases is responsible for most of the increase in human longevity over the past two centuries.*

lucid (adjective) clear and understandable. *Hawking's* A Short History of the Universe *is a lucid explanation of modern scientific theories about the origin of the universe.* **lucidity** (noun).

lurid (adjective) shocking, gruesome. *While the serial killer was on the loose, the newspapers were filled with lurid stories about his crimes.*

M

malediction (noun) curse. *In the fairy tale "Sleeping Beauty," the princess is trapped in a death-like sleep because of the malediction uttered by an angry witch.*

malevolence (noun) hatred, ill will. *Critics say that Iago, the villain in Shakespeare's* Othello, *seems to exhibit malevolence with no real cause.* **malevolent** (adjective).

malinger (verb) to pretend incapacity or illness to avoid a duty or work. *During the labor dispute, hundreds of employees malingered, forcing the company to slow production and costing it millions in profits.*

malleable (adjective) able to be changed, shaped, or formed by outside pressures. *Gold is a very useful metal because it is so malleable. A child's personality is malleable and deeply influenced by the things her parents say and do.* **malleability** (noun).

mandate (noun) order, command. *The new policy of using only organic produce in the restaurant went into effect as soon as the manager issued his mandate about it.* **mandate** (verb), **mandatory** (adjective).

maturation (noun) the process of becoming fully grown or developed. *Free markets in the former Communist nations are likely to operate smoothly only after a long period of maturation.* **mature** (adjective and verb), **maturity** (noun).

mediate (verb) to act to reconcile differences between two parties. *During the baseball strike, both the players and the club owners were willing to have the president mediate the dispute.* **mediation** (noun).

mediocrity (noun) the state of being middling or poor in quality. *The New York Mets finished in ninth place in 1968 but won the world's championship in 1969, going from horrible to great in a single year and skipping mediocrity.* **mediocre** (adjective).

mercurial (adjective) changing quickly and unpredictably. *The mercurial personality of Robin Williams, with his many voices and styles, made him perfect for the role of the ever-changing genie in Aladdin.*

meticulous (adjective) very careful with details. *Repairing watches calls for a craftsperson who is patient and meticulous.*

mimicry (noun) imitation, aping. *The continued popularity of Elvis Presley has given rise to a class of entertainers who make a living through mimicry of "The King."* **mimic** (noun and verb).

misconception (noun) a mistaken idea. *Columbus sailed west with the misconception that he would reach the shores of Asia.* **misconceive** (verb).

mitigate (verb) to make less severe; to relieve. *Wallace certainly committed the assault, but the verbal abuse he'd received helps to explain his behavior and somewhat mitigates his guilt.* **mitigation** (noun).

modicum (noun) a small amount. *The plan for your new business is well designed; with a modicum of luck, you should be successful.*

mollify (verb) to soothe or calm; to appease. *Carla tried to mollify the angry customer by promising him a full refund.*

morose (adjective) gloomy, sullen. *After Chuck's girlfriend dumped him, he lay around the house for a couple of days, feeling morose.*

mundane (adjective) everyday, ordinary, commonplace. *Moviegoers in the 1930s liked the glamorous films of Fred Astaire because they provided an escape from the mundane problems of life during the Great Depression.*

munificent (adjective) very generous; lavish. *Ted Turner's billion-dollar donation to the United Nations was one of the most munificent acts of charity in history.* **munificence** (noun).

mutable (adjective) likely to change. *A politician's reputation can be highly mutable, as seen in the case of Harry Truman—mocked during his lifetime, revered afterward.*

N

narcissistic (adjective) showing excessive love for oneself; egoistic. *Andre's room, decorated with photos of himself and the sports trophies he has won, suggests a narcissistic personality.* **narcissism** (noun).

nocturnal (adjective) of the night; active at night. *Travelers on the Underground Railroad escaped from slavery to the North by a series of nocturnal flights. The eyes of nocturnal animals must be sensitive in dim light.*

nonchalant (adjective) appearing to be unconcerned. *Unlike the other players on the football team who pumped their fists when their names were announced, John ran on the field with a nonchalant wave.* **nonchalance** (noun).

nondescript (adjective) without distinctive qualities; drab. *The bank robber's clothes were nondescript; none of the witnesses could remember their color or style.*

notorious (adjective) famous, especially for evil actions or qualities. *Warner Brothers produced a series of movies about notorious gangsters such as John Dillinger and Al Capone.* **notoriety** (noun).

novice (noun) beginner. *Lifting your head before you finish your swing is a typical mistake committed by the novice at golf.*

nuance (noun) a subtle difference or quality. *At first glance, Monet's paintings of water lilies all look much alike, but the more you study them, the more you appreciate the nuances of color and shading that distinguish them.*

nurture (verb) to nourish or help to grow. *The money given by the National Endowment for the Arts helps nurture local arts organizations throughout the country.* **nurture** (noun).

O

obdurate (adjective) unwilling to change; stubborn, inflexible. *Despite the many pleas he received, the governor was obdurate in his refusal to grant clemency to the convicted murderer.*

objective (adjective) dealing with observable facts rather than opinions or interpretations. *When a legal case involves a shocking crime, it may be hard for a judge to remain objective in his rulings.*

oblivious (adjective) unaware, unconscious. *Karen practiced her oboe with complete concentration, oblivious to the noise and activity around her.* **oblivion** (noun), **obliviousness** (noun).

obscure (adjective) little known; hard to understand. *Mendel was an obscure monk until decades after his death, when his scientific work was finally discovered. Most people find the writings of James Joyce obscure; hence the popularity of books that explain his books.* **obscure** (verb), **obscurity** (noun).

obsessive (adjective)   haunted or preoccupied by an idea or feeling. *His concern with cleanliness became so obsessive that he washed his hands twenty times every day.* **obsess** (verb), **obsession** (noun).

obsolete (adjective)   no longer current; old-fashioned. *W. H. Auden said that his ideal landscape would include water wheels, wooden grain mills, and other forms of obsolete machinery.* **obsolescence** (noun).

obstinate (adjective)   stubborn, unyielding. *Despite years of effort, the problem of drug abuse remains obstinate.* **obstinacy** (noun).

obtrusive (adjective)   overly prominent. *Philip should sing more softly; his bass is so obtrusive that the other singers can barely be heard.* **obtrude** (verb), **obtrusion** (noun).

ominous (adjective)   foretelling evil. *Ominous black clouds gathered on the horizon, for a violent storm was fast approaching.* **omen** (noun).

onerous (adjective)   heavy, burdensome. *The hero Hercules was ordered to clean the Augean Stables, one of several onerous tasks known as "the labors of Hercules."* **onus** (noun).

opportunistic (adjective)   eagerly seizing chances as they arise. *When Princess Diana died suddenly, opportunistic publishers quickly released books about her life and death.* **opportunism** (noun).

opulent (adjective)   rich, lavish. *The mansion of newspaper tycoon Hearst is famous for its opulent decor.* **opulence** (noun).

ornate (adjective)   highly decorated, elaborate. *Baroque architecture is often highly ornate, featuring surfaces covered with carving, sinuous curves, and painted scenes.*

ostentatious (adjective)   overly showy, pretentious. *To show off his wealth, the millionaire threw an ostentatious party featuring a full orchestra, a famous singer, and tens of thousands of dollars' worth of food.*

ostracize (verb)   to exclude from a group. *In Biblical times, those who suffered from the disease of leprosy were ostracized and forced to live alone.* **ostracism** (noun).

P

pallid (adjective)   pale; dull. *Working all day in the coal mine had given him a pallid complexion. The new musical offers only pallid entertainment: the music is lifeless, the acting dull, the story absurd.*

parched (adjective)   very dry; thirsty. *After two months without rain, the crops were shriveled and parched by the sun.* **parch** (verb).

pariah (noun)   outcast. *Accused of robbery, he became a pariah; his neighbors stopped talking to him, and people he'd considered friends no longer called.*

partisan (adjective)   reflecting strong allegiance to a particular party or cause. *The vote on the president's budget was strictly partisan: every member of the president's party voted yes, and all others voted no.* **partisan** (noun).

pathology (noun)   disease or the study of disease; extreme abnormality. *Some people believe that high rates of crime are symptoms of an underlying social pathology.* **pathological** (adjective).

pellucid (adjective)   very clear; transparent; easy to understand. *The water in the mountain stream was cold and pellucid. Thanks to the professor's pellucid explanation, I finally understand relativity theory.*

penitent (adjective)   feeling sorry for past crimes or sins. *Having grown penitent, he wrote a long letter of apology, asking forgiveness.*

penurious (adjective)   extremely frugal; stingy. *Haunted by memories of poverty, he lived in penurious fashion, driving a twelve-year-old car and wearing only the cheapest clothes.* **penury** (noun).

perceptive (adjective)   quick to notice, observant. *With his perceptive intelligence, Holmes was the first to notice the importance of this clue.* **perceptible** (adjective), **perception** (noun).

perfidious (adjective)   disloyal, treacherous. *Although he was one of the most talented generals of the American Revolution, Benedict Arnold is remembered today as a perfidious betrayer of his country.* **perfidy** (noun).

perfunctory (adjective)   unenthusiastic, routine, or mechanical. *When the play opened, the actors sparkled, but by the thousandth night their performance had become perfunctory.*

permeate (verb)   to spread through or penetrate. *Little by little, the smell of gas from the broken pipe permeated the house.*

persevere (adjective)   to continue despite difficulties. *Although several of her teammates dropped out of the marathon, Laura persevered.* **perseverance** (noun).

perspicacity (noun)   keenness of observation or understanding. *Journalist Murray Kempton was famous for the perspicacity of his comments on social and political issues.* **perspicacious** (adjective).

peruse (verb)   to examine or study. *Mary-Jo perused the contract carefully before she signed it.* **perusal** (noun).

pervasive (adjective)   spreading throughout. *As news of the disaster reached the town, a pervasive sense of gloom could be felt.* **pervade** (verb).

phlegmatic (adjective)   sluggish and unemotional in temperament. *It was surprising to see Tom, who is normally so phlegmatic, acting excited.*

placate (verb)   to soothe or appease. *The waiter tried to placate the angry customer with the offer of a free dessert.* **placatory** (adjective).

plastic (adjective)   able to be molded or reshaped. *Because it is highly plastic, clay is an easy material for beginning sculptors to use.*

plausible (adjective)   apparently believable. *According to the judge, the defense attorney's argument was both powerful and plausible.* **plausibility** (noun).

polarize (verb)   to separate into opposing groups or forces. *For years, the abortion debate polarized the American people, with many people voicing extreme views and few trying to find a middle ground.* **polarization** (noun).

portend (verb)   to indicate a future event; to forebode. *According to folklore, a red sky at dawn portends a day of stormy weather.*

potentate (noun)   a powerful ruler. *The Tsar of Russia was one of the last hereditary potentates of Europe.*

pragmatism (noun) a belief in approaching problems through practical rather than theoretical means. *Roosevelt's approach to the Great Depression was based on pragmatism: "Try something," he said. "If it doesn't work, try something else."* **pragmatic** (adjective).

preamble (noun)   an introductory statement. *The preamble to the Constitution begins with the famous words, "We the people of the United States of America . . ."*

precocious (adjective)   mature at an unusually early age. *Picasso was so precocious as an artist that, at nine, he is said to have painted far better pictures than his teacher.* **precocity** (noun).

predatory (adjective)   living by killing and eating other animals; exploiting others for personal gain. *The tiger is the largest predatory animal native to Asia. Microsoft has been accused of predatory business practices that prevent other software companies from competing with it.* **predation** (noun), **predator** (noun).

predilection (noun) a liking or preference. *To relax from his presidential duties, Kennedy had a predilection for spy novels featuring James Bond.*

predominant (adjective)   greatest in numbers or influence. *Although hundreds of religions are practiced in India, the predominant faith is Hinduism.* **predominance** (noun), **predominate** (verb).

prepossessing (adjective)   attractive. *Smart, lovely, and talented, she has all the prepossessing qualities that mark a potential movie star.*

presumptuous (adjective)   going beyond the limits of courtesy or appropriateness. *The senator winced when the presumptuous young staffer addressed him as "Chuck."* **presume** (verb), **presumption** (noun).

pretentious (adjective)   claiming excessive value or importance. *For a shoe salesman to call himself a "Personal Foot Apparel Consultant" seems awfully pretentious.* **pretension** (noun).

procrastinate (verb)   to put off, to delay. *If you habitually procrastinate, try this technique: never touch a piece of paper without either filing it, responding to it, or throwing it out.* **procrastination** (noun).

profane (adjective)   impure, unholy. *It is inappropriate and rude to use profane language in a church.* **profane** (verb), **profanity** (noun).

proficient (adjective)   skillful, adept. *A proficient artist, Louise quickly and accurately sketched the scene.* **proficiency** (noun).

proliferate (verb)   to increase or multiply. *Over the past twenty-five years, high-tech companies have proliferated in northern California, Massachusetts, and Seattle.* **proliferation** (noun).

prolific (adjective)   producing many offspring or creations. *With more than 300 books to his credit, Isaac Asimov was one of the most prolific writers of all time.*

prominence (noun)   the quality of standing out; fame. *Barack Obama rose to political prominence after his keynote address to the 2004 Democratic National Convention.* **prominent** (adjective).

promulgate (verb)   to make public, to declare. *Lincoln signed the proclamation that freed the slaves in 1862, but he waited several months to promulgate it.*

propagate (verb)   to cause to grow; to foster. *John Smithson's will left his fortune for the founding of an institution to propagate knowledge, without saying whether that meant a university, a library, or a museum.* **propagation** (noun).

propriety (noun)   appropriateness. *The principal questioned the propriety of the discussion the teacher had with her students about another instructor's gambling addiction.*

prosaic (adjective)   everyday, ordinary, dull. *"Paul's Case" tells the story of a boy who longs to escape from the prosaic life of a clerk into a world of wealth, glamour, and beauty.*

protagonist (noun)   the main character in a story or play; the main supporter of an idea. *Leopold Bloom is the protagonist of James Joyce's great novel* Ulysses.

provocative (adjective)   likely to stimulate emotions, ideas, or controversy. *The demonstrators began chanting obscenities, a provocative act that they hoped would cause the police to lose control.* **provoke** (verb), **provocation** (noun).

proximity (noun)   closeness, nearness. *Neighborhood residents were angry over the proximity of the sewage plant to the local school.* **proximate** (adjective).

prudent (adjective)   wise, cautious, and practical. *A prudent investor will avoid putting all of her money into any single investment.* **prudence** (noun), **prudential** (adjective).

pugnacious (adjective)   combative, bellicose, truculent; ready to fight. *Ty Cobb, the pugnacious outfielder for the Detroit Tigers, got into more than his fair share of brawls, both on and off the field.* **pugnacity** (noun).

punctilious (adjective)   very concerned about proper forms of behavior and manners. *A punctilious dresser like James would rather skip the party altogether than wear the wrong color tie.* **punctilio** (noun).

pundit (noun)   someone who offers opinions in an authoritative style. *The Sunday morning talk shows are filled with pundits, each with his or her own theory about the week's political news.*

punitive (adjective)   inflicting punishment. *The jury awarded the plaintiff one million dollars in punitive damages, hoping to teach the defendant a lesson.*

purify (verb)   to make pure, clean, or perfect. *The new plant is supposed to purify the drinking water provided to everyone in the nearby towns.* **purification** (noun).

Q

quell (verb)   to quiet, to suppress. *It took a huge number of police to quell the rioting.*

querulous (adjective)   complaining, whining. *The nursing home attendant needed a lot of patience to care for the three querulous, unpleasant residents on his floor.*

R

rancorous (adjective) expressing bitter hostility. *Many Americans are disgusted by recent political campaigns, which seem more rancorous than ever before.* **rancor** (noun).

rationale (noun) an underlying reason or explanation. *Looking at the sad faces of his employees, it was hard for the company president to explain the rationale for closing the business.*

raze (verb) to completely destroy; demolish. *The old Coliseum building will soon be razed to make room for a new hotel.*

reciprocate (verb) to give and take mutually. *If you'll watch for my kids tonight, I'll reciprocate by taking care of yours tomorrow.* **reciprocity** (noun).

reclusive (adjective) withdrawn from society. *During the last years of her life, actress Greta Garbo led a reclusive existence, rarely appearing in public.* **recluse** (noun).

reconcile (verb) to make consistent or harmonious. *FDR's greatness as a leader can be seen in his ability to reconcile the demands and values of the varied groups that supported him.* **reconciliation** (noun).

recrimination (noun) a retaliatory accusation. *After the governor called his opponent unethical, his opponent angrily replied with recriminations that the governor was a hypocrite.* **recriminate** (verb), **recriminatory** (adjective).

recuperate (verb) to regain health after an illness. *Although she left the hospital two days after her operation, it took her a few weeks to fully recuperate.* **recuperation** (noun), **recuperative** (adjective).

redoubtable (adjective) inspiring respect, awe, or fear. *Johnson's knowledge, experience, and personal clout made him a redoubtable political opponent.*

refurbish (verb) to fix up; renovate. *It took three days' work by a team of carpenters, painters, and decorators to completely refurbish the apartment.*

refute (verb) to prove false. *The company invited reporters to visit their plant in an effort to refute the charges of unsafe working conditions.* **refutation** (noun).

relevance (noun) connection to the matter at hand; pertinence. *Testimony in a criminal trial may be admitted only if it has clear relevance to the question of guilt or innocence.* **relevant** (adjective).

remedial (adjective) serving to remedy, cure, or correct some condition. *Affirmative action can be justified as a remedial step to help minority members overcome the effects of past discrimination.* **remediation** (noun), **remedy** (verb).

remorse (noun) a painful sense of guilt over wrongdoing. *In Poe's story* The Tell-Tale Heart, *a murderer is driven insane by remorse over his crime.* **remorseful** (adjective).

remuneration (noun) pay. *In a civil lawsuit, the attorney often receives part of the financial settlement as his or her remuneration.* **remunerate** (verb), **remunerative** (adjective).

renovate (verb) to renew by repairing or rebuilding. *The television program* This Old House *shows how skilled craftspeople renovate houses.* **renovation** (noun).

renunciation (noun) the act of rejecting or refusing something. *King Edward VII's renunciation of the British throne was caused by his desire to marry an American divorcee, something he couldn't do as king.* **renounce** (verb).

replete (adjective) filled abundantly. *Graham's book is replete with wonderful stories about the famous people she has known.*

reprehensible (adjective) deserving criticism or censure. *Although Pete Rose's misdeeds were reprehensible, not all fans agree that he deserves to be excluded from the Baseball Hall of Fame.* **reprehend** (verb), **reprehension** (noun).

repudiate (verb) to reject, to renounce. *After it became known that Duke had been a leader of the Ku Klux Klan, most Republican leaders repudiated him.* **repudiation** (noun).

reputable (adjective) having a good reputation; respected. *Find a reputable auto mechanic by asking your friends for recommendations based on their own experiences.* **reputation** (noun), **repute** (noun).

resilient (adjective) able to recover from difficulty. *A professional athlete must be resilient, able to lose a game one day and come back the next with confidence and enthusiasm.* **resilience** (noun).

resplendent (adjective) glowing, shining. *In late December, midtown New York is resplendent with holiday lights and decorations.* **resplendence** (noun).

responsive (adjective) reacting quickly and appropriately. *The new director of the Internal Revenue Service has promised to make the agency more responsive to public complaints.* **respond** (verb), **response** (noun).

restitution (noun) return of something to its original owner; repayment. *Some Native American leaders are demanding that the U.S. government make restitution for the lands taken from them.*

revere (verb)   to admire deeply, to honor. *Millions of people around the world revered Mother Teresa for her saintly generosity.* **reverence** (noun), **reverent** (adjective).

rhapsodize (verb)   to praise in a wildly emotional way. *That critic is such a huge fan of Toni Morrison that she will surely rhapsodize over the writer's next novel.* **rhapsodic** (adjective).

S

sagacious (adjective)   discerning, wise. *Only a leader as sagacious as Nelson Mandela could have united South Africa so successfully and peacefully.* **sagacity** (noun).

salvage (verb)   to save from wreck or ruin. *After the earthquake destroyed her home, she was able to salvage only a few of her belongings.* **salvage** (noun), **salvageable** (adjective).

sanctimonious (adjective)   showing false or excessive piety. *The sanctimonious prayers of the TV preacher were interspersed with requests that the viewers send him money.* **sanctimony** (noun).

scapegoat (noun)   someone who bears the blame for others' acts; someone hated for no apparent reason. *Although Buckner's error was only one reason the Red Sox lost, many fans made him the scapegoat, booing him mercilessly.*

scrupulous (adjective)   acting with extreme care; painstaking. *Disney theme parks are famous for their scrupulous attention to small details.* **scruple** (noun).

scrutinize (verb) to study closely. *The lawyer scrutinized the contract, searching for any sentence that could pose a risk for her client.* **scrutiny** (noun).

secrete (verb)   to emit; to hide. *Glands in the mouth secrete saliva, a liquid that helps in digestion. The jewel thieves secreted the necklace in a tin box buried underground.*

sedentary (adjective)   requiring much sitting. *When Officer Samson was given a desk job, she had trouble getting used to sedentary work after years on the street.*

sequential (adjective)   arranged in an order or series. *The courses for the chemistry major are sequential; you must take them in order, since each course builds on the previous ones.* **sequence** (noun).

serendipity (noun)   the act of lucky, accidental discoveries. *Great inventions sometimes come about through deliberate research and hard work, sometimes through pure serendipity.* **serendipitous** (adjective).

servile (adjective)   like a slave or servant; submissive. *The tycoon demanded that his underlings behave in a servile manner, agreeing quickly with everything he said.* **servility** (noun).

simulated (adjective)   imitating something else; artificial. *High-quality simulated gems must be examined under a magnifying glass to be distinguished from real ones.* **simulate** (verb), **simulation** (noun).

solace (verb)   to comfort or console. *There was little the rabbi could say to solace the husband after his wife's death.* **solace** (noun).

spontaneous (adjective)   happening without plan. *When the news of Kennedy's assassination broke, people everywhere gathered in a spontaneous effort to share their shock and grief.* **spontaneity** (noun).

spurious (adjective)   false, fake. *The so-called Piltdown Man, supposed to be the fossil of a primitive human, turned out to be spurious, although who created the hoax is still uncertain.*

squander (verb)   to use up carelessly, to waste. *Those who had made donations to the charity were outraged to learn that its director had squandered millions on fancy dinners and first-class travel.*

stagnate (verb)   to become stale through lack of movement or change. *Having had no contact with the outside world for generations, Japan's culture gradually stagnated.* **stagnant** (adjective), **stagnation** (noun).

staid (adjective)   sedate, serious, and grave. *This college is no "party school"; the students all work hard, and the campus has a reputation for being staid.*

stimulus (noun)   something that excites a response or provokes an action. *The arrival of merchants and missionaries from the West provided a stimulus for change in Japanese society.* **stimulate** (verb).

stoic (adjective)   showing little feeling, even in response to pain or sorrow. *A soldier must respond to the death of his comrades in stoic fashion, since the fighting will not stop for his grief.* **stoicism** (noun).

strenuous (adjective)   requiring energy and strength. *Hiking in the foothills of the Rockies is fairly easy, but climbing the higher peaks can be strenuous.*

submissive (adjective)   accepting the will of others; humble, compliant. *At the end of Ibsen's play* A Doll's House, *Nora leaves her husband and abandons the role of submissive housewife.*

substantiate (verb)   verified or supported by evidence. *The charge that Nixon had helped to cover up crimes was substantiated by his comments about it on a series of audio tapes.* **substantiated** (adjective), **substantiation** (noun).

sully (verb)   to soil, stain, or defile. *Nixon's misdeeds as president did much to sully the reputation of the American government.*

superficial (adjective)   on the surface only; without depth or substance. *Her wound was superficial and required only a light bandage. His superficial attractiveness hides the fact that his personality is lifeless and his mind is dull.* **superficiality** (noun).

superfluous (adjective)   more than is needed, excessive. *Once you've won the debate, don't keep talking; superfluous arguments will only bore and annoy the audience.*

suppress (verb)   to put down or restrain. *As soon as the unrest began, thousands of helmeted police were sent into the streets to suppress the riots.* **suppression** (noun).

surfeit (noun)   an excess. *Most American families have a surfeit of food and drink on Thanksgiving Day.* **surfeit** (verb).

surreptitious (adjective)   done in secret. *Because Iraq avoided weapons inspections, many believed it had a surreptitious weapons development program.*

surrogate (noun)   a substitute. *When the congressman died in office, his wife was named to serve the rest of his term as a surrogate.* **surrogate** (adjective).

sustain (verb)   to keep up, to continue; to support. *Because of fatigue, he was unable to sustain the effort needed to finish the marathon.*

T

tactile (adjective) relating to the sense of touch. *The thick brush strokes and gobs of color give the paintings of van Gogh a strongly tactile quality.* **tactility** (noun).

talisman (noun) an object supposed to have magical effects or qualities. *Superstitious people sometimes carry a rabbit's foot, a lucky coin, or some other talisman.*

tangential (adjective) touching lightly; only slightly connected or related. *Having enrolled in a class on African-American history, the students found the teacher's stories about his travels in South America of only tangential interest.* **tangent** (noun).

tedium (noun) boredom. *For most people, watching the Weather Channel for 24 hours would be sheer tedium.* **tedious** (adjective).

temerity (noun)   boldness, rashness, excessive daring. *Only someone who didn't understand the danger would have the temerity to try to climb Everest without a guide.* **temerarious** (adjective).

temperance (noun)   moderation or restraint in feelings and behavior. *Most professional athletes practice temperance in their personal habits; too much eating or drinking, they know, can harm their performance.* **temperate** (adjective).

tenacious (adjective)   clinging, sticky, or persistent. *Tenacious in pursuit of her goal, she applied for the grant unsuccessfully four times before it was finally approved.* **tenacity** (noun).

tentative (adjective)   subject to change; uncertain. *A firm schedule has not been established, but the Super Bowl in 2012 has been given the tentative date of February 5.*

terminate (verb)   to end, to close. *The Olympic Games terminate with a grand ceremony attended by athletes from every participating country.* **terminal** (noun), **termination** (noun).

terrestrial (adjective)   of the Earth. *The movie* Close Encounters of the Third Kind *tells the story of the first contact between beings from outer space and terrestrial humans.*

therapeutic (adjective)   curing or helping to cure. *Hot-water spas were popular in the nineteenth century among the sickly, who believed that soaking in the water had therapeutic effects.* **therapy** (noun).

timorous (adjective)   fearful, timid. *The cowardly lion approached the throne of the wizard with a timorous look on his face.*

toady (noun)   someone who flatters a superior in hopes of gaining favor; a sycophant. *"I can't stand a toady!" declared the movie mogul. "Give me someone who'll tell me the truth—even if it costs him his job!"* **toady** (verb).

tolerant (adjective)   accepting, enduring. *San Franciscans have a tolerant attitude about lifestyles: "Live and let live" seems to be their motto.* **tolerate** (verb), **toleration** (noun).

toxin (noun)   poison. *DDT is a powerful toxin once used to kill insects but now banned in the United States because of the risk it poses to human life.* **toxic** (adjective).

tranquillity (noun)   freedom from disturbance or turmoil; calm. *She moved from New York City to rural Vermont seeking the tranquillity of country life.* **tranquil** (adjective).

transgress (verb)   to go past limits; to violate. *No one could fathom why the honor student transgressed by shoplifting hundreds of dollars of merchandise from her favorite clothing store.* **transgression** (noun).

transient (adjective)   passing quickly. *Long-term visitors to this hotel pay a different rate than transient guests who stay for just a day or two.* **transience** (noun).

transitory (adjective) quickly passing. *Public moods tend to be transitory; people may be anxious and angry one month but relatively content and optimistic the next.* **transition** (noun).

translucent (adjective) letting some light pass through. *Panels of translucent glass let daylight into the room while maintaining privacy.*

transmute (verb) to change in form or substance. *In the Middle Ages, the alchemists tried to discover ways to transmute metals such as iron into gold.* **transmutation** (noun).

treacherous (adjective) untrustworthy or disloyal; dangerous or unreliable. *Nazi Germany proved to be a treacherous ally, first signing a peace pact with the Soviet Union, then invading. Be careful crossing the rope bridge; parts are badly frayed and treacherous.* **treachery** (noun).

tremulous (adjective) trembling or shaking; timid or fearful. *Never having spoken in public before, he began his speech in a tremulous, hesitant voice.*

trite (adjective) boring because of over-familiarity; hackneyed. *Her letters were filled with trite expressions, like "All's well that ends well" and "So far so good."*

truculent (adjective) aggressive, hostile, belligerent. *Hitler's truculent behavior in demanding more territory for Germany made it clear that war was inevitable.* **truculence** (noun).

truncate (verb) to cut off. *The poor copying job truncated the playwright's manuscript: the last page ended in the middle of a scene, halfway through the first act.*

turbulent (adjective) agitated or disturbed. *The night before the championship match, Martina was unable to sleep, her mind turbulent with fears and hopes.* **turbulence** (noun).

U

unheralded (adjective) little known, unexpected. *In a year of big-budget, much-hyped, mega-movies, this unheralded foreign film has surprised everyone with its popularity.*

unpalatable (adjective) distasteful, unpleasant. *Although I agree with the candidate on many issues, I can't vote for her, because I find her position on capital punishment unpalatable.*

unparalleled (adjective) with no equal; unique. *Tiger Woods's victory in the Masters golf tournament by a full twelve strokes was an unparalleled accomplishment.*

unstinting (adjective)   giving freely and generously. *Eleanor Roosevelt was much admired for her unstinting efforts on behalf of the poor.*

untenable (adjective)   impossible to defend. *The theory that this painting is a genuine van Gogh became untenable when the artist who actually painted it came forth.*

untimely (adjective)   out of the natural or proper time. *The untimely death of a youthful Princess Diana seemed far more tragic than Mother Teresa's death of old age.*

unyielding (adjective)   firm, resolute, obdurate. *Despite criticism, Cuomo was unyielding in his opposition to capital punishment; he vetoed several death penalty bills as governor.*

usurper (noun)   someone who takes a place or possession without the right to do so. *Kennedy's most devoted followers tended to regard later presidents as usurpers, holding the office they felt he or his brothers should have held.* **usurp** (verb), **usurpation** (noun).

utilitarian (adjective)   purely of practical benefit. *The design of the Model T car was simple and utilitarian, lacking the luxuries found in later models.*

utopia (noun)   an imaginary, perfect society. *Those who founded the Oneida community dreamed that it could be a kind of utopia—a prosperous state with complete freedom and harmony.* **utopian** (adjective).

V

validate (verb)   to officially approve or confirm. *The election of the president is validated when the members of the Electoral College meet to confirm the choice of the voters.* **valid** (adjective), **validity** (noun).

variegated (adjective)   spotted with different colors. *The brilliant, variegated appearance of butterflies makes them popular among collectors.* **variegation** (noun).

venerate (verb)   to admire or honor. *In Communist China, Chairman Mao Zedong was venerated as an almost god-like figure.* **venerable** (adjective), **veneration** (noun).

verdant (adjective)   green with plant life. *Southern England is famous for its verdant countryside filled with gardens and small farms.* **verdancy** (noun).

vestige (noun)   a trace or remainder. *Today's tiny Sherwood Forest is the last vestige of a woodland that once covered most of England.* **vestigial** (adjective).

vex (verb)   to irritate, annoy, or trouble. *It vexes me that she never helps with any chores around the house.* **vexation** (noun).

vicarious (adjective)   experienced through someone else's actions by way of the imagination. *Great literature broadens our minds by giving us vicarious participation in the lives of other people.*

vindicate (verb)   to confirm, justify, or defend. *Lincoln's Gettysburg Address was intended to vindicate the objectives of the Union in the Civil War.*

virtuoso (noun)   someone very skilled, especially in an art. *Vladimir Horowitz was one of the great piano virtuosos of the twentieth century.* **virtuosity** (noun).

vivacious (adjective)   lively, sprightly. *The role of Maria in* The Sound of Music *is usually played by a charming, vivacious young actress.* **vivacity** (noun).

volatile (adjective)   quickly changing; fleeting, transitory; prone to violence. *Public opinion is notoriously volatile; a politician who is very popular one month may be voted out of office the next.* **volatility** (noun).

W

whimsical (adjective)   based on a capricious, carefree, or sudden impulse or idea; fanciful, playful. *Dave Barry's* Book of Bad Songs *is filled with the kind of goofy jokes that are typical of his whimsical sense of humor.* **whim** (noun).

Z

zealous (adjective)   filled with eagerness, fervor, or passion. *A crowd of the candidate's most zealous supporters greeted her at the airport with banners, signs, and a marching band.* **zeal** (noun), **zealot** (noun), **zealotry** (noun).

NOTES

NOTES

NOTES

NOTES

NOTES

NOTES

NOTES

abstain	adversity	alleviate
abridge	adulation	alacrity
abbreviate	acrimonious	affected

(*verb*) to refrain, to hold back.

After his heart attack, he was warned by the doctor to <u>abstain</u> from smoking, drinking, and overeating.

(*verb*) to shorten, to reduce.

The Bill of Rights is designed to prevent Congress from <u>abridging</u> the rights of Americans.

(*verb*) to make briefer, to shorten.

Because time was running out, the speaker had to <u>abbreviate</u> his remarks.

(*noun*) misfortune.

It's easy to be patient and generous when things are going well; a person's true character is revealed under <u>adversity</u>.

(*noun*) extreme admiration.

Few young actors have received greater <u>adulation</u> than did Marlon Brando after his performance in *A Streetcar Named Desire*.

(*adjective*) biting, harsh, caustic.

The election campaign became <u>acrimonious</u>, as the candidates traded insults and accusations.

(*verb*) to make lighter or more bearable.

Although no cure for AIDS has been found, doctors are able to <u>alleviate</u> the suffering of those with the disease.

(*noun*) promptness, speed.

Thrilled with the job offer, he accepted with <u>alacrity</u>—"Before they can change their minds!" he thought.

(*adjective*) false, artificial.

At one time, Japanese women were taught to speak in an <u>affected</u> high-pitched voice, which was thought girlishly attractive.

anachronistic

arable

astute

amicable

antiseptic

ascetic

ambivalent

anomaly

arbitrary

(adjective) out of the proper time.

The reference, in Shakespeare's *Julius Caesar*, to "the clock striking twelve" is anachronistic, since there were no striking timepieces in ancient Rome.

(adjective) able to be cultivated for growing crops.

Rocky New England has relatively little arable farmland.

(adjective) observant, intelligent, and shrewd.

His years of experience in Washington and his personal acquaintance with many political insiders make him an astute commentator on politics.

(adjective) friendly, peaceable.

Although they agreed to divorce, their settlement was amicable and they remained friends afterward.

(adjective) fighting infection; extremely clean.

A wound should be washed with an antiseptic solution. The all-white offices were bare and almost antiseptic in their starkness.

(adjective) practicing strict self-discipline for moral or spiritual reasons.

The so-called Desert Fathers were hermits who lived an ascetic life of fasting, study, and prayer.

(adjective) having two or more contradictory feelings or attitudes; uncertain.

She was ambivalent toward her impending marriage; at times she was eager to go ahead, while at other times she wanted to call it off.

(noun) something different or irregular.

The tiny Pluto, orbiting next to the giant planets Jupiter, Saturn, and Neptune, has long appeared to be an anomaly.

(adjective) based on random or merely personal preference.

Both computers cost the same and had the same features, so in the end I made an arbitrary decision about which to buy.

belated

bourgeois

caustic

auspicious

bereft

capricious

audacious

benevolent

camaraderie

(*adjective*) delayed past the proper time.

She called her mother on January 5th to offer her a belated "Happy New Year."

(*adjective*) middle-class or reflecting middle-class values.

The Dadaists of the 1920s produced art deliberately designed to offend bourgeois art collectors, with their taste for respectable, refined, uncontroversial pictures.

(*adjective*) burning, corrosive.

No one was safe when the satirist H. L. Mencken unleashed his caustic wit.

(*adjective*) promising good fortune; propitious.

The news that a team of British climbers had reached the summit of Everest seemed an auspicious sign for the reign of newly crowned Queen Elizabeth II.

(*adjective*) lacking or deprived of something.

Bereft of parental love, orphans sometimes grow up to be insecure.

(*adjective*) unpredictable, willful, whimsical.

The pop star Madonna has changed her image so many times that each new transformation now appears capricious rather than purposeful.

(*adjective*) bold, daring, adventurous.

Her plan to cross the Atlantic single-handed in a 12-foot sailboat was audacious, if not reckless.

(*adjective*) wishing or doing good.

In old age, Carnegie used his wealth for benevolent purposes, donating large sums to found libraries and schools.

(*noun*) a spirit of friendship.

Spending long days and nights together on the road, the members of a traveling theater group develop a strong sense of camaraderie.

cloying

competent

condolence

circumvent

collaborate

concise

circumlocution

cognizant

composure

(adjective) overly sweet or sentimental.

The deathbed scenes in the novels of Dickens are famously cloying; as Oscar Wilde said, "One would need a heart of stone to read the death of Little Nell without laughing."

(verb) to get around.

When Jerry was caught speeding, he tried to circumvent the law by offering the police officer a bribe.

(noun) speaking in a roundabout way; wordiness.

Legal documents often contain circumlocutions which make them difficult to understand.

(adjective) having the skill and knowledge needed for a particular task; capable.

Any competent lawyer can draw up a will.

(verb) to work together.

To create a truly successful movie, the director, writers, actors, and many others must collaborate closely.

(adjective) aware, mindful.

Cognizant of the fact that it was getting late, the master of ceremonies cut short the last speech.

(noun) pity for someone else's sorrow or loss; sympathy.

After the sudden death of Princess Diana, thousands of messages of condolence were sent to her family.

(adjective) expressed briefly and simply; succinct.

Less than a page long, the Bill of Rights is a concise statement of the freedoms enjoyed by all Americans.

(noun) calm, self-assurance.

The president managed to keep his composure during his speech even when the teleprompter broke down, leaving him without a script.

curtail

contemporary

conformity

debunk

convoluted

consolation

decry

criterion

consummate

(noun) agreement with or adherence to custom or rule.

In my high school, conformity was the rule: everyone dressed the same, talked the same, and listened to the same music.

(adjective) modern, current; from the same time.

I prefer old-fashioned furniture rather than contemporary styles. The composer Vivaldi was roughly contemporary with Bach.

(verb) to shorten.

Because of the military emergency, all soldiers on leave were ordered to curtail their absences and return to duty.

(noun) relief or comfort in sorrow or suffering.

Although we miss our dog very much, it is a consolation to know that she died quickly, without suffering.

(adjective) twisting, complicated, intricate.

Tax law has become so convoluted that it's easy for people to accidentally violate it.

(verb) to expose as false or worthless.

Magician James Randi loves to debunk psychics, mediums, clairvoyants, and others who claim supernatural powers.

(verb) to complete, finish, or perfect.

The deal was consummated with a handshake and the payment of the agreed-upon fee.

(noun) a standard of measurement or judgment.

In choosing a design for the new taxicabs, reliability will be our main criterion.

(verb) to criticize or condemn.

Cigarette ads aimed at youngsters led many to decry the marketing tactics of the tobacco industry.

diligent

destitute

delegate

discern

diffident

demure

discomfit

digress

derivative

(*verb*) to give authority or responsibility.

The president delegated the vice president to represent the administration at the peace talks.

(*adjective*) very poor.

Years of rule by a dictator who stole the wealth of the country had left the people of that country destitute.

(*adjective*) working hard and steadily.

Through diligent efforts, the townspeople were able to clear away the debris from the flood in a matter of days.

(*adjective*) modest or shy.

The demure heroines of Victorian fiction have given way to today's stronger, more opinion-ated, and more independent female characters.

(*adjective*) hesitant, reserved, shy.

Someone with a diffident personality should pursue a career that involves little public contact.

(*verb*) to detect, notice, or observe.

I could discern the shape of a whale off the starboard bow, but it was too far away to determine its size or species.

(*adjective*) taken from a particular source.

When a person first writes poetry, her poems are apt to be derivative of whatever poetry she most enjoys reading.

(*verb*) to wander from the main path or the main topic.

My high school biology teacher loved to digress from science into personal anecdotes about his college adventures.

(*verb*) to frustrate, thwart, or embarrass.

Discomfited by the interviewer's unexpected question, Peter could only stammer in reply.

disparity

diverge

divulge

discrepancy

dissipate

divisive

discredit

disruptive

divination

(noun) difference in quality or kind.

There is often a disparity between the kind of high-quality television people say they want and the low-brow programs they actually watch.

(verb) to move in different directions.

Frost's poem *The Road Less Traveled* tells of the choice he made when "Two roads diverged in a yellow wood."

(verb) to reveal.

The people who count the votes for the Oscar awards are under strict orders not to divulge the names of the winners.

(noun) a difference or variance between two or more things.

The discrepancies between the two witnesses' stories show that one of them must be lying.

(verb) to spread out or scatter.

The windows and doors were opened, allowing the smoke that had filled the room to dissipate.

(adjective) causing disagreement or disunity.

Throughout history, race has been the most divisive issue in American society.

(verb) to cause disbelief in the accuracy of some statement or the reliability of a person.

Although many people still believe in UFOs, among scientists the reports of "alien encounters" have been thoroughly discredited.

(adjective) causing disorder, interrupting.

When the senator spoke at our college, angry demonstrators picketed, heckled, and engaged in other disruptive activities.

(noun) the art of predicting the future.

In ancient Greece, people wanting to know their fate would visit the priests at Delphi, supposedly skilled at divination.

egoism

empirical

ephemeral

eclectic

emollient

engender

durable

elusive

encroach

(*noun*) excessive concern with oneself; conceit.

Robert's egoism was so great that all he could talk about was the importance—and the brilliance—of his own opinions.

(*adjective*) based on experience or personal observation.

Although many people believe in ESP, scientists have found no empirical evidence of its existence.

(*adjective*) quickly disappearing; transient.

Stardom in pop music is ephemeral; most of the top acts of ten years ago are forgotten today.

(*adjective*) drawn from many sources; varied, heterogeneous.

The Mellon family art collection is an eclectic one, including works ranging from ancient Greek sculptures to modern paintings.

(*noun*) something that softens or soothes.

She used a hand cream as an emollient on her dry, work-roughened hands.

(*verb*) to produce, to cause.

Countless disagreements over the proper use of national forests have engendered feelings of hostility between ranchers and environmentalists.

(*adjective*) long lasting.

Denim is a popular material for work clothes because it is strong and durable.

(*adjective*) hard to capture, grasp, or understand.

Though everyone thinks they know what "justice" is, when you try to define the concept precisely, it proves to be quite elusive.

(*verb*) to go beyond acceptable limits; to trespass.

By quietly seizing more and more authority, Robert Moses continually encroached on the powers of other government leaders.

exculpate

expropriate

exuberant

exacerbate

expiate

extricate

euphoric

expedite

extenuate

(*verb*) to free from blame or guilt.

When someone else confessed to the crime, the previous suspect was <u>exculpated</u>.

(*verb*) to seize ownership of.

When the Communists came to power in China, they <u>expropri-ated</u> most businesses and turned them over to government-appointed managers.

(*adjective*) wildly joyous and enthusiastic.

As the final seconds of the game ticked away, the fans of the winning team began an <u>exuberant</u> celebration.

(*verb*) to make worse or more severe.

The roads in our town already have too much traffic; building a new shopping mall will <u>exacerbate</u> the problem.

(*verb*) to atone for.

The president's apology to the survivors of the notorious Tuskegee experiments was his attempt to <u>expiate</u> the nation's guilt over their mistreatment.

(*verb*) to free from a difficult or complicated situation.

Much of the humor in the TV show *I Love Lucy* comes in watching Lucy try to <u>extricate</u> herself from the problems she creates by fibbing or trickery.

(*adjective*) a feeling of extreme happiness and well-being; elation.

One often feels <u>euphoric</u> during the earliest days of a new love affair.

(*verb*) to carry out promptly.

As the flood waters rose, the governor ordered state agencies to <u>expedite</u> their rescue efforts.

(*verb*) to make less serious.

Karen's guilt is <u>extenuated</u> by the fact that she was only twelve when she committed the theft.

florid

frivolity

gratuitous

feral

fraternize

genial

fallacy

fractious

fugitive

(*adjective*) flowery, fancy; reddish.

The grand ballroom was decorated in a <u>florid</u> style. Years of heavy drinking had given him a <u>florid</u> complexion.

(*adjective*) wild.

The garbage dump was inhabited by a pack of <u>feral</u> dogs that had escaped from their owners and become completely wild.

(*noun*) an error in fact or logic.

It's a <u>fallacy</u> to think that "natural" means "healthful"; after all, the deadly poison arsenic is completely natural.

(*noun*) lack of seriousness; levity.

The <u>frivolity</u> of the Mardi Gras carnival is in contrast to the seriousness of the religious season of Lent that follows.

(*verb*) to associate with on friendly terms.

Although baseball players aren't supposed to <u>fraternize</u> with their opponents, players from opposing teams often chat before games.

(*adjective*) troublesome, unruly.

Members of the British Parliament are often <u>fractious</u>, shouting insults and sarcastic questions during debates.

(*adjective*) given freely or without cause.

Since her opinion was not requested, her harsh criticism of his singing seemed a <u>gratuitous</u> insult.

(*adjective*) friendly, gracious.

A good host welcomes all visitors in a warm and <u>genial</u> fashion.

(*noun*) someone trying to escape.

When two prisoners broke out of the local jail, police were warned to keep an eye out for the <u>fugitives</u>.

hierarchy	impinge	inconsequential
hackneyed	impeccable	incisive
guileless	iconoclast	impute

(noun) a ranking of people, things, or ideas from highest to lowest.

A cabinet secretary ranks just below the president and vice president in the hierarchy of the executive branch.

(verb) to encroach upon, touch, or affect.

You have a right to do whatever you want, so long as your actions don't impinge on the rights of others.

(adjective) of little importance.

When the stereo was delivered, it was a different shade of gray than I expected, but the difference was inconsequential.

(adjective) without originality, trite.

When someone invented the phrase, "No pain, no gain," it was clever, but now it is so commonly heard that it seems hackneyed.

(adjective) flawless.

The crooks printed impeccable copies of the Super Bowl tickets, making it impossible to distinguish them from the real ones.

(adjective) expressed clearly and directly.

Franklin settled the debate with a few incisive remarks that summed up the issue perfectly.

(adjective) without cunning; innocent.

Deborah's guileless personality and complete honesty make it hard for her to survive in the harsh world of politics.

(noun) someone who attacks traditional beliefs or institutions.

Comedian Stephen Colbert enjoys his reputation as an iconoclast, though people in power often resent his satirical jabs.

(verb) to credit or give responsibility to; to attribute.

Although Sarah's comments embarrassed me, I don't impute any ill will to her; I think she didn't realize what she was saying.

indistinct

innate

insurgency

indeterminate

ingenious

insolence

incorrigible

induce

inoculate

(adjective) unclear, uncertain.

We could see boats on the water, but in the thick morning fog their shapes were <u>indistinct</u>.

(adjective) inborn, native.

Not everyone who takes piano lessons becomes a fine musician, which shows that music requires <u>innate</u> talent as well as training.

(noun) uprising, rebellion.

The angry townspeople had begun an <u>insurgency</u> bordering on downright revolution.

(adjective) not definitely known.

The college plans to enroll an <u>indeterminate</u> number of students; the size of the class will depend on the number of applicants and how many accept offers of admission.

(adjective) showing cleverness and originality.

The Post-It note is an <u>ingenious</u> solution to a common problem—how to mark papers without spoiling them.

(noun) an attitude or behavior that is bold and disrespectful.

Some feel that news reporters who shout questions at the president are behaving with <u>insolence</u>.

(adjective) impossible to manage or reform.

Lou is an <u>incorrigible</u> trickster, constantly playing practical jokes no matter how much his friends complain.

(verb) to cause.

The doctor prescribed a medicine that was supposed to <u>induce</u> a lowering of the blood pressure.

(verb) to prevent a disease by infusing with a disease-causing organism.

Pasteur found he could prevent rabies by <u>inoculating</u> patients with the virus that causes the disease.

intuitive

irrational

lethargic

intrepid

inveterate

laudatory

interlocutor

invariable

languid

malediction	mercurial	mundane
lucid	mediate	mollify
lithe	malinger	mimicry

(*noun*) curse.

In the fairy tale "Sleeping Beauty," the princess is trapped in a death-like sleep because of the maledICTION uttered by an angry witch.

(*adjective*) changing quickly and unpredictably.

The mercurial personality of Robin Williams, with his many voices and styles, made him perfect for the role of the ever-changing genie in *Aladdin*.

(*adjective*) everyday, ordinary, commonplace.

Moviegoers in the 1930s liked the glamorous films of Fred Astaire because they provided an escape from the mundane problems of life during the Great Depression.

(*adjective*) clear and understandable.

Hawking's *A Short History of the Universe* is a lucid explanation of modern scientific theories about the origin of the universe.

(*verb*) to act to reconcile differences between two parties.

During the baseball strike, both the players and the club owners were willing to have the president mediate the dispute.

(*verb*) to soothe or calm; to appease.

Carla tried to mollify the angry customer by promising him a full refund.

(*adjective*) flexible and graceful.

The ballet dancer was almost as lithe as a cat.

(*verb*) to pretend incapacity or illness to avoid a duty or work.

During the labor dispute, hundreds of employees malingered, forcing the company to slow production and costing it millions in profits.

(*noun*) imitation, aping.

The continued popularity of Elvis Presley has given rise to a class of entertainers who make a living through mimicry of "The King."

nondescript	objective	obtrusive
nocturnal	nurture	obsolete
mutable	novice	obscure

(adjective) without distinctive qualities; drab.

The bank robber's clothes were nondescript; none of the witnesses could remember their color or style.

(adjective) dealing with observable facts rather than opinions or interpretations.

When a legal case involves a shocking crime, it may be hard for a judge to remain objective in his rulings.

(adjective) overly prominent.

Philip should sing more softly; his bass is so obtrusive that the other singers can barely be heard.

(adjective) of the night; active at night.

Travelers on the Underground Railroad escaped from slavery to the North by a series of nocturnal flights. The eyes of nocturnal animals must be sensitive in dim light.

(verb) to nourish or help to grow.

The money given by the National Endowment for the Arts helps nurture local arts organizations throughout the country.

(adjective) no longer current; old-fashioned.

W. H. Auden said that his ideal landscape would include water wheels, wooden grain mills, and other forms of obsolete machinery.

(adjective) likely to change.

A politician's reputation can be highly mutable, as seen in the case of President Harry Truman—mocked during his lifetime, revered afterward.

(noun) beginner.

Lifting your head before you finish your swing is a typical mistake committed by the novice at golf.

(adjective) little known; hard to understand.

Mendel was an obscure monk until decades after his death, when his scientific work was finally discovered.

ostentatious

penitent

persevere

opulent

pathology

perfunctory

onerous

pariah

perceptive

To show off his wealth, the millionaire threw an ostentatious party featuring a full orchestra, a famous singer, and tens of thousands of dollars worth of food.

(*adjective*) overly showy, pretentious.

The mansion of newspaper tycoon Hearst is famous for its opulent decor.

(*adjective*) rich, lavish.

The hero Hercules was ordered to clean the Augean Stables, one of several onerous tasks known as "the labors of Hercules."

(*adjective*) heavy, burdensome.

Having grown penitent, he wrote a long letter of apology, asking forgiveness.

(*adjective*) feeling sorry for past crimes or sins.

Some people believe that high rates of crime are symptoms of an underlying social pathology.

(*noun*) disease or the study of disease; extreme abnormality.

Accused of robbery, he became a pariah; his neighbors stopped talking to him, and people he'd considered friends no longer called.

(*noun*) outcast.

Although several of her teammates dropped out of the marathon, Laura persevered.

(*adjective*) to continue despite difficulties.

When the play opened, the actors sparkled, but by the thousandth night their performance had become perfunctory.

(*adjective*) unenthusiastic, routine, or mechanical.

With his perceptive intelligence, Holmes was the first to notice the importance of this clue.

(*adjective*) quick to notice, observant.

plastic

predatory

procrastinate

phlegmatic

preamble

presumptuous

peruse

potentate

predominant

(*noun*) appropriateness.

Some people had doubts about the <u>propriety</u> of the congress-man discussing his underwear on the late-night talk show.

(*adjective*) producing many offspring or creations.

With more than 300 books to his credit, Isaac Asimov was one of the most <u>prolific</u> writers of all time.

(*adjective*) skillful, adept.

A <u>proficient</u> artist, Louise quickly and accurately sketched the scene.

(*noun*) someone who offers opinions in an authoritative style.

The Sunday morning talk shows are filled with <u>pundits</u>, each with his or her own theory about the week's political news.

(*noun*) closeness, nearness.

Neighborhood residents were angry over the <u>proximity</u> of the sewage plant to the local school.

(*noun*) the main character in a story or play; the main supporter of an idea.

Leopold Bloom is the <u>protagonist</u> of James Joyce's great novel *Ulysses*.

(*noun*) an underlying reason or explanation.

Looking at the sad faces of his employees, it was hard for the company's president to explain the <u>rationale</u> for closing the business.

(*adjective*) complaining, whining.

The nursing home attendant needed a lot of patience to care for the 3 <u>querulous</u>, unpleasant residents on his floor.

(*verb*) to make pure, clean, or perfect.

The new plant is supposed to <u>purify</u> the drinking water provided to everyone in the nearby towns.

recuperate	remorse	resilient
reconcile	relevance	replete
reciprocate	refurbish	renovate

(verb) to regain health after an illness.

Although she left the hospital two days after her operation, it took her a few weeks to fully recuperate.

(noun) a painful sense of guilt over wrongdoing.

In Poe's story "The Tell-Tale Heart," a murderer is driven insane by remorse over his crime.

(adjective) able to recover from difficulty.

A pro athlete must be resilient, able to lose a game one day and come back the next with confidence and enthusiasm.

(verb) to make consistent or harmonious.

Roosevelt's greatness as a leader can be seen in his ability to reconcile the demands and values of the varied groups that supported him.

(noun) connection to the matter at hand; pertinence.

Testimony in a criminal trial may be admitted only if it has clear relevance to the question of guilt or innocence.

(adjective) filled abundantly.

Graham's book is replete with wonderful stories about the famous people she has known.

(verb) to make a return for something.

If you'll watch my kids tonight, I'll reciprocate by taking care of yours tomorrow.

(verb) to fix up; renovate.

It took three days' work by a team of carpenters, painters, and decorators to completely refurbish the apartment.

(verb) to renew by repairing or rebuilding.

The television program *This Old House* shows how skilled craftspeople renovate houses.

sagacious

secrete

solace

revere

scrupulous

servile

responsive

sanctimonious

sequential

(*adjective*) discerning, wise.

Only a leader as sagacious as Nelson Mandela could have united South Africa so successfully.

(*verb*) to emit; to hide.

Glands in the mouth <u>secrete</u> saliva, a liquid that helps in digestion.

(*verb*) to comfort or console.

There was little the neighbors could say to <u>solace</u> him after his loss.

(*verb*) to admire deeply, to honor.

Millions of people around the world revered Mother Teresa for her generosity.

(*adjective*) acting with extreme care; painstaking.

Disney theme parks are famous for their <u>scrupulous</u> attention to small details.

(*adjective*) like a servant; submissive.

The tycoon demanded that his underlings behave in a <u>servile</u> manner, agreeing quickly with everything he said.

(*adjective*) reacting quickly and appropriately.

The new director of the Internal Revenue Service has promised to make the agency more <u>responsive</u> to public complaints.

(*adjective*) showing false or excessive piety.

The <u>sanctimonious</u> pleas of the TV preacher were interspersed with requests that the viewers send him money.

(*adjective*) arranged in an order or series.

The courses for the chemistry major are <u>sequential</u>; you must take them in the order, since each course builds on the previous ones.

stimulus

superficial

sustain

stagnate

substantiated

surreptitious

spurious

strenuous

suppress

(noun) moderation or restraint in feelings and behavior.

Most professional athletes practice temperance in their personal habits; too much eating or drinking, they know, can harm their performance.

(adjective) fearful, timid.

The cowardly lion approached the throne of the wizard with a timorous look on his face.

(adjective) passing quickly.

Long-term visitors to this hotel pay at a different rate than transient guests who stay for just a day or two.

(noun) boredom.

For most people, watching the Weather Channel for 24 hours would be sheer tedium.

(adjective) of the Earth.

The movie Close Encounters of the Third Kind tells the story of the first contact between beings from outer space and terrestrial humans.

(noun) freedom from disturbance or turmoil; calm.

She moved from New York City to rural Vermont seeking the tranquillity of country life.

(noun) an object supposed to have magical effects or qualities.

Superstitious people sometimes carry a rabbit's foot, a lucky coin, or some other talisman.

(adjective) subject to change; uncertain.

A firm schedule has not been established, but the Super Bowl in 2013 has been given the tentative date of February 2.

(adjective) accepting, enduring.

His neighbors have a tolerant attitude about lifestyles: "Live and let live" seems to be their motto.

trite

unparalleled

utilitarian

treacherous

unheralded

unyielding

translucent

truncate

untenable

(*adjective*) boring because of over-familiarity; hackneyed.

Her letters were filled with trite expressions, like "All's well that ends well" and "So far so good."

(*adjective*) untrustworthy or disloyal; dangerous or unreliable.

Nazi Germany proved to be a treacherous ally, first signing a peace pact with the Soviet Union, then invading.

(*adjective*) letting some light pass through.

Blocks of translucent glass let daylight into the room while maintaining privacy.

(*adjective*) with no equal; unique.

Tiger Woods's victory in the Masters golf tournament by a full twelve strokes was an unparalleled accomplishment.

(*adjective*) little known, unexpected.

In a year of big-budget, much-hyped mega-movies, this unheralded foreign film has surprised everyone with its popularity.

(*verb*) to cut off.

The manuscript of the play appeared truncated; the last page ended in the middle of a scene, halfway through the first act.

(*adjective*) purely of practical benefit.

The design of the Model T car was simple and utilitarian, lacking the luxuries found in later models.

(*adjective*) firm, resolute, obdurate.

Despite criticism, Cuomo was unyielding in his opposition to capital punishment; he vetoed several death penalty bills as governor.

(*adjective*) impossible to defend.

The theory that this painting is a genuine van Gogh became untenable when the artist who actually painted it came forth.

vestige

virtuoso

zealous

venerate

vindicate

whimsical

validate

vicarious

volatile

(noun) a trace or remainder.

Today's tiny Sherwood Forest is the last vestige of a woodland that once covered most of England.

(verb) to admire or honor.

In Communist China, Chairman Mao Zedong was venerated as an almost god-like figure.

(verb) to officially approve or confirm.

The election of the president is validated when the members of the Electoral College meet to confirm the choice of the voters.

(noun) someone very skilled, especially in an art.

Vladimir Horowitz was one of the great piano virtuosos of the twentieth century.

(verb) to confirm, justify, or defend.

Lincoln's *Gettysburg Address* was intended to vindicate the objectives of the Union in the Civil War.

(adjective) experienced through someone else's actions by way of the imagination.

Great literature broadens our minds by giving us vicarious participation in the lives of other people.

(adjective) filled with eagerness, fervor, or passion.

A crowd of the candidate's most zealous supporters greeted her at the airport with banners, signs, and a marching band.

(adjective) based on a capricious, carefree, or sudden impulse or idea; fanciful, playful.

Dave Barry's *Book of Bad Songs* is filled with the kind of goofy jokes that are typical of his whimsical sense of humor.

(adjective) quickly changing; fleeting, transitory; prone to violence.

Public opinion is notoriously volatile; a politician who is very popular one month may be voted out of office the next.